HARRISBURG *in*
WORLD WAR I
and the
1918 PANDEMIC

HARRISBURG *in*
WORLD WAR I
·········· *and the* ··········
1918 PANDEMIC

R ODNEY R OSS

THE
History
PRESS

Published by The History Press
Charleston, SC
www.historypress.com

First published 2024

Manufactured in the United States

ISBN 9781467156011

Library of Congress Control Number: 2023947105

To three wonderful women: Mildred M. Ross, my mother;
Aida G. Ross, my spouse; and Christine L.G. Ross, my daughter.

CONTENTS

PREFACE

This writing redresses a void. No narrative exists chronicling Harrisburg's World War I home front and pandemic ordeal during the nineteen months between April 1917 and November 1918.

Harrisburgers did their bit and prevailed. They mustered offices, churches, clubs and corporations, as well as fraternal and sororal societies. War veterans, old folks, schoolchildren and Boy Scouts stepped forward. Women volunteered for the Red Cross. They sought industrial employment and cultivated war gardens.

Newspapers furnished wholehearted support, printing war news, maps, advisories, film reviews, correspondence, cartoons, comic strips, poems and advertisements.

The municipality enforced federal guidelines for draft calls, food conservation, fuel savings and arms production. Residents gladly embraced Liberty loans.

Harrisburg braved wartime tribulations. Soldiers and laborers thronged the community, intensifying housing shortages, traffic congestion, criminal mischief and immoral goings-on. War plants and railroads suffered numerous accidents.

The city revealed an ill temperament. Residents feared espionage and sabotage. They suspected foreigners and demanded loyalty. Teutonophobia cast aspersions on anything German.

My research encompassed books, newspapers, journals, scholarly reviews and internet findings. Residents' observations provided piquancy.

There is much to learn about the city on the Susquehanna River's eastern shore. Hopefully this volume will whet appetites.

ACKNOWLEDGEMENTS

I am grateful to many for their assistance.

Without the Dauphin County Library's online newspapers, this book could not have been researched. Also, librarian Christine Lauver kindly provided images of value.

Joe Hermit at PennLive promptly approved reprint privileges.

As always, the professional management and active support of Banks Smither at The History Press were mightily valued.

I thank Nancy Sheets at the Market Square Presbyterian Church for her quick reply giving permission to use photographs from Dr. William Sisson's *Serving Christ and Community: A History of Market Square Presbyterian Church, 1794–1992*.

Church historian Kenneth C. Hays's image of the Pine Street Presbyterian Church and information about a member killed in France were greatly appreciated.

I value the interest and support of Raechel Albright.

David J. Morrison at the Historic Harrisburg Association cordially accommodated an image request.

I commend Ken Frew of the Historical Society of Dauphin County for his diligent toil and ready response to my inquiry.

My gratitude goes to my late parents for their perceptions and memories of early twentieth-century Harrisburg.

My stalwart spouse, Aida, was always accommodating, tolerating my remoteness and absorption.

This book is a combined venture. The labor would have gone unfinished without my daughter Christine's typing, graphic design, editing and computer expertise.

Chapter 1

WAR

April 1917

Harrisburgers expected the United States' entry in the European conflict. President Woodrow Wilson's war message and Congress's declaration in April 1917 followed repeated violations of neutral rights by Imperial Germany's submarines. The city set out to cope with home front exigencies.

Some opposed involvement. The Harrisburg Peace Society sent a letter to the White House decrying "aggressive warfare" as a "weapon of despotism and un-American." The message continued, "There is absolutely no excuse at this time for a declaration of war against Germany." Hummel Street's Church of the Brethren displayed a notice discouraging military enlistment. Its Reverend William K. Connor entertained the conviction that "the rules of the church discourage the carrying of arms and that he will back up everything he says by a statement from the Bible."

Internal threats preoccupied officials. Susquehanna River bridges needed security. Suspicious characters lurked about the Cumberland Valley span. Authorities pursued them, and gunfire erupted. The culprits fled by boat. Later, railroad officers discovered explosives.

The Cumberland Valley Railroad enforced restrictions. It barred employees from the bridges and prohibited patrons from occupying passenger car platforms when going over spans. Guards even stopped the company's president during a routine inspection.

Municipal chief of police J. Edward Wetzel announced additional commands. Bridges received more guards and more nighttime lighting.

Harrisburg's doughboy statue ("Lest we forget"). *Courtesy of PennLive.*

Regulations required watercraft to move under the spans via inscribed piers, or they risked being fired on. "Any persons loitering about the bridges or passing near the bridges on the Island will be shot at," Wetzel warned. "There are to be no exceptions to this order and unless it is obeyed, it will result in the slaughter of some of the citizens of Harrisburg."

During the daylight, Old Glory hung from the spans, including the Market Street and Walnut Street crossings.

Wartime restrained water recreation. Railroad executives prohibited trespassing on Dauphin County's Powell's and Clark's Creeks, effectively preventing fishing. In the Park Department, the Greater Harrisburg Navy met. Its committee, arranging the canoeists' yearly outing from Mifflin to the city via the Juniata and Susquehanna Rivers, believed bridge sentinels might shoot its boaters.

Within Harrisburg, vital installations received added protection. Commonwealth police patrolled the capitol complex. The city guarded its waterworks. Recognizing the reservoir's significance, Commissioner William H. Lynch forbid visits. The chamber of commerce pressed the employment of "every measure to safeguard the city's water supply and its distribution system against plots that may be hatched."

War's advent stirred suspicions. A Boy Scout told police about those he suspected. A railroad employee entrained to Lancaster stopped a person from snapping a photo of Steelton's Bethlehem Steel Company. A Harrisburg student experienced arrest in Weehawken, New Jersey, for taking a picture of a trolley. Authorities detained two Mexican women, concluding their Biblical quotations in Spanish translation might be "part of a new form of secret code."

Police ordered enemy nationals to relinquish specified belongings or suffer arrest within twenty-four hours. They must hand over military hardware, explosives and "any paper, document or book, written or printed in cipher, or in which there may be invisible writing."

Motorcyclists offered their services, volunteering to protect sections of the city. The Keystone Motorcycle Club, gathering at Cameron and Paxton Streets, pondered the idea.

Citizens dealt harshly with contrary leanings. A teacher took exception to a student's presentation opposing hostilities against Germany and, in reprimand, remarked, "We don't want any pacifists…in our public speaking classes." The youth risked "vengeance" by classmates. Groups introduced resolves to quash sedition and to rally: "He who is not for us is against us." Area physicians, up for military service, renounced any inclination toward pacificism. An African American at the Pennsylvania Railroad Station, drunk and offensive, profaned "the United States and the flag and called himself 'a black German.'" Police lodged him in the Dauphin County Prison for thirty days. The *Evening News* carried a photograph of pacifists' signboards awash in yellow stain.

Newspapers aroused support for belligerency. The *Harrisburg Telegraph* proclaimed, "WAR!"—lending editorial endorsement. Its cartoon strip *Bringing Up Father* referenced preparedness and Father volunteering. The *Evening News* declared, "WE FIGHT NOW—NOT FOR SORDID GAIN OF ANY SORT, BUT TO PUT DOWN UNRESTICTED MURDER ON THE HIGH SEAS."

Industrial employees chimed love of country. Flag-waving music reverberated from the Moorhead Knitting Company's recreation hall. Patriotic oratory and songs attended flag ceremonies at the Elliot-Fisher plant. Workers mustered at the Chestnut Street Hall, and the Central Labor Union exhorted national solidarity.

Clergy evoked the divine and explained war's impact. Reverend Dr. George Edward Hawes thought fighting Germany was "significant" and recalled, "1,900 years ago today the Savior paid the demand for the redemption of the world." The *Evening News* echoed Billy Sunday: "I believe Christ would

Camp Curtin Memorial Church. *Courtesy of the Historic Harrisburg Association.*

expect his followers to go to war in a righteous cause." At the Camp Curtin Memorial Methodist Church, the Reverend A.S. Williams pointed out the reasons for intervention and "why it was necessary." An audience at Grace Methodist Episcopal heard Dr. Robert Bagnell preach "The Meaning of the War," asserting, "We have no real quarrel with the German people"; instead, "our battle was with the Hohenzollern dynasty and the ruling class of Prussia." Sermons stressed duty and loyalty: "Our Country's Call and the Answer We Should Give," "The Nation's Call" and "Doing Our Bit."

Old soldiers sought to serve. Post 58 of the Grand Army of the Republic (GAR) came forward, and ten thousand members of Howard L. Calder, No. 31, Veterans of Foreign Wars made known their availability.

Various organizations made themselves available. The Harrisburg Rifle Club offered its services. The West End Democratic Association stood firm for President Wilson. The Harrisburg Chapter of the Daughters of the American Revolution (DAR) flag waved and sang patriotic numbers. The Historical Society of Dauphin County heard speeches "to show the spirit of the people at the outbreak of the Revolutionary and the Civil War." In the Masonic Temple, the Perseverance Lodge, No. 21, Free and Accepted Masons dined and vocalized their love-of-country tunes. The Central Pennsylvania Homeopathic Medical Society volunteered.

Loyalty presented no dilemmas among Harrisburg's diverse elements, foreign-born or native. Serbians attending mass at South Second Street's Greek Orthodox church pledged adherence. On North Third Street, the Star of America, No. 113, Ancient and Illustrious Order Knights of Malta gave support. At the Pocoson tribe's wigwam, members of Native American clans gathered and shaped preparations for a patriotic parade.

The city anticipated "a great outburst of patriotism" when the onetime American ambassador to Berlin arrived. Arranged by the chamber of commerce, James W. Gerard's speech followed a parade. Charging that Germany schemed to strike the United States, he declared the country "owes it to humanity to plant the principles of democracy where they have been stamped out by Prussian militarism." An *Evening News* editorial, "The Facts from Mr. Gerard," confirmed "his confident conviction that America must go to war."

Harrisburg held a large procession on April 23 "to stimulate patriotism and recruiting," organized by civic clubs. An invitation went to former president Theodore Roosevelt. Led by marching bands, the 13,550 participants included veterans, state employees, women and high school students. The demonstration began at Front and Market Streets, advanced on Market to Fourth and, in turn, to Sixth, Seneca, Third, Hamilton and Second and ended at Chestnut. The *Evening News* opined the march might have been the greatest expression of fidelity to the country bestowed by city residents.

At war's outbreak, an excited city witnessed a hurry to the colors. Potential recruits numbered 13,835 in Harrisburg and 26,000 throughout Dauphin County. The army station at 325 Market Street attracted volunteers as young as fifteen and sixteen, as well as a mother delivering her son. Soon, area recruiting led the state, bestirred by a ballyhoo of whistles and bells. The *Evening News* demanded, "YOU! ENLIST TODAY! YOUR COUNTRY NEEDS YOU!" Harking to Lexington's skirmish and Paul Revere's ride, the city drew 26 volunteers within twenty-four hours. *The Scribb Family—They Live Right Here in Harrisburg* cartooned a child desiring to join the navy. Unfortunately, many enlistees failed physicals. They suffered disqualification. The *Evening News* looked to the inevitable. It editorialized support for conscription.

In response to the national emergency, the Red Cross established headquarters in the Hunter building at 206 Walnut Street. Amid pledges of aid, it met with national preparedness officials to unite under their leadership. The Civic Club volunteered its facilities. The Harrisburg Academy of Medicine extended affiliation. The Madrigal Club held a

Above: Patriotic parade promotes Red Cross recruitment. *From the* Evening News. *Courtesy of PennLive.*

Left: A summons from Uncle Sam. *From the* Evening News. *Courtesy of PennLive.*

Women seek Red Cross memberships. *From the* Evening News. *Courtesy of PennLive.*

fundraiser in Fahnestock Hall, inspired by the lyrisms "Comrades in Arms," "Sailor's Song" and "Cossack's War Song." A Bowman's store advertisement reminded the community, "When a catastrophe menaces...the world turns to the Red Cross...[to] lend support."

The Cross launched a membership drive. The Civic Club manned a booth to register joiners. Boy Scouts blanketed the area with placards and went door to door. A "flying squadron" of cars supporting "district captains" expedited the campaign that included "industrial canvassers." The press printed application forms and gave editorial backing. The *Evening News* implored Harrisburgers to affiliate and "do your 'bit.'" The *Telegraph*'s editorial "RED CROSS SLACKERS" scolded, "There is no age limit to enlistment in the Red Cross and there are none who are exempt for any other reason, except that they are too poor to join."

By April's end, the membership push had surpassed its goal. A patriotic parade gave the campaign a lift. Pennsylvania Railroad employees, 180 of them, signed on, as did 100 workers at the Blough Manufacturing Company. Spokespersons encouraged students to join. Contrary to hearsay that they would be unwelcome, African Americans could enroll. The Red Cross's ranks reached 5,500.

Throughout April, Harrisburg boosted the Cross. Retailers helped. Claster's Jewelry Store gifted a percentage of ten days' income. The Keeney's Cut Rate Flower Shops donated part of its gross earnings. Dives, Pomeroy and Stewart sold a cloth-enclosed speech by President Wilson for the organization's good. Others chipped in. The Keystone Chapter of the United States Daughters of 1812 promised contributions. The Authors' Club anticipated, "This year, on account of the war, very few big social functions will be given…for there is little doubt but that society will give all its time and energy to…Red Cross work." At a benefit, the John Harris Lodge, No. 193, Knights of Pythias traded packaged sugar at a reduced price. The Moorhead Knitting Company set up a group to fashion surgical needs. Church sermons held Cross-themed activities.

The Red Cross stepped up its services. It taught first aid and held hygienic sessions. In addition to classes, "women work[ed], making surgical supplies… rolling bandages [and] sewing hospital garments."

Wartime spending necessitated government borrowing. Twenty-four hours after the United States entered the conflict, the Commonwealth Trust Company on Market Street pitched, "We will gladly forward all such subscriptions." City sheets solicited public attention. The *Courier* prompted, "Your country needs you now…buy a bond or two." The *Telegraph* favored loans for partial payment of the war's cost and stated, "There is no question as to the desire of Americans to 'do their bit' in this way toward financing the war, and doubtless they will come forward as they have done before." The *Telegraph* also thought balancing bonds and taxes represented "good business," since upcoming "generations should bear their share of a debt to be incurred primarily for their benefit."

An emblem-studded city exuded a patriotic ambience. Mayor Ezra S. Meals designated "April 4, as Harrisburg Flag Day," asked for the banner's exhibition and proclaimed, "Ours is really ONE nation, devoted only to ONE flag and inhabited by a citizenry willing to pay whatever price may be necessary in order to protect the honor and maintain the dignity of our land."

Citizens came out for Flag Day. Retailers experienced a sudden demand for the colors. Railroaders adorned their work clothes with the Stars and Stripes. Students displayed Old Glory while vocalizing flag-waving lyrics. Emblem-draped automobiles and motorcycles roamed the roadways.

Workers loft flag at Central Iron and Steel. *From the* Harrisburg Telegraph. *Courtesy of PennLive.*

Newspapers urged the banner's showing. Prior to Flag Day, the *Courier* beckoned, "Show Your Colors." The *Evening News* repeated the sentiment four days later. The *Telegraph* instructed, "Here's Way to Fly Flag."

Old Glory propped for the foreign-born to demonstrate Americanism. The *Evening News* headlined: a naturalized Dane "Climbs 80-Foot Pole on Round House to Get Kink Out of Stars and Stripes." Italian railroaders elevated a flag in the Pennsylvania yards.

Flag raisings became common. Hoistings sprouted at the Central Iron and Steel Company, the Swift firm, the Lalance-Grosjean works, the Fort Hunter estate and the Public Service Bureau. Banner pitchmen exploited the market. The Kaufman store barked, "FLAGS FLAGS FLAGS for sale." Near the Market Street Subway, the Stationer and News Dealer yelped, "Flags! Show Your Patriotism" and "Carry a Flag in the Big Parade!"— adding, "We have them in all sizes—at all prices."

The Stars and Stripes seemed pervasive. It provided a love-of-country feeling at a Masonic temple dance. It ornamented veils, stockings and gloves. It highlighted a preacher's sermon. *The Scribb Family—They Live Right Here in Harrisburg* pictured a home flying a banner and a purchase reminder.

Verses enlisted Old Glory. Berton Braley poeticized:

Up with the flag! Up with the flag!
Up with the flag we love!
Till its colors flutter from every roof
And merge with the skies above,
And our eyes shall fill and our hearts shall thrill
With the joy that is always new
At the grand old sight of the red and white
And the stars in a field of blue.

And John Kemble chanted:

Unfurl! Unfurl!
Oh, Flag of Mine!
And let the wide world take
This message from your flapping folds,
"America's awake!"

"The Star-Spangled Banner" imbued patriotic feeling. The *Courier* printed a front-page copy accompanied by Francis Scott Key's portrait. The *Evening News* followed with the anthem's lyrics and notes. Before the Bowman's store's employees, the Reverend Bagnell called Harrisburgers to arms, and a performance of Key's composition "keyed the audience to a high pitch of enthusiasm."

The symbolic Uncle Sam joined the fray. A cartoon titled "Aroused" showed him determined.

Throwbacks inspired. The Spirit of '76 invoked the Revolution. The United States Daughters of 1812 heard a speech about the presidents "Washington and Lincoln." The *Evening News* recalled Admiral David Farragut and, on a take-off of the Spanish-American War's *Maine*, suggested, "Remember the *Lusitania!*" for the British liner sunk by a German U-boat. The paper hawked *America: The Land We Love* as a "great, patriotic, American book" and promised, "It takes you from the days of the discovery of America in 1492, through every phase of its progress and development up to the present day."

Music told of duty's summons. The *Telegraph* thought the patriotic parade should revive "Tramp, Tramp, Tramp, the Boys Are Marching." J.H. Troup Music House on Market Square sold Columbia's recordings of "America," "The Star-Spangled Banner," "Story of Old Glory," "Call of a Nation," "Uncle

Sammy's Boys in Camp," "Rally to the Call Boys" and "American Patrol." The *Telegraph* carried the "Battle Hymn of the Republic" on its front page.

Harrisburg, an integral element in the national economy, suffered scarcities. Industry begged for labor and tried to entice workers. Hard-pressed railroads failed to deliver. Coal came up short, and its dealers wanted customers to request their needs. H.M. Kelley and Company warned, "Order whatever coal you need now—don't wait and run the risk of not being able to get any." "Under no circumstances," cautioned the United Ice and Coal Company, "should the holdholder wait."

Agriculture lacked hands. Dauphin County and the chamber of commerce, trying to recruit, sloganized, "Do a day's work on the farm." Suffragists and students promised aid. Pleas went to the Rotary Club to enroll tillers. The *Evening News* queried, "Why not a vacation on a farm, working? [Since] the days of indolence and senseless luxury are past in America [and] the war has demanded its 'bit' of the people." In late April, public school teachers met to consider employing upper-grade youth on unoccupied plots and neighboring farmlands.

Harrisburg awoke to the necessity of agricultural productivity. "In modern war," affirmed an *Evening News* editorial, "the plow is as potent a weapon as the 16-inch gun." Newspapers spearheaded a war garden program. The *Telegraph* promised the Harrisburg Benevolent Association seed for tillage, declaring it was time to act and not talk: "Plant a food garden and do your part otwards [*sic*] the economic victory." Advice suggested vegetables, row separation and cultivation deepness. The paper urged high yields, imploring residents to "help feed yourself" and "waste no food." The comic strip Scribb family started a potato garden and warded off marauding chickens. The *Evening News* chipped in, printing plot applications and running "Your Own Garden," a series. The columnist, pen-named A. Gardner, advised about fertilizer, crops and hoeing.

The chamber of commerce hummed. Its Agricultural Committee, chaired by Donald McCormick, sought unused land for transfer to city cultivators. Unfortunately, some landholders slowed the release of their property. Nevertheless, businesses helped. The Harrisburg Silk Mill and the Capital City Realty contributed ground. Miller Brothers and Company, another realtor, listed a Bellevue Park dwelling "with garden plot." Tractor dealerships donated plowing services.

Through the chamber, Shirley Watts, war garden superintendent, parceled allotments. He assigned 150 plots. To meet the crisis, Watts intended residents to cut living expenses, enjoy physical activity and save foodstuffs. In

Overalled woman cultivates war garden. *From the* Evening News. *Courtesy of PennLive.*

stipulating ground regulations, he ruled applicants must furrow in less than a week and supply their own seedlings. Weeding and tilling slackness, Watts added, "forfeits the right to [the] plot." The Agriculture Committee had to approve parcel transfers.

Thieves plagued the cultivators. A letter to the *Evening News* asked "Is [there] not a stronger law to punish offenders who steal another man's crops?"

War gardeners needed assistance. The *Telegraph* lobbied for federal "daylight savings" legislation "to pass as a war emergency measure," since when "home-gardening…light is essential." The sheet inquired, "Who will come forward with money enough to pay for an instructor in backyard gardening for the people of Harrisburg who want to help increase the supply of vegetables the coming summer?" Expertise did come when the Pennsylvania State College's J.B. Scherrer scheduled a talk at the Tech High School.

Crops conferred attributes. Caloric peas and beans built brawn. Potatoes reigned as expense economizers with the "food problem, one of the greatest of the war." Eugene H. Grubb and W.S. Guilford's *The Potato* and Edith Loring Fullerton's *How to Make a Vegetable Garden* published spud tips for patriots.

Prohibitionists lambasted grain's conversion to drink. "The greatest waste to-day in America," charged the Women's Christian Temperance Union's (WCTU) Ella Broomell, "is the waste which is brought about by the liquor traffic." She claimed, "It brings crime, insanity, disease, inefficiency and degeneracy in its train and it will take many generations to overcome its curse and blight." Cereal conservers desired signees to make the wagon pledge. In a letter to the *Telegraph*, a mother wrote, "I have wondered why this Nation, which already is greatly concerned about its food supply, should keep on wasting its grain in the manufacture of liquor." She mused, "Is this country run and dominated by the brewers and liquor men?"

Food prices spiked as stocks shrank. Grocers warned against laying up and sloganed, "Buy as you eat." A woman accused producers of withholding provisions from markets: "It is bad enough that the price of food should be increased through a possible shortage of supply, but it is outrageous that selfish men will endeavor to corner the market by offering a somewhat higher price no [*sic*] that they may profit by a still higher price a few months hence, buyers say." The *Telegraph* begged, "Don't hoard food," heeding the "result of housekeepers piling up huge quantities of salt, meats, canned goods, sugar, flour, etc., will be to make provision supplies even lower than they are and force prices higher."

Newspapers mustered homemakers. The *Evening News* stressed food conservation and concluded, "In the final analysis it is up to the women of the nation." War offered the moment to avoid waste and exercise saving. After all, "The housewife largely controls the home budget and expenditures, and the women of the United States can save millions of dollars for the common good," echoed the *Courier*.

Wartime appeals summoned teens. Mrs. William Henderson, president of the Harrisburg Civic Club, spoke for Red Cross enlistment. Mrs. Maurice E. Finney decried sickly military recruits and pleaded "for both boys and girls to have clean thoughts in order that they may have clean and healthy bodies." She hoped girls would glance away from "a boy who did not try to lead such a life that would make him an asset and not a liability to his country." Captain H.M. Stine counseled maidens to scorn pacifists. He also encouraged Red Cross enrollment and food preparation study. Instructors taught Harrisburg Academy pupils marching drill, a precursor for military camp.

War altered children's garb and games. Dives, Pomeroy and Stewart retailed seaman caps for imaginary military play. The store likewise advertised Boy Scouts' footgear "to better enable the youngsters to render the service that their young hearts and enthusiasm prompt." Cartoons illustrated kids marching and executing a spy.

Pooches paraded their patriotism. The *Telegraph* segmented their fidelity. "Kaiser," a bulldog, pouted until his owner changed his ignominious name. "Miss Patsy," a red-and-white spaniel, wore a blue bow to embody national colors. "Teddy," a fox terrier, shunned sauerkraut and switched to a milky broth. "Yankee Doodle," a dalmatian, cut a rug to the ditty of his name.

America encountered "a German problem." The 1910 census counted eight million Germanics. Their answer to the country's call remained dubious. An anti-German hysteria erupted nationwide and engulfed Harrisburg. Gossip spread about the city concerning German residents. Police rescued a tipsy devotee of Teutons from an angry crowd. Another, Peter Hoffman, owner of an Uptown bakery, "denied that he had exhibited a picture of the German Kaiser in the window of his store, that he had pulled a young girl's ears for twitting him about Germany, and that his absence from his market stand last Saturday was the result of his being in jail." He declared "full sympathy with the United States" and volunteered himself and his bakery for service. The accusations tormented his Mrs. into sickness.

The press stirred the enmity. Editorials denounced Berlin's Hohenzollern rulers, backed their demise and favored democracy. Cartoons foretold dynastic doom. A drawing of Napoléon Bonaparte and Kaiser Wilhelm suggested they looked alike and would experience the same end.

Teutonic inklings received rebukes. A physician claimed state-proposed health insurance "was devised by [a] German-obsessed propagandist" and endorsed by "the academic class known as sociologists—a Germany-obsessed class of theorists." An out-of-town restaurateur removed the term *Hamburgers* from his menu. To eliminate the Germanic tinge, he introduced "Harrisburgers." The *Telegraph* reduced the German ruler to an insect. Demeaning the Kaiser as fly-like, it portrayed him strewing calamity and cataclysm in his wake. "Treat him kindly and he plots your ruin," appended the paper, and "so does the fly, with his poisoned feet and his germ-laden wings." Adding to the alarm, Washington's local Department of Justice reported disturbing news. In central Pennsylvania, there had been "a surprising [*sic*] large number of acts of disloyalty."

While jeering Germans, Harrisburgers fraternized with Frenchmen. Pennsylvania proclaimed April 26 "France Day." The Tricolor flew beside the Stars and Stripes to commemorate the Marquis de Lafayette's arrival in America to espouse the Revolution. The occasion bore witness "to the sincere friendship and deep obligation its citizens feel for France." At Central High,

Time elapsing for Germany. *From the* Evening News. *Courtesy of PennLive.*

the French War Orphan Fund gathered moneys. The poem "To France" by Corrine Roosevelt Robinson, published in *Collier's*, set a comradely tone:

We, who have loved the France of old,
The France that gave us Lafayette
Now deeper still our poignant
And tenderer tenthousandfold.
Our youth has shed its blood for you
Because your valor wrung the heart,
You, who have borne so brave a part—
You builded better than you knew.
If we, of alien race and tongue,
Shall face once more the God of War,
What you have been and what you are
Shall be the flame before us flung
Your gallant heart shall strengthen ours
To reach unswerving toward the goal;
Through you, perchance, a newborn soul,
Unrecognized within us flokers
Ah, France, who gave us Lafayette,
When we were scarred as you are now,
Before your wounds we humbly bow
And bless you for our deeper debt!

The war brought forth literature. Recalling the nation's Russian ally, Dives, Pomeroy and Stewart carried Rolland Romain's *Tolstoy* and the novelist's *Anna Karenina*. Fernand van Langenhove's *The Growth of a Legend* related German atrocities in Belgium. War readiness and military routine filled the pages of Arthur Bullard's *Mobilizing America*; J.W. Muller's *The A.B.C. of National Defense*, *Field Service Regulations United States Army* and *Infantry Drill Regulations United States Army*; Ralph Earle's *Life at the U.S. Naval Academy*; and Colonel Jennings C. Wise's *The Call of the Republic*, which favored universal military training.

Historical works appeared. Residents could scan *With Americans of Past and Present Days* by J.J. Jusserand and *Moderning the Monroe Doctrine* by Charles H. Sherrill.

Dissimilar decisions greeted the national emergency. The Motor Club of Harrisburg shelved its yearly banquet, yet the community scheduled track meets.

Surprisingly, heads turned to the postwar. Speaking before the Salesmanship Club of Harrisburg, B.F. Sprankle alerted merchants "to train every saleperson [*sic*] up to the highest possible efficiency, because the competition will be unusually keen when the energies of Europe are again diverted into the commercial channels." In the spirit of Orrine's pharmaceutical—advertised in the press as a home cure for habitual drinking that "destroys all desire for whiskey, beer, or other alcoholic stimulants"—H.R. Bender, a pastor, "declared that national prohibition will surely follow the close of the world-wide war."

Warfare had become total. Countries mobilized all their resources. Civilians as well as combatants served. In a summons, the *Telegraph* prompted everyone to "do his bit," informing readers "that the safety of the nation does not lie solely with the government, but as well with the individuals that make up the government." In a speech to Bowman's workers, Dr. Bagnell stressed, "This is not a war fought alone by soldiers but it is a war of the people."

Nevertheless, the *Courier* encouraged Harrisburgers to exist as before. Admitting the necessity of economizing, the paper recommended unaltered everyday living: "We must live a little more closely, and work a little harder and save a little more, and be a little more thoughtful of the other fellow," and yet "continue…as nearly as possible as we do during normal times."

Chapter 2

SUMMONS

May–July 1917

Harrisburg pivoted into action, facilitating federal and local war measures. Organizations and citizens volunteered. Entrepreneurs pitched in. Arms contracts boomed its economy. Meanwhile, residents adjusted to the emergency as officials confronted attendant problems.

The initial Liberty loan, a bond campaign, got under way. National authorities targeted the $2 billion mark. The city aimed for $2 million, later increased to $4 million. By mid-June, it had exceeded the $4 million goal.

Spearheaded by the chamber of commerce, businesses displayed posters, hoping to attract the "small investor." The Harrisburg Clearing House Association met with out-of-town brokers to establish soliciting committees "in every local store and factory, in churches and fraternities, and from house to house throughout the city." The Rotary Club gave support. The clergy sermonized assistance.

Ads boosted bonds. The Commonwealth Trust Company questioned, "Are you patriotic?" Livingston's on Market Square announced, "Our government is about to issue bonds," and "it is a duty of citizenship…to buy." Kaufman's store implored, "Buy a Liberty bond," and Dives, Pomeroy and Stewart jingled:

> *You believe in liberty, don't you?*
> *Well this is the land of liberty*
> *So buy a Liberty bond.*

A choice: fetters or freedom. *From the* Harrisburg Telegraph. *Courtesy of PennLive.*

Slogans peppered Harrisburg. An appeal for bond salesmen admonished, "Don't be a slacker." Helped along by "flying squadron" hawkers and department store booths, the campaign's message gave a dire warning: "If you don't come across the Germans will."

Promoters touted a Liberty loan's advantages. The Clearing House Association's Donald McCormick claimed it was the most secure venture. The *Harrisburg Telegraph*'s "Evening Chat," a regular column, approved of many families buying their children bonds.

The community turned out. Mayor Charles A. Miller issued a proclamation. The Zembo Temple; the Harrisburg Aeria, No. 122; the Fraternal Order of Eagles; the Reily Hose Company No. 10; the Hamilton School; the Firemen's Union; the West End Social Club; and the Harrisburg Ladies' Nest of Owls No. 1930 subscribed. The Dauphin County Bar Association endorsed bond investments. The Boy Scouts scurried about selling.

Industry contributed. The Bethlehem Steel Company, the Harrisburg Pipe and Pipe Bending Company, the Central Iron and Steel Company, the Pennsylvania Railroad and other firms eased the way for employee bond purchases. The Bell Telephone Company promised to handle subscriptions. At the Elliott-Fisher plant, 199 workers invested in Liberty loans.

The bond push entered theaters. With daily movie attendance at 10 percent of the nation's population, film ads reached a large audience.

The *Telegraph* branded anti-war advocates treasonous during the Liberty loan push, akin to Civil War–era "copperheads." The paper wanted their names made public and believed "concentration camps for alien enemies are the place for such."

Levity came in for rebuke. Charles E. Murray, a Third Ward alderman, jokingly questioned why he should purchase a bond. He then remarked "that he would rather use the money to buy an automobile and then smash it up than subscribe to the loan." After being reported to federal authorities, he publicly asked forgiveness, pledged his loyalty and procured $1,000 in bonds.

Frank V. Vanderlip, a New York banker visiting to encourage subscriptions, extolled the city's effort: "Your organization is the best I have seen anywhere." The *Evening News* editorialized self-gratulation with the headline "Harrisburg Shows the Nation."

Near the drive's end, a commotion took place. Fire station alarms sounded simultaneously with Philadelphia's Liberty Bell to call the citizenry to support the war and buy bonds.

In early May, brisk military volunteering set a record for the city's region. A North Front Street resident, Russell T. Whitson, informed former president

Military recruiting at the Majestic Theater. *From the* Harrisburg Telegraph. *Courtesy of PennLive.*

Theodore Roosevelt "that he is willing and ready to join the division of the army the Colonel is preparing to take to France." Student athletes dropped out of school to enter the navy. Recruiters turned away two thirteen-year-old girls offering their service.

Fanfare accompanied recruiting. On Market Square, the state band enticed through instrumental allure. Spokesmen added flag-waving rhetoric. As a consequence, the Market Street recruiting center received an onrush for the reserves.

The city was, at one point, seen as a recruitment hub, but enlistments experienced ups and downs. Nevertheless, local motorists found the national guard's truck unit attractive. "Recruiting Week," with ample patriotic music and an excited assembly, endeavored to promote enrollments. In fact, many youths of the Steven's Memorial Bible class planned to enlist. Recruiters realized the national draft would offset their efforts.

Recruitment aid came from many directions. The Orpheum Theater hosted the Rotary Club's support. The Regent Theater screened *The Man Who Was Afraid*, a film about a "slacker" transformed into a hero once he joined the army. The City Grays' Veteran Association promised to look after recruits' kin. The *Evening News* publicized recruiting station sites, and the *Telegraph*'s *Bringing Up Father* illustrated a youth considering military service. A song reminded, "It's time for every boy to be a soldier."

Voluntary enlistments failed to satisfy manpower needs. A draft became necessary. On May 18, President Wilson approved the Selective Service Act.

The legislation, carried out by local volunteers, registered men ages twenty-one to thirty.

Harrisburg encouraged registration. The press editorialized backing and opined the threatening, "There's a COME-BACK for those who HANG-BACK." Protestant and Catholic churches urged compliance. The mayor issued a proclamation, citizens offered to serve and employers released their employees. High school students debated conscription and resolved in its favor. Saloonkeepers shut their doors in support.

Registration succeeded. City fire bells sounded, calling young men. Railroad workers and baseball players signed up. Registrants included the imprisoned, the insane, the "deaf and dumb" and "hoboes." Interpreters helped with the foreign-born. Dauphin County counted 14,193 enlistees, and Harrisburg listed nearly 7,000.

Registrars administered without interference. But some enrollees gave false residences. Authorities warned dodgers of arrest and incarceration. A North Street youth swallowed acid, fearing the draft's impact on his mother's health.

Selective service provided exemptions. Quaker brethren qualified for deferrals. However, Democrats charged Governor Martin G. Brumbaugh, a Republican, of misusing his appointive authority by assigning "party hacks" to exemption panels. Brumbaugh appeared to enact an intentional strategy

Draft registration at an uptown fire station. *From the* Evening News. *Courtesy of PennLive.*

"of fastening Republican dominated boards on all the state's most loyally Democratic counties."

The law deferred those with dependents. Several regions saw a rush to the altar. Yet Harrisburg recorded a meager rise in nuptials, demonstrating "that there are not many 'slacker' marriages here."

The city had installed draft boards by early July. Selectee serial numbers emanated from the press and postings. But local youths escaped the first call, since voluntary enlistments met the area's manpower quota.

Harrisburg mulled over a nickname for the soldier. The *Evening News* asked for ideas. The well-regarded "Sammies" (a descriptive disliked by General John Pershing, commander of the American Expeditionary Force) became preferred. Suggestions included "Yanks" and "Braves," as well as "the Boys of the U.S.A.," "the Patriotic Sons of the American World," "Bravo Boys," "Yellowjackets" and "Liberty Boys."

Harrisburg's economy took off. Industry, transportation and retail thrived. Financial clearings rose by the millions. Demand for goods and labor outstripped supply. Chamber of commerce chief executive David E. Tracy (also president of the Harrisburg Pipe and Pipe Bending Company) remarked, "We are very busy and have been and there are many unfilled orders."

Government contracts spurred the boom. The Harrisburg Manufacturing and Boiler Company agreed to build a sixty-ton turbine for the Panama Canal. The Central Iron and Steel Company manufactured steel plates for the navy, the Bethlehem Steel plant signed an accord for firearms and Tracy's Pipe and Pipe Bending firm produced four-inch shells. The Lochie works hired over sixty workers to satisfy the ferro-manganese market. With its many companies, including Elliott-Fisher, South Harrisburg emerged as a manufacturing axis.

The growth necessitated augmentation. The Bell Telephone Company of Pennsylvania financed extensions to augment the upgraded Central Iron and Steel mill. Still, the Harrisburg Pipe and Pipe Bending executives rejected competing for an aircraft contract, since retooling would be expensive. Instead, it would concentrate on existing obligations.

Construction sagged. Builders encountered expense add-ons, material shortages and labor deficiencies aggravated by wartime. Nonetheless, heavy machinery broke ground for the Walnut Street's Penn-Harris Hotel.

Harrisburg upheld its patriotic reputation. To ensure loyalty, citizens who were too young or too old for the military established a home guard of over two hundred men in four companies. Reportedly, "The object of the organization will be to support the administration and make it dangerous to indulge in any pro-German talk or activity." The city also requested state financing for an armory to aid the raising of national guard units.

Officials paid heed to home front cleanliness. Plans developed to collect wintertime's trash. Citing sanitary and health sources, the *Telegraph* advanced a "call for municipal ownership and operation." The *Evening News* seconded this with, "There is no question whatever that the city should assume direct control of the collection and disposal of garbage and ashes."

By early May, the chamber of commerce had assigned hundreds of garden lots. Tillers received land at Third and Emerald Streets and at Sixth beyond Division. Wildwood Park contained five acres of plots. By mid-June, six hundred gardeners farmed twenty-six acres, exhausting the available land.

Encouragement abounded. The *Telegraph* publicized tips "giving expert advice on garden work." It advertised the Schell's Seed Store as the "headquarters for the patriotic army of the garden and farm." The paper made known *How to Make the Garden Pay*, a book by Edward Morrison and Charles Thomas Brues, and Idea D. Bennett's *The Vegetable Garden*.

Food called to duty. *From the* Harrisburg Telegraph. *Courtesy of PennLive.*

Harrisburgers stepped up. Pupils and teachers green-thumbed. Stevens Church boys cultivated. Women and families came out. Boy Scouts volunteered, and Anna Hamilton Wood composed "The Scout with the Hoe":

> *His voice is as music to mothering ears,*
> *It was lately we comforted baby-boy tears,*
> *Yet behold, over night this young stripling appears,*
> *This lad with the hoe!*
> *He has sternly discarded the little-boy ways*
> *For these are important and red letter days*
> *A Boy Scout gives of labor and service that pays,*
> *This lad with the hoe!*
> *The country needs food? Then the young back will bend*
> *To seeding and weeding, a means to an end,*
> *And old Mother Nature is even a friend*
> *To the lad with the hoe.*
> *Young muscles grow firmer, young characters true*
> *And simple and wholesome the deeds that they do.*
> *Life teachers her meaning while God's face shines through*
> *On the lad with the hoe.*
> *Sturdy and straight he becomes, clean of limb,*
> *And clean is the tender young spirit of him*
> *Withheld from the snare of the street corner sin,*
> *This Scout with the hoe.*

Given the national emergency, Sunday gardening seemed warranted. A Lexington, Massachusetts minister shut his chapel to allow tilling by his brethren. A man working eleven hours daily Monday through Saturday should "be permitted, and in fact encouraged, to spend as much of the Sabbath in his garden 'doing his bit' as his conscience dictates."

Unshielded plots faced hazards. Bugs, dogs and chickens trespassed. Heavy rains drenched gardens. Weeds sprouted. Drunks damaged, and vandals thieved. The hoers welcomed protection. Residents considered recruiting garden watchers. Quail and blackbirds gobbled insects. Schell's Seed Store marketed a louse-eradicating spray. The *Evening News*'s "Doing My Bit" and the *Telegraph*'s "Crop Pest Letter," regular columns, clued readers in about bug banishment. The latter paper and the Harrisburg Benevolent Association offered rewards for the capture of looters. Governor Brumbaugh sanctioned legislation fining or jailing predators.

Through the chamber of commerce's oversight, Shirley Watts reported a large output. Potatoes led in quantity. Harrisburgers escaped the high dealers' prices that cornered the spud supply.

Wartime needs and poor yields squeezed the food supply. In May, President Wilson selected Herbert Hoover to run the Food Administration. Hoover repudiated rationing but established prices. Hoping to exploit patriotic volunteerism, he urged abnegation and teamwork: "We propose to mobilize the spirit of self-denial and self-sacrifice in this country." His agency created regulations that determined earnings at each market level.

Harrisburg expressed backing for victuals saving. Newspaper editors, a columnist, a cartoon and a sugar company messaged belt-tightening. Grocers, restaurants, hotels, bakers and the library lent support. Pastors sermonized "Food Shortage and War Bullets," "Food Conservation" and "Helping Win with Bread."

Stopgaps alleviated scarcities. Consumers prioritized food products over tobacco crops. They employed dishes without meat, oleomargarine for butter, cheese for steak and honey for sugar. Makeshifts included "war cake" (without butter and eggs), rusk and dandelion soup. Self-restraint dictated slicing only the bread one intended to consume, restaurant "war portions" (limited amounts) and canning without sugar.

Jane Gilbert suggested the "Herbert Hoover Sandwich":

The latest kind of sandwich—
An appetite improver—
For use in meatless, wheatless homes,
Is called the "Herbert Hoover."
Slice thin the bread of idleness
(The less of it the better)
And toast on patriotic fire—
The spirit and the letter.
For butter, which for present use
Is very much disputed,
The oil of gladness you will find
Can well be substituted.
Spread with some conservative jam—
This nice economixture
Will also spread on Uncle Sam
The grin that is a fixture.
Favor enthusiastically;

Garnish red, white and blue;
It's easy to make and to digest—and
Washington likes it, too.

Canning saved foodstuffs. A campaign prompted residents to collect containers "for putting up fruits, preserves, jellies, jams and fruit juices." The Civic Club's Red Cross organization scheduled an educational exhibition, as did the Dauphin County agricultural office in association with the chamber of commerce. The *Telegraph* alerted homemakers to a federal Department of Agriculture farm report, "Home Canning by the One-Period Cold-Pack Method." For the general welfare, the paper pushed women to mail their "favorite receipts and methods to the editor and they will be placed before thousands of other housewives."

Bakeries trading stale bread for fresh loaves wasted wheat. National agencies prodded bakers to stop the exchange. Schmidt's promised compliance. Bakery owners met in the Columbus Hotel and discussed the relationship between middlemen and retailers. The attendees sought the means of baking "the correct amount so that it will be unnecessary…for the baker to take back from the grocer all bread which the latter is unable to sell." They decided to do away with the practice.

The Civic Club. *Courtesy of the Historical Society of Dauphin County, Harrisburg, Pennsylvania.*

The food-saving push enlisted women. Ward captains picked precinct lieutenants to distribute pledges door to door, aided by Boy Scouts, Red Cross units, Camp Fire Girls and car owners. Housewives promised to cut wastage and reduce snacking. Obligations called for dining wheatless once a day, saving a bread loaf weekly and limiting meat servings. Officials discouraged cooking with butter and promoted produce and fish consumption. They urged food purchases from neighborhood retailers and believed cutbacks could lower expenses. Signees rallied behind the "gospel of the clean plate."

A columnist favored a military-style regimen. Albert Barrett Sayres proposed housekeepers establish a seven-day allotment, not to be violated, then persevere by knowing the means to impose the lines of conduct to eating routines. Reflection and regard for particulars would ration the family intake. Enrollment began on July 9, helped by Boy Scouts distributing hundreds of placards with the dictum, "I need you, too." By July 21, enlistees numbered 11,160 from the thousands who had pledged.

A resident complained about wives carrying the whole onus, since men wasted more, adding, "Let the men sign a pledge to give up, not necessaries, but the harmful things, such as tobacco, cigars, pool playing, Coca-Cola and beer, and turn that money into the family purse."

The food crisis energized drys. *Telegraph* editorials deplored drink's "waste of food" and endorsed congressional restraints on manufacturing cereals into alcohol. It printed a letter asking, "Why should any considerable quantity of grain be made into 'booze' during the war—or any time for that matter?" The WCTU joined the chorus of protest, denouncing sustenance's diversion into brew.

Harrisburg's Fink Brewing Company countered, stating that France thought beer possessed health qualities and England licensed spirits, but it failed to dissuade. Women's pledge cards carried dry convictions:

> *Liquor, tobacco and chewing gum are the first three things that ought to be done away with.*

> *Will stop waste in our home without hesitation if you'll stop grinding grain into liquid damnation!*

> *I sign this card with an earnest protest against any grain being used in making beer!*

> *Always have I conserved food. Would the government conserve by prohibition the Lord would bless us.*

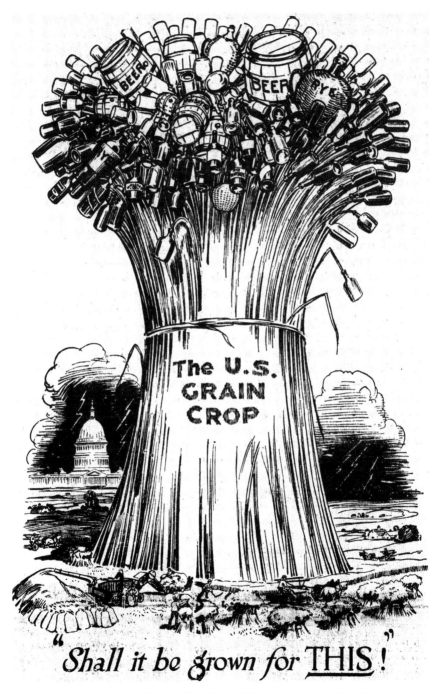

Don't waste grain on booze. *From the* Harrisburg Telegraph. *Courtesy of PennLive.*

Harrisburg Public Library. *Courtesy of Christine Lauver at the Dauphin County Library System.*

The Harrisburg Public Library on Front and Walnut Streets circulated food facts. It carried reading material concerning canning and cultivation. It also collected advisories, such as Alfred W. McCann's *Thirty-Cent Bread*, which warned, "Without regulation…we shall have bread cards and soup kitchens within a year," and Mary S. Brown's *Three Reasons for a Vegetarian Diet*, a pamphlet anticipating days without meat.

A patriotic halo topped sauerkraut. Considering cabbage's bountiful harvest, the state agricultural department recommended its consumption. Sauerkraut stood as a treat in Pennsylvania and served its food-preserving goals: "Beating back the German efforts to starve us out with waves of steam from pots of boiling sauerkraut is our idea of combining patriotism with pleasure."

The Red Cross made ready. A membership drive, aided by a booth at the Pennsylvania Railroad Station and augmented by Elliott-Fisher workers, swelled sign-ons to eleven thousand by June. Repeated pleas reached out for volunteers. Hundreds of women answered the call.

The Cross needed funds. On June 2's Tag Day, 1,500 schoolchildren canvassed. Donors received lapel markers. Silk banners ornamented classrooms soliciting the most money. Youngsters pocketed rewards of as much as fifty cents. The collections financed surgical bandages.

On June 21, Red Cross officials mounted a three-day fundraiser, aiming to realize $100,000 as the local contribution for the national organization's kitty. President Wilson proclaimed a Red Cross Week, beginning on June

18, and the *Telegraph* relabeled a Sunday's "Bunker Hill Day" as "Red Cross Sunday." The *Evening News* sloganized, "Be a backer, not a slacker," and advised, "Every Harrisburg dollar put into the Red Cross fund is as good as a bullet." Liberty loan campaigners and Boy Scout teams tramped door to door. The Doutrich's store promoted the drive, and the Harrisburg Trust offered a dividend. By June 23, the undertaking had attained $37,406 beyond its goal.

Innovations smoothed Red Cross operations. The local chapter assigned women motorists to its messenger service. These women, garbed in khaki, took car repair classes scheduled with automobile dealers. They chauffeured personnel and materials to neighboring subsidiaries. In addition, the Harrisburg Light and Power Company gifted electrical engine connections to sewing machines, thereby easing the labor of seamsters.

Red Cross activities multiplied. The organization gathered books and magazines for the military, requesting help in collecting clipped press and periodical articles about recent events, comics, illustrations and athletics and suggesting "that the 'lighter vein' be sought rather than the serious." Volunteers produced hundreds of medical dressings and contemplated fashioning soldiers' kits. First aid classes continued, and food seminars began. The Red Cross's Committee on Civilian Aid, or "War Friends," planned relief for servicemen's kin. Finally, aware of sentries' discomfort in stormy weather, the chapter provided a shelter for bridge sentinels.

The Red Cross auto corps dressed in newly fashioned outfits. *From the* Evening News. *Courtesy of PennLive.*

The Red Cross auto unit learns mechanics. *From the* Evening News. *Courtesy of PennLive.*

Churches threw themselves into war work. For instance, they programed Red Cross benefits. The Ohev Sholom Temple held a dance, Grace Methodist Episcopal put on a concert highlighting Joseph Haydn's "Creation" and the Otterbein United Brethren performed "Onward Christian Soldiers" and the "Red Cross Scarf Drill," the latter synchronized by a dozen girls. The Lutheran Woman's League created a Red Cross unit. The Stevens Memorial Methodist congregation planned Cross lectures and assistance, while its women intended to stitch.

Churches stood behind the chapter's $100,000 push. Ministers resurrected Luke's parable of the Good Samaritan to spirit donations. The Society of Friends, despite its exemption from military service, gave support.

Clergy kept in mind the advent of war, preaching sermons about "The Patriot at Home," "My Country," "America and the Brotherhood of Nations," "The Gospel in War Times" and "The Faith of a Soldier." The Sixth and Forster Streets' Messiah Lutheran parish offered "a special service of prayer for 'Our Country,' in the present crisis."

Pine Street Presbyterian Boy Scouts did a good deed. They unexpectedly delivered tasty pastries to sentries at the Rockville Bridge.

The national emergency activated the grassroots. Diverse groups and individuals contributed to the city's war efforts. The business-oriented demonstrated patriotism. The chamber of commerce met to explore manifold duties. The Pennsylvania Railroad café donated fabric to the Red Cross. Its women's war relief unit planned a dance.

Public-minded associations responded. The Civic Club advanced Red Cross membership in the schools and contributed funds to the Young Men's Christian Association (YMCA). The Cross likewise benefited from the monetary generosity of the Author's Club, the Story Telling League's library event and the Knights of Pythias's sewing machine gift. A Cubical Club gathering voiced a love of patriotic music. Penn State alumni heard loyalty talks. The Rotary Club gave "wrist watches, dollar bills, cigars, cigarettes and chewing gum" to military camp departees.

Welfare organizations bustled. The Young Women's Christian Association (YWCA) scheduled first aid classes. Its Commonweal Club stopped programs to make room for Red Cross activities. A reading and musical performance in the YWCA's John Y. Boyd Hall aided the Cross. At the behest of the Civic Club and through the bestowal of residents, the YMCA garnered nearly $7,000 for its "National Three Million Dollar War Work Fund." At the Fifteenth and Vernon Streets school, the East Harrisburg WCTU established a Red Cross adjunct.

The school district got involved. Forney Elementary participated in a Colonial Dames of America competition speaking to "what it means to be a true American." Central High started a first aid class. Camp Curtin and Tech High helped the Red Cross.

Young lassies showed their love of country. Camp Fire Girls raised funds for an ambulance. At the Cross's urging, women solicited money to purchase tobacco for soldiers.

Minorities came through. Jews contributed $5,100 for their famished kindred in Europe. The Carlo Alberto Lodge, No. 272, of the Order of the Sons of Italy joined the Red Cross.

Individuals stepped forward. Charles H. Crampton recruited African American women for the Cross. Mrs. T. Edward Munce labored on materials, and Mrs. Howard E. Moses held a fete, earning thirty-one dollars for the local chapter.

Entertainment lent enthusiasm to endeavors. The Pennsylvania Railroad Woman's Division of War Relief organized its July dance at the Nineteenth and Derry Streets home of Mr. and Mrs. Samuel F. Dunkle. On the Red Cross's behalf, the Edna Santamaria School of Dancing and the Moorhead

Harrisburg's Tech High. *From the* Sunday Patriot-News. *Courtesy of PennLive.*

Choral Society staged shows. The Cross similarly benefited from a baseball game, a golf tournament and a gun shoot. At a North Second Street residence, card playing also supported the chapter.

Harrisburg befriended soldiers. Baseball games welcomed them free of charge. The YMCA invited them its washroom and rest areas without payment. It also entertained troops at Fahnestock Hall. Its women prepared a festive sendoff. The Harrisburg Newsboy's Association bid farewell to one of their own, Sam Koplovitz, and, from their home, Mr. and Mrs. C.S. Wilson of Linden Street celebrated the departure of their son, Ray. An Ammunition Train Truck Company set out amid a procession and much fanfare.

Newspapers carried suggested amenities. Dives, Pomeroy and Stewart advertised the useful: toilet packs, sewing bags, first aid kits, mirrors and money belts. The *Telegraph* thought its secondhand issues might be given to lonesome sentries. The *Evening News* column "Doing My Bit" urged correspondence and tobacco.

Women answered the call. The labor shortage offered employment opportunities. The Pennsylvania Railroad hired women for office work. The Harrisburg Railways Company maintained male-manned trolleys but thought the opposite sex might eventually substitute. Nurse graduates found hospital work. The Auto Transportation School taught women motoring and automobile upkeep. Large numbers took classes. The South Market Square School of Commerce pitched, "Your country needs you, too," in an appeal to the "daughters of America." The military attracted one. Penn Street's Helen Schaeffer joined the naval reserve, thinking women "should share with men the burdens of war as well as alleviate their wounds and make them comfortable."

Yet officials disallowed women marching in parades. Some wondered why.

Women performed war tasks. They toiled in gardens. They helped the Red Cross. Comic strips pictured them taking an interest in flying and joining local defense. Nevertheless, an *Evening News* editorial, conceding women's "bravery and sacrifices," suggested their frailty. Proclaiming, "Standing in street cars is good for men [but] it isn't good for women," the paper proposed, "Let's organize a Strap-Hangers' League for Patriotic Service, with the slogan 'Have my seat, madam!'" Regardless, women became assertive. Some wanted the right to vote.

Soldiers and sailors craved correspondence. Columnist Annie Laurie discouraged writing to people one was unacquainted with by curtly asking, "Are you just silly girls?" She added, "Yes, I fear you are." However, a sketch of a woman corresponding with a soldier was captioned, "This is the MOST important duty of their day."

Women sewed, nursed and tilled. They agonized over departed progeny. Anna Hamilton Wood poetized their obligation:

> *The cross is for your bearing,*
> *Mothers of men!*
> *The grief is for your sharing,*
> *Mothers of men!*
> *The fated hour at last has come*
> *That wrings your souls with anguish dumb*
> *And ye must foot the mighty sum,*
> *Mothers of men!*
>
> *Other hearts were crucified,*
> *Mothers of men!*
> *Other sons have bled and died,*
> *Mothers of men!*
> *The mother holds but second place*
> *When scourge of war attacks a race*

And hearts would break but for God's grace,
Mothers of men!
God is in His Heav'n still,
Mothers of men!
Hard the ruling of His will,
Mothers of men?
Once, Mary stood on Calvary
And are not ye as brave as she
To see your lad bring victory,
Mothers of men?
Our flag has never known defeat,
Mothers of men!
And home and peace are very sweet,
Mothers of men!
But these cannot be ours to-day
While tyrant's bloody rule holds sway.
YOUR SONS! There is no other way,
Mothers of men!

Harrisburg appreciated America's allies. Residents readied for the stopover of France's Field Marshal Joseph Jacques Césaire, an occasion that would rekindle memories of the 1778 alliance and the Marquis de Lafayette's visit. Bands rehearsed the "Marsellaise." Kaufman's store sold French flags, and they flew throughout the city. Unfortunately, the marshal's train derailed, leading to the event's cancellation. Joffre did reach the city and slept there during a short layover. In a gesture, the *Telegraph* sent him "a handsomely mounted and inscribed facsimile of the Harrisburg City Flag." A comic strip noticed Joffre. The *Telegraph*'s *Nebby Neighbors* clashed about the correct pronunciation of the marshal's surname. The *Evening News* recognized the Tricolor's hoisting nationwide and its symbolizing human freedom and advancement. "Liberty, Equality, Fraternity" radiated from its colors.

Belgium's plight—invaded by Germany—tugged the heartstrings. The kaiser's army "beheld something that was fair and turned it into the semblance of hell." Looking forward, Americans embraced Belgium's liberation, restoration and healing "to make it as nearly as possible the wonderful, busy, happy little country it was." In response, Mrs. John C. Kunkel Jr. and neighbors on South Front Street collected clothes and shoes for Belgian youth.

A mother's sacrifice. *From the* Evening News. *Courtesy of PennLive.*

The chamber of commerce prepared for the Royal Italian Mission's visit. Italy's banners adorned structures and vehicles in expectation. But the Italians lingered less than eight minutes as they passed through the city.

Harrisburgers borrowed from Britain, whose "win-the-war cook-book" suggested formulas for conserving food, such as scalloped parsnips, oatcake and barley bread and broth.

The war solemnized and subdued Memorial Day. The Daughters of the American Revolution (DAR) advocated a reverent ceremony without frivolity. The Pine Street Presbyterian Church sermonized "Our Debt to the Past" and messaged about "The Swordsman." The *Telegraph* explained

Pine Street Presbyterian Church. *Courtesy of Kenneth C. Hays, church historian.*

the flag-display standard. The *Courier* lamented, "Next year there will be fresh graves to mark." Dignity capped the observance. The GAR marched, church chimes pealed and community citizens commemorated.

Old Glory shined. The emblem was pinned to lapels and hats. It bedecked a YWCA dinner that included little souvenir replicas.

The flag's alleged misemployment provoked. When the Victoria theater's playbill featured Old Glory with "The Star-Spangled Banner," its management faced arrest for exploiting the flag in print for promotional purposes. In defense, the manager claimed "he was using the American flag…purely for patriotic reasons."

Harrisburg prepared for Flag Day. The Elks invited the DAR, Kaufman's sold banners and officials mapped a march line. The *Telegraph* noted, "Never within the history of the anniversary has Flag Day meant so much," and it encouraged the populace to "show your colors."

Ceremonies took place on June 15. At Reservoir Park, a band saluted Old Glory. On South Front Street, the Dauphin County Historical Society listened to its president pay homage to the flag. Events intensified emotions as Harrisburg unified in an encomium to the Stars and Stripes.

Flag rites became common. Raisings lifted colors over Foose Elementary, Central Iron and Steel and Maennerchor's German club. At Pine Street Presbyterian, the agenda included a speech about the banner's hues and Dr. L.S. Mudge speaking to their significance. At program's end, attendants unfolded a flag while the audience aired the national anthem.

The war resuscitated a musical rendering. The *Telegraph* reminded residents of George M. Cohan's "You're a Grand Old Flag":

You're a grand old flag tho' you're torn to a rag,
And for-ev-er in peace may you wave.
You're the emblem of the land I love,
The home of the free and the brave.
Ev-'ry heart beats true under Red, White and Blue.

"This work," according to the paper, "is the only one that seems to fire the patriotism of the masses and possesses the catchiest melody."

Harrisburg ramped up for July Fourth. Stores hawked war toys: cannons at Goldsmith's and guns at Globe Boy's Clothing Department. Dives, Pomeroy and Stewart pushed the Stars and Stripes and flagpoles. The *Patriot-Evening News* scheduled park band performances. The courthouse arranged a flag raising. The Messiah Lutheran Church planned devotions. But officials banned explosion-producing devices.

Disregard for "The Star-Spangled Banner" rankled. The city solicitor considered making it unlawful to ignore its communal performance. Harrisburgers would have to remain upright, and men would need to take off headgear. The inattention entered a cartoon titled "*Does Your Club Contain One of These?*" in which a father instructs his son to know the anthem's lyrics yet fails to recall them himself when attempting their rendition.

The city dissuaded commotion on the Fourth. Weapons discharged blanks, bells rang, whistles tooted, bands played and athletes competed. Still, sober ceremonies and chapel worship marked the holiday. It seemed, recorded the *Telegraph*, that "the seriousness of the present situation with the country at war is felt by everyone."

Affronts tagged the flag. A banner's theft roused a ten-dollar bounty for the culprit's capture. Authorities removed miniature facsimiles from the overcoat of a Turk who offended an enlisted man. He faced a twenty-dollar fine or thirty days' jailtime. The *Evening News* chided, "A man who will make such remarks is not fit to wear the American flag." The *Telegraph* published a letter deploring the emblem's image trimming clothes and hankies as unpatriotic, "a desecration [that] shows a very improper appreciation for the boys and men of our country who…gave their lives."

As if to exalt the banner, the *Telegraph* printed a twelve-year old's honorary, "Our Flag":

Thirteen stripes of red and white,
What do they stand for but pureness and might?
Thirteen stripes of red and white,
What do they stand for but victory and power
Over the foe in the crisis hour?
Thirteen stripes and the field of blue,
Standing for things that are always true;
The field of blue with its stars of white,
Meaning the states that will always fight
For victory in the crisis hour.

So fling out the banner red, blue, and white.
Fling out the banner of freedom and might.
Our nation's flag, oh, long may it wave
O'er a land that is true, and a land that is brave.
When the county calls in the crisis hour.

Downtown theaters booked war fare. *Darkest Russia*, at the Victoria, portrayed an ally in upheaval. The theater's management screened British propaganda and the English *Moral Courage. America First* and *Mothers of France* likewise promoted the cause, the latter showing a woman's dedication to France after sacrificing kin. *Yankee Pluck* and *The Star Spangled Banner* resounded patriotically. *Womanhood, the Glory of the Nation* fantasized about Americans fending off an enemy invasion. At the Regent, *The Little American* pictured a survivor of a torpedoed vessel returning to her French homeland and bearing witness to German inhumanity. The Colonial marqueed *Our Fighting Forces.* It also screened *The Great Power*, in which patriotic characters give an explosive-producing formula to the government.

Music waxed patriotic. J.H. Troup retailed the newly released Victor recordings of "The Star Spangled Banner," "America," "Columbia, the Gem of the Ocean" and "Battle Hymn of the Republic." Newspapers published the latter's score, as well as that of "The Marines' Hymn." In a presented flag's ceremony, Grace Methodist Church trolled "Onward Christian Soldiers," "The Nation," "The Battle Hymn of the Republic," "Loyalty" and "America." For July 4, the Victrola Talking Machine Company advertised "music that stirs your patriotism," marketing, among others, "Hail Columbia," "America, Here's My Boy," "Let's All Be Americans Now" and "Dixie." Municipal and military bands conducted concerts.

Sassafras Street's Harry Wolfe composed "Sure, We Are Some Big America," a work warning, "Our country is in danger from a fierce invading foe." Its sheet cover illustrated Uncle Sam encircled by airplanes and fronted by an eagle with a background of blue and red sparkling and spotlighting the elderly icon. City stores and Wolfe sold the song's prints.

Literature enlisted. Dives, Pomeroy and Stewart retailed patriotism with Edward Everett Hale's *The Man Without a Country*. The store also carried the *President's War Message* and the *Stars and Stripes*, the soldiers' newspaper. The National Americanization Committee circulated over "one million copies" of *Your Flag and Mine* and *Song of Our Country*.

Authors acknowledged the allies. Charlotte Kellogg's *Women of Belgium* paid praise. Alexander Powell's *Brothers in Arms* acquainted Harrisburgers with the French. George Louis Beer's *The English-Speaking Peoples: Their Future Relations and Joint International Obligations* spoke to a growing comity. Dives, Pomeroy and Stewart offered narratives concerning China.

Notoriety scribed the Germans. D. Thomas Curtin's *The Land of Deepening Shadow* analyzed Germany after three years of conflict. Albert Rhys Williams's *In the Claws of the German Eagle* told of the author's espionage trial at Germanic hands in Belgium. Arthur Gleason's *Our Part in the Great War* elucidated Germany's war crimes against the French. In his *The Will to Freedom*, John Neville Figgis pontificated that Nietzsche has "done much to produce that modern monster known as the German Kultur which is now bathing the world in blood in order to realize its insane dream of the 'Blood Beast' enthroned in the place of God." Hermann Fernau's *The Coming Democracy* summoned Germany's people to seek redemption by rejecting the Hohenzollerns.

Why the United States went to war and the desired outcome received scrutiny. Leonard Magnus penned *Pros and Cons of the Great War*. The *Patriot* and the *Evening News* extended without cost to readers President Wilson's explanation for entry and hopes for result.

Publications informed the public about the military and the war. The *Patriot* and the *Evening News* tendered, free of charge, a pictorial relating army experiences. The Harrisburg Library lent numerous titles about the armed services. A critic acclaimed John Curtis Underwood's *War Flames* as a "vivid insight into war." In *Open Boats*, Alfred Neyes described what followed a submarine attack. J.S. Smith contributed *Trench Warfare*.

The war breathed consequences and promise. *Papers from Picardy* by T.W. Pym and Geoffrey Gordon recorded the conflict's theological impact on soldiers. Will Irwin's *The Latin at War* chronicled the ordeal's sociological and economical tendencies. Hermann Hagedorn's *You Are the Hope of the World* looked to America's younger generation, "pointing out that in view of the slaughter of the youth of Europe, they are largely the 'hope of the world' in the years to come and indicating the ideals by which they should be guided in the face of this responsibility."

Contagion stalked Harrisburg. Authorities cautioned about typhus, infantile paralysis, tuberculosis and smallpox. Contaminants lurked in ice cream, milk, soda fountains, conduits and drinking water. From Europe, wartime afflictions enhanced the alarm. Outsiders entering the city added to the peril. A common insect became a bête noire. The *Evening News* singled out the housefly by asking, "Are you prepared for this enemy?" It editorialized, "This foe to all mankind will soon be carrying the germs of measles, scarlet fever, the fatal typhoid or, perhaps, even the hideous infantile paralysis." The "Doing My Bit" column advised, "Never let a fly escape."

Countermeasures grappled with pestilence. Draftees' health examinations detected tuberculosis. An official suggested preventive measures for households and military installations and believed nutrition combated disease. The Gately and Fitzgerald Supply Company on South Second Street advertised belligerency against bacteria, declaring, "Get the refrigerator working." The United Ice and Coal Company on Forster and Cowden pushed coolant to preserve foodstuffs and prevent spoilage. When soldiers reported a dirty and unhealthy café, the health office ordered it closed. The comic strip *That Son-In-Law of Pa's* spoke of a chicken pox quarantine. The *Evening News* advised that, like in the army, all should receive vaccinations.

Disease broke out in June. Neighboring Steelton reported smallpox. Harrisburg recorded typhoid. Pneumonia accounted for deaths two months prior. The need for a Dauphin County sanitary hospital became apparent. Epidemics threatened the military. The county organized to check tuberculosis. The *Evening News* publicized a nationwide expansion of infectious meningitis. The Civic Club sponsored fly-killing, offering money and prizes. When a count was made in late July, the campaign had exterminated 2,464,000 flies. A youth who submitted 138 pints of dead flies won first place.

Aviation excited interest. Flight attracted Harrisburg's youth, and many joined the air corps. The comic strip *Polly and Her Pals* illustrated a girl desiring to fly. The infatuation with flying became "a grim and expensive romance." An editorial damned German raids killing Londoners. City officials detained a woman, "temporarily unbalanced," who fled New York out of fear of an air attack.

The war brought soldiers to Harrisburg. Some misbehaved. They thieved, boozed and assaulted. Crime soared. Police pounced repeatedly on Cowden Street fleshpots. Offenses occurred frequently on Island Park. Authorities chided youths for dawdling. The *Courier* reported merrymaking at Hargest Island and Rockville on the Susquehanna River. Tales of uninhibited behavior and late night "orgies," where inebriated women commingled with soldiers, shamed the community. The revelries "included undress bathing parties, tangoes on the sand and some free-for-all fights."

Wartime soon began disturbing daily life. Commodity shortages coupled with cost-of-living jumps prompted frugality. Schools taught children thrift. Clergy warned of speculation. Authorities planned additional food markets and urged residents to conserve. The *Evening News* preached a "duty" to economize and avoid dissipation, adding, "Modern war means sacrifice by everybody."

Youth faced loss and exploitation. Military enlistments deprived the city of playground attendants, thus curbing recreation. Educators called for pupils considering employment to remain in the classroom. The editorial "Conserving Childhood" cautioned about ignoring limits on youngsters' drudgery: "It would be nothing less than suicide for the United States to risk the flower of her manhood in the trenches of blood-soaked France, while at home we were subjecting our future men and women to a killing blight that would break down their bodies, blunt their minds and abate their morals."

Despite the war, residents needed time off. Employee vacations enhanced rather than reduced their productivity, and, "If we are to have effective working people during the coming period of great stress every one of them should be given at least a short vacation this summer," advised the *Courier*.

Harrisburgers altered routines. Riverfront walkers strolled but at some distance from guarded bridges. The Elks canceled a yearly outing to Boston. To help retailers economize, the chamber of commerce gave shoppers tips. For limiting deliveries, it advised customers to bear acquisitions and returns themselves. It further suggested putting off "C.O.D. purchases whenever possible" and shopping "early in the day."

The *Evening News*'s headline "Hep! Hep! Hep!" clued residents to exercise. Walking after garden labor instead of sitting invigorated the body. In fact, "physical fitness is patriotic, these days." For those with neurasthenia, a malady brought on by the war, medicine promoted an ameliorative: "Dr. Williams' Pink Pills act directly…and have proved of the greatest benefit."

Chapter 3

RALLY

August–October 1917

Harrisburg stepped up. Citizens mustered and industry bustled as the city responded to the call.

Military volunteers came forward. In mid-August, most appeared healthy. A band and parade aided recruiting. At month's end, enlistments dropped off, but then they shot up in September. The city reputedly led the nation. Fifteen-year-old twins and a sixteen-year-old attempted to enroll. An imprisoned offender promised to join if released. Large draft numbers could be avoided with bountiful volunteering.

The draft encountered snags. Most enlisters submitted correct information, yet a few gave incorrect residences, such as an empty lot or a fake household. Authorities counted more than one hundred slackers, mainly foreign-born and African American men. Numerous call-ups flunked physicals. At the suburban Paxtang station, "contagious disease," "bad teeth," "underweight," "bunions" and "bad eyes" disqualified many. In September, examinations disclosed some with "mental and nervous disorders."

The Selective Service Act allowed deferments. Following registration, draft officials heard exemption requests founded on religion, health, kin and employment. Members of the Society of Friends avoided combat by assignment to "camps." A singer claimed cold weather pained his ears, and a youth pleaded that "bare ground" disturbed his "constitution." Authorities placed the former in the navy and the latter in the air corps. One registrant had unnecessary tooth extractions to avoid conscription but was told, "What are you hanging around here for? We don't want you. You've got flat feet."

Draft registrants report for physical examinations. *From the* Evening News. *Courtesy of PennLive.*

Family dependency challenged the local board. Men unsupportive of a wife, living out of wedlock and alleging care for a dependent aunt faced induction, as did a married man not living with his mate and a bartender asserting sole upkeep of his spouse. No sympathy was extended to those adopting or marrying on the spot.

The Colonial screened *The Slacker*, portraying a fiancé who delays his wedding but suddenly decides to go through with it once war breaks out. His wife, realizing his intention, converts him to patriotic service. The movie house ad asked, "Is the man next door a coward at heart?"

Labor excuses ran the gamut. Steel, railroad and coal firms requested employees' immunity. The board heard petitions from a blacksmith, a shell maker, a farmer and a carpenter. Pleas came from a telephone and telegraph pole laborer, a lime manufacturer and an apple butter boiler.

In October, a York County rustic attempted his seventh draft evasion. He argued religion, farming and spousal dependency as justification.

Soon, the army's character became perceptible. Recruiters rejected German aliens yet accepted others who were unnaturalized. The multi-tongued military homogenized Americanism for a diverse society. The army likewise sought the adept, wanting foreign language interpreters, motorcyclists and tool-skilled workmen. The failure to get volunteers for engineer details rankled.

Men entering combat thought the nickname "Sammy" inappropriate and laughable. Officers chuckled at the tag. At West Point, it meant "hand over the molasses" when at chow.

Harrisburg went to bat for the military. Through War Department cooperation, the *Harrisburg Telegraph* published a "Home Reading Course for Citizen-Soldiers," a public-spirited gesture designed for draftees' comfort. Initial entries were titled "Your Post of Honor" and "Making Good as a Soldier." The newspaper also mailed specially designed editions to the uniformed. In one, called "*GREATEST NEED THE TELEGRAPH*," a onetime employee revealed soldiers' craving for the hometown sheet's supplement.

The civic-minded believed literature sustained the troops. Hoping to direct them down the straight and narrow, the Harrisburg and Dauphin County Christian Endeavor Union bought over one thousand copies of *Make Christ King*, a hymn collection for the Eighth Regiment stationed on City Island.

The community gathered books for army cantonments. The Harrisburg Public Library requested writings "in fair condition" by novelists, poets and dramatists. It welcomed French-language primers, technological texts, ethical briefs and magazines. The nationwide campaign spearheaded by the American Library Association, the Red Cross and the YMCA planned a $1 million fundraiser. Local organizers asked each resident to contribute a dollar. The Catholic diocese's Bishop Philip R. McDevitt gave twenty-five dollars, "the first person to make a donation." The Knights of Columbus and the Young Men's Hebrew Association (YMHA) helped. Librarian Alice R. Eaton coined the catchphrase "Give such books as you would give to your friend." Aided by the War Department, the money drive's decreed Liberty War Fund Week began on September 24 and ended on October 2.

The Harrisburg Public Library headquartered the push. Officials pressed residents for $6,000 and desired French-subject volumes in particular. A poster supported the campaign. The *Evening News* warned "of providing proper diversions for the soldiers in the periods of their leisure" because "dangers…lurk in these idle hours," such as "temptations and debasing influences… and if they are not offset by influences of an

Librarian Alice Eaton. *Courtesy of Christina Lauver at the Dauphin County Library System.*

opposite nature they will contribute a direct menace to the morale and stamina of our fighting forces."

The library fund made some progress. Donations arrived from local organizations. High school students helped. The Boy Scouts sloganed, "A million dollars for a million books for a million men." Still, donations lagged. Despite the state librarian's generous contribution, the city failed to meet its promise.

The Commission on Training Camp Activities (CTCA), a federal office, aimed, with the assistance of benevolent societies, to rule the troops' sensual activities. Determined to prevent vice in cantonments, the government shut down over one hundred red-light bailiwicks and detained fifteen thousand convicted harlots, the majority of whom were imprisoned two years beyond the war's end. As soon as the United States entered the conflict, "both the army and civilian moral reformers attempted to enhance the public image of the United States and the U.S. Army by making soldiers models of virtue and sexual abstention."

Newspapers and the silver screen publicized behavioral concerns. For example, the *Telegraph* editorialized, associations had energized "to safeguard the morals of the citizen soldiers" and urged readers to back them. Its "Time to Tell the Truth," another opinion piece, applauded frank speech about "delicate subjects," aiding "our boys in France [to] escape the perils that have dragged so many sturdy young soldiers to ruin" and desiring "them to come back clean and pure." The Grand Theater showed the War Department's *Who Leads the National Army*, heralding the military leadership as "highly trained, efficient officers who are capable of taking care of the men under them in every exigency."

Smokes heartened soldiers. The *Telegraph* initiated "Our Boys in France Tobacco Fund" and asserted, "There's nothing like a good old pipe to make a soldier forget his troubles." The medical profession agreed. Doctors reporting from combat commended smokes for troops: "Nothing they say, so quiets the nerves under the stress of trench life as tobacco." Physicians approved the fund, stating, "It would be the height of folly, both from the medical and a military standpoint, to deny tobacco to the men at the front." A Civil War veteran gave to the fund, recalling, "I once craved a good smoke" and empathizing, "The boys over there are likely to be feeling the same way." The *Telegraph* joked, "Send tobacco to France and help American soldiers 'smoke out' the Hun." United States military leadership espoused cigarette firms' claims of tobacco's "physiological" values. Smokes enhanced soldiering. The YMCA and others endorsed tobacco as a psychological uplift.

Madison Avenue twisted wants to fit wartime. Cuticura Soap and Ointment vaunted "the soldier's ever-ready friends for eczemas, rashes, itchings, irritations, cuts, wounds, bruises, bites and stings of insects, sunburn and windburn." The Gillette Safety Razor Company reminded folks, "Your fighting man's only luxury is in keeping fit-shaved every day." The Gorgas "Rexall" Stores pushed snapshots, claiming Kodaks "let him see familiar faces and places." The Kellberg Studio questioned, "Does your soldier boy have your photograph?" Wrigley's Spearmint targeted women, boasting its gum instilled gusto and provided "comfort and refreshment" for your warrior. "Doing My Bit" advised asking enlistees their desires and discouraged unexpected gifts.

Harrisburg looked out for doughboys. A letter to the *Courier* suggested free trolley rides because of their low income. Soon, motorists' lifts for enlistees caught on. Island festivities raised money for their encampments. Thanks went to Tech High for a donated football. The *Evening News* began a Pennsylvania Boys' Christmas Fund. Texans stationed at Middletown appreciated the city's cordiality.

The city responded to insults against the uniformed. When individuals demeaned guardsmen as "slackers," a near riot ensued. An African American woman spent time in jail for allegedly offending a serviceman's spouse and then pulling a blade when he attempted to defend her.

War complicated relationships. Mentors instructed girls to quiz men, inoffensively, about their civilian status and refrain from discouraging enlistment. For those at camp, frequent letters served as the "best kind of tonic." Avoid a "gloomy, tearful screed," advisors steered, and correspond cheerfully of "jolly good news," asking the soldier what he needs. Under the right "circumstances," a girl was told, "there should be no bar to an early wedding."

Departures triggered an "open season" of kissing. Its propriety became an issue. A smooch proved acceptable if the man desired one or if shared between the betrothed, counselors claimed. Otherwise, a "cordial handshake and a smiling good-bye" would do. When fashion models tossed affections during a parade, a soldier remarked, "Gee, its worth while going to war to have those kind of peaches throw kisses at you."

In a letter to the *Telegraph*, a mother proffered tidbits of wisdom. Concerned about excessive pampering, she dismissed "pity, doubt or fear," which hindered soldier sons and advantaged the enemy. Rather, mothers should inculcate "courage, health, strength, right, justice," which aided virtue and produced readiness. She requested a regular column for mothers,

Give the soldier a lift. *From the* Harrisburg Telegraph. *Courtesy of PennLive.*

Draftees depart for camp. *From the* Evening News. *Courtesy of PennLive.*

"where she can daily find some helpful thought of courage to direct her aright in thinking of her boy that she may not hinder, but help him."

Servicemen captivated young girls. Two, sixteen and seventeen, tried to elope with doughboys. Three damsels, chasing soldiers while staying out at night, received fines and "little sympathy" for their "improper conduct."

Winona Wilcox's column in the *Evening News* warned about the idolized uniform, illustrated with a maiden and a shield marked "WOMENS VIRTUE." Wilcox called to mind the idea that "a uniform does not necessarily make over the nature of man."

A few soldiers bared troublesome behaviors. An army private gulped poison following a falling-out with a female companion. The Harrisburg Hospital ministered first aid. Another disturbed a busy Market Street diner by yelling, "I've got a bomb. Watch this place go up!" Police arrested the soldier. On investigation, the supposed explosive turned out to be a light bulb filled with pitchy ink. Authorities scheduled a mental exam.

Mingling soldiers succumbed to misconduct. Many bargained with bootleggers for booze. Drunken doughboys ended up in jail. One collected cash for a bogus benefit. Another attacked a young woman while imbibing. Police apprehended streetwalkers vamping their wiles on the Mulberry Street Bridge and corralled girls and soldiers on a raid at Dewberry Alley. Two Penbrook prostitutes, Fudge and Fury, plied their trade.

Drafted men march off for training. *From the* Evening News. *Courtesy of PennLive.*

Ostentatious farewells released sentiments. Christian Endeavorers and others paraded to City Island from Market Square for an enlistee send-off that included a minister's solemn, "Let not your heart be troubled," recitation of the Lord's Prayer, distribution of the hymn volume *Make Christ King*, singing of "My Country Tis of Thee" and a concluding blessing. Retailers shut their doors, fire bells rang and a parade along with a four-hour ceremony preceded the departure of Company D, Eighth Regiment, capped by the emotional burial of the unit's canine. A parade accompanied a quartermaster detail's leaving, and throngs bid adieu to Troop C, a cavalry detachment. As it headed out, military songs sounded, handshaking bustled, mothers' eyes watered and soldiers delighted in clutches like the "Sammie Hug." Troop C's parting also touched the animal kingdom. The unit's mascot, a bulldog, passed away, anguished over the separation.

Stores serenaded the decamped. Doutrichs fortified:

> *"Courage!" Soldier, "Courage!"*
> *Day—After—Day*
> *There are new problems to face*
> *but if you have courage you*
> *can WIN THE FIGHT...*

William Strouse looked forward to reunion:

> *GOOD BYE, BOY!*
> *On This Eventful Day*
> *you will march through*
> *the streets, amid applause*

and tears—music and flags—
and we all join in.
Good Luck to the Gallant Eight
May You All Return
Home in Good Health.

Harrisburg's Percy Vinton Ritter honored Troop C:

O, Cavalrymen who so nobly answer your country's crying needs.
How we will miss you and your dashing prancing steeds
Our streets which rang with your boyish glee and cheer,
Will be silent as you pass, into the yesteryear.

No more will we hear the echoing hoofbeats in this lonesome lonely land
In memory's sacred chambers only will we see you and your loyal band.
Our loss is the gain of nations in distress
And God for your sacrifices will more than bless.

His benediction, "Well Done" will be wafted on the breeze,
To you, "most noble Troopers" in those lands beyond the seas.
When carnage days are over and in your coming from the quest.
We will salute you with all homage—pride of the State—"OUR BEST."

Songs expressed soldiers' melancholy and sacrifice. "Send Me Away with a Smile," "So Long, Mother," "It's a Long Way Back to Mother's Knee" and "I Wonder How the Old Folks Are at Home" conjured leave-taking and longing, while "Your Country Needs You Now" invoked obligation with the rhythmic "They love you, I know, but they want you to go."

Moreover, music beat the drum for separation. Farewells inspired "The Ragtime Volunteers Are Off to War," "Over There" and "Laddie Boy." Revivals harmonized: the Civil War's "Tenting Tonight on the Old Camp Ground" and "I Wish I Was in Dixie," as well as the Spanish-American War's "Break the News to Mother." Heavy hearts melodized "There's a Long, Long Trail," "I'm Lonesome," "Longing for My Dixie Home" and "Somewhere in France Is Daddy."

The war vicariously entered Harrisburg homes. William G. Shepherd put forward *Confessions of a War Correspondent*. Captain Bruce Bairnsfather's *Fragments from France* revealed "indescribable pictures of life in the trenches" with "amusing captions." The *Telegraph*'s series "Letters from the Front"

Initial unit sets out for France. *From the* Harrisburg Telegraph. *Courtesy of PennLive.*

described the ambulance corps' adventures. The Red Cross's Dr. Albert Parker Fitch spoke of battlefield vistas concerning the Western Front.

The War Department envisioned an air depot in Middletown. Covering over twenty acres of the Keystone State Fair Association grounds, a large warehouse priced at thousands of dollars would consolidate military hardware. Its construction anticipated a skilled worker influx, a local employment boom and the state capitol's regular flyover.

Air units continued to appeal. Many volunteered, and the government planned an aviation training center. *Polly and Her Pals* referred to joining the "Flying Corps," and Wrigley's puffed that pilots gnawed its chew like clockwork because "it steadies stomach and nerves."

Middletown's readiness quickened. By mid-September, over one hundred trainees had settled in. Housing erection began for the billeting of thousands. In early October, authorities announced plans to build an aircraft factory.

According to the *Evening News,* "America will lead in the air." Congress set aside $600 million for aircraft production. The country developed the best aeronautic motor and projected six pilot schools. Steel and wood stocks would meet supply requirements for plane manufacture at home and abroad.

A Soldiers' Christmas Fund gained support. The Knights of Columbus aimed to garner $3 million in conjunction with the Committee on War Activities. Children contributed pennies. Movie houses offered percentages of their proceeds for touted showings of the Victoria's *The Tanks* and the Regent's *The Woman God Forgot*. Dances at Market Square's Winterdale and Race Street's Harrisburg Cigar Company bolstered the sum, as did a recital by the Augsburg Lutheran Church's youth.

In August, the Lever Act became effective. The war measure called for food and fuel conservation and disallowed the distillation of foodstuffs into liquor. By early September, hundreds of distillers had stopped operations, affecting thousands of employees. A speaker of Dauphin County's WCTU "predicted whiskey never would be manufactured again…being banished by…science and religion, education…and legislation." The Pennsylvania State Prohibition Committee, headquartered in Harrisburg, begged President Wilson to have Congress prevent the conversion of eatables into alcohol permanently.

The city took on food conservation. Over eight thousand households promised to save, and newspapers pressed for changed cravings. An editorial argued, "Applebutter bread in one hand and a coffee cup in the other beats dining without meat and wheat." The column "Doing My Bit" urged preparing meals differently in an appealing fashion to lure, advising, "Serve it in small portions, garnish it and present it in such a way that it will attract the eye." Another commentary preached we should "start training our finicky appetites right away quick!" It added, "That will be a long and important step in food conservation and of immeasurable assistance to our Allies, in sore need of the food which will keep body and soul together."

Savings necessitated sacrifices and safeguards. The Franklin Sugar Refining Company, requesting its sweetener's conservation, declared, "Two spoonsful a day saved by each American will keep France in sugar." "Doing My Bit" thought butter could be nursed in diners. Hotels pledged meatless Tuesdays, and the Bolton observed Wednesdays without wheat. Homeowners needed to caution domestic help about wastage, said to be "the greatest duty many a woman can perform for the country she loves and wishes with all her heart to serve."

Harrisburg abstained from wastage. Garbage cans showed no evidence of scraps. The *Evening News* directed homemakers and eating houses to assign odds and ends to "their oldtime place at the table." Leftovers ought to be utilized instead of tossed.

Creativity and thrift altered foodways. Bread and soup could be produced from skim milk, and sour milk could make "crowdie," or Scottish cottage cheese. One recipe called for peanut soup. Housewives could conserve by frying cornmeal instead of wheat, preparing French toast from stale bread, fixing meat turnovers and using one meal's gravy for a second time. By October, suggestions were coming forward on cooking at a large scale, to serve as many as forty-five to fifty persons.

Programs, posters and publications propagandized food salvage. Many girls registered for a cuisine study at Central High. A train, sponsored by a Pennsylvania Railroad council, toured the state advising housewives and spent two days in the city. The area's Food Supply Committee distributed placards for homemakers' kitchens, preaching:

1. *Buy it with thought.*
2. *Cook it with care.*
3. *Serve just enough.*
4. *Save what will keep.*
5. *Eat what would spoil.*
6. *Home-grown is best.*

The Patriot-News Company offered to mail free of charge federal literature promoting staple savings, asserting its release "shows how every home can help; how every woman can save enough food to assure some American boy in France of three square meals a day."

Substitutes moderated restrictions. Cornmeal mush, hominy and potatoes replaced wheat. Isabel Brands's regular column "Kitchen Economies" suggested the concoctions "Spiced Bread Pudding," "Chocolate Bread Pudding" and "Crumb Bread." "Doing My Bit" featured half-and-half breads made by utilizing "two cups of either cornmeal, soy bean flour, finely crushed peanuts or rice flour for each two cups of wheat flour." A Grape-Nuts ad touted barley as a wheat saver, but despite the war, Shredded Wheat hawked its grain-based cereal.

Alternatives surfaced for meat. The *Telegraph* bellowed, "EAT FISH," adding that it was inexpensive and plentiful. The *Evening News* served up *Fish Recipes*, a booklet containing over sixty prescriptions. For a week's meatless days, the Manhattan Restaurant prepared denizens of the deep. Cheeses likewise took the place of beef. For a seven-day stretch, Brands provided "variety" and "nourishment" with, among others, "Vegetable Soup," "Cheese Souffle Rice with Tomato Sauce," "String Bean Salad" and "Cream of Corn Soup."

Stopgaps saved sweetener and butter. "Doing My Bit" informed readers, "A loaf cake costs less than a layer cake, for it goes further and requires less sugar for filling and frosting." A letter to the *Telegraph* urged production of oleomargarine. Oak Grove margarine's ad argued its commodity "enables you to save on your butter bill and at the same time supply your family with a high grade butter equivalent."

Recommendations went out for staples. Encouraging residents to be innovative, "Doing My Bit" favored dasheen and soybeans. The *Telegraph* pushed sweet potatoes.

Wartime created demand for cabbage. Over one hundred Harrisburg Topographical Union fellows munched a sauerkraut meal in Maennerchor Hall, oblivious of any disloyalty.

Canning complemented and supplemented food savings. Franklin Sugar offered health, taste and economic benefits. The *Telegraph* explained the wisdom of readying timeworn receptacles and rallied homemakers to share their formulas. "Doing My Bit" offered tips for putting up late produce. The YWCA offered a course through the Red Cross. Its preserved vegetables went to military families.

Household waste yielded uses. The *Telegraph* discerned its value and commanded, "Harrisburg…should look toward the conservation of its garbage" since the planet "is too short of fats, fertilizers and pork to permit a continuance of the frightful wastage." Observers approved of the state hospital's feeding its pigs refuse. "Doing My Bit" characterized scraps as "excellent fertilizing material."

Harrisburgers seemed dilatory about food strictures. The Red Cross reported only a few attending a domestic dietetics program. Bakers noted white bread's continued consumption, and despite federal Food Administration requests, little demand came for flour replacements like rye and other dark ingredients.

Authorities asked for the clergy's help. Pastors scrutinized their congregations, recording their weekly wheat and meat meals. Eateries inaugurated restrictions. Tuesdays became meatless in railroad dining cars— even "tongue and oxtails" were banned. With hotels serving poultry instead of beef and corn and rye breads rather than wheat derivations, observers thought limits "will not cause much dieting or work a severe hardship on the good citizens of this community." Since diners and hotels expended only a small percentage of consumables, "if any real good is to come from these food conservation days it is up to the housewife."

Wartime tamed Halloween. The *Telegraph* deplored food's misuse, favored prohibited frolics and capers and thought their disallowance should be binding. The paper approved the arrest of those tossing corn and cabbage heads at housefronts. The *Evening News* reiterated, "America cannot squander its food resources to make hideous an antiquated custom." Officials messaged schoolchildren to be responsible, while police forbid the use of "ticklers" and the custom "of boys following girls and young women to dark places and then tying them with rope." Harrisburg did observe calm trick-or-treating, confined to one day.

War garden harvests offset foreign exports and domestic consumption. Tillers worked hundreds of plots, many located in the Tenth Ward on Allison Hill and in the Thirteenth Ward below Derry Street. The chamber of commerce, through its Agricultural Committee, spearheaded the gardening effort, costing over $1,600 yet producing crops valued at thousands of dollars. To ease expenditure, members suggested a $1.50 deposit per plot. The program was "so popular that more than one-hundred persons applied for crop raising space after the twenty-seven acres available in the spring had been disposed of," according to the *Evening News*.

Kids participated. On Fifteenth and Vernon Streets, an eight-year-old grew "beets, cabbage and tomatoes of superior quality." The Children's Industrial Home pitched in. War garden directors figured public school youth cultivated crops worth $2,607.34.

Anticipating additional gardens in the future, the *Telegraph* deemed them "one of the best things that the war has brought to Pennsylvania." Husbandry made residents hardworking and land-caring. Some marketed surpluses, garnering income and reducing prices. Health benefits ensued. Men ailing "devoted themselves to digging and delving in their gardens," and "they are only giving the doctors a passing smile instead of their pulse to feel," reported the *Harrisburg Telegraph*.

Cultivators breached the Sabbath. Laboring on Sunday jounced the city's propriety. Still, when considering the extended hours of factory, farm and social obligations, brought on by contemporary warfare, the lapse seemed tolerable. "The man with the Sunday morning hoe probably violates fewer tenets than the Sunday automobile tourist," opined the *Telegraph*.

Forney School pupils till a war garden. *From the* Harrisburg Telegraph. *Courtesy of PennLive.*

Ongoing thefts plagued war gardens. If gardeners' laborious efforts went for naught, they could be disheartened. To deter thieves, draconian measures fit. The *Courier* dismissed reluctance to apprehend and prosecute: "Give a few of the culprits a full dose of the law and it will go a long way toward breaking up the practice." Two adults and an adolescent were arraigned for taking tomatoes from a Sixteenth and Herr plot. They admitted their misdeeds. The state's agriculture department gave notice of "severe penalties" for those guilty of spoiling beds. A law called for fines or incarceration of the convicted.

Gardeners benefited from enticements. For a completed form mailed to a Philadelphia firm, residents secured its *Mid-summer Garden Book*, prescribing the late growth of produce. For those contemplating the succeeding season, the federal agricultural office prepared *Farmers' Bulletin No. 255: The Home Vegetable Garden*. "Doing My Bit" proposed the assemblage of garden gangs for 1918.

Harrisburgers readied for the forthcoming year. Tillers chose, weeded and enriched grounds. Weeding prevented bugs from nestling. Poultry coops supplied fertile droppings. Shops reported a market for fruit saplings. The *Evening News* recommended spraying peach plants in the fall. The Thirteenth Ward voiced high expectations: "[The] number of persons who are to be seen covering up their tracts of land for the winter or tearing up the cabbage stumps and clearing away the corn indicates that gardening is going to be a serious business next summer."

The city permitted war gardeners to transact sidewalk sales, intended to get rid of excess. These "curb markets" operated on Tuesdays and Fridays between six and eleven o'clock in the morning. They went unregulated and untaxed. Police were to shoo regular city grocers away. Surprisingly, no cultivators appeared on the first day.

Officials prepared for the nation's second Liberty loan and promised that "the coming campaign will be a hummer." The four-week effort pursued individuals in all walks of life. Housed in the Dauphin Building's chamber of commerce quarters, a committee carried out their duties in the city which was partitioned into seven sections and subsectioned into sixths. Publicizing a loan's preferability to taxes, over five hundred volunteers planned to solicit thirty thousand residents. In early September, Boy Scouts readied their part.

Newspapers promoted the loan push. The *Evening News* tendered awards to youngsters composing top-notch responses to queries about bonds. It editorialized, "If any single soul failed or refused to buy all that he or she was able, Harrisburg has 'slacked.'" A *Telegraph* article titled "A Great Investment" reminded readers of the gains to country and self. Cartoons shamed the nonsubscriber and ridiculed the German monarch, one directing, "Hook der kaiser."

Businesses signalized war loans. Full-page ads by merchants plastered dailies in late October. Harrisburg Pipe and Pipe Bending Works ran a one-sheet spread. Kaufman's touted trade advantages, and Witmer, Bair and Witmer jingled, "Buy buy the Liberty bonds and bye bye the kaiser." The Dauphin Deposit Trust Company hailed the Statue of Liberty.

Regalia prompted sales. Signboards glistened on Market Street and Market Square. A larger streamer dangled above the former. Stickers and placards bedecked automobiles. Army pilots dropped red, white and blue leaflets, while "Four-Minute Men," volunteer speakers of the federal Committee on Public Information sloganized, "Shoot U.S. bonds."

Throughout October, officials pressed for purchases. Six hundred pitchmen scrounged for buyers. The campaign asked women to exercise their sway. A Civic Club spokesman "recalled the important part played in the history of the country at all times, how…women have always been at the front of big movements and how much depends on their co-operation with the national committee." The Harrisburg Ministerial Association lauded the loan and promised pastoral support. Congregations heard the Grace Methodist Episcopal's sermon "Investment and Democracy" and the Pleasant View Church of God's "The Liberty Bond." The Reverend Bagnell made a rousing appeal. Concerts, dancing and President Wilson's "Liberty Day" proclamation for October 24, endorsed by the city, publicized the endeavor.

Schools got going. The *Evening News* applauded their work and editorialized, "The children of this generation have a right to know why their country has gone to war." Students wrote compositions about the loan. Open Air School pupils bought a bond. High schools competed for sales. By October 25, Central announced $12,000 collected.

The community turned out. The Bell Telephone Company and the Wharton School backed the drive. Attesting their loyalty, the German-Maennerchor Society's membership and President Edward Moeslein, a veteran of the Franco-Prussian War, "pledged themselves to aid the local campaign." Officers recorded bond buys by the city council, Pennsylvania Railroad workers, silk mill laborers, restaurant employees, military recruiters and hotel guests. A four-year-old boy made a purchase. The Warrior Eagle Tribe, No. 340, Improved Order of Red Men subscribed. A German submarine's sinking of the *Antilles*, an American troop vessel, on October 17 with the loss of sixty-seven souls might have spiked loan sales. Both

Alien railroaders purchase Liberty bonds. *From the* Harrisburg Telegraph. *Courtesy of PennLive.*

city and country oversubscribed. A thankful President Wilson recognized Harrisburgers "hit" on "the barbarian."

The Red Cross maintained a steady pace. It collected books for soldiers and linens for hospitals. It added work hours as it pleaded for more help. Chapter activities intensified. Workers aided soldiers' families in need and troops in transit. They provided instruction on care for the sick, fundamental hygiene and first aid. They also gathered blankets for Belgian tots and clothing for French babies. Cross girls and supplies went to the front. A Tech High composition topic hallowed "Angels of Mercy—The American Red Cross."

Knitting became a priority. An appeal asked for one thousand volunteers. The city lagged behind its assigned needlework; additional "knitters are needed and every one is requested to knit, knit, knit." A YWCA high school group considered starting stitching classes. For the novice, the *Patriot* and the *Evening News* made available, without cost, *The Knitting Book*. Stitchers labored at Cross headquarters and in private households. An elderly man of eighty-four residing on Market Square darned "nightingales," threadbare garments for recovering hospital patients.

Despite the Red Cross's good works, allegations jabbed. Hearsay charged workers with selling or self-use of produced garments. Manager Charles Scott of the society's Pennsylvania unit discounted the gossip, and the *Evening News* dismissed such accusations as "absurd."

Ministers growled about Sunday stitching during sermons. The Episcopal Church's Bishop James Henry Darlington feared distraction and inattention would "interfere with our worship of God." The Messiah Church's H.W.A. Hanson thought congregants' misbehavior would increase. The First Baptist Church's William J. Lockhart wanted devotions on the Sabbath and knitting "done some other time." Grace Methodist's Pastor Bagnell opined, "There are plenty of chances for women to knit in other places than their church." Park Street United Evangelical Church's A.E. Hangen believed his holding forth would lose its spark, since "a minister gets his inspiration from a congregation." The Pine Street Presbyterian's Lewis Seymour Mudge pontificated, "I do not regard the church as a proper place to do other than worship."

Putting aside clerical grumbles, "The Knitters" poeticized the needle loopers' steadfastness and preoccupation:

> *Oh the womenfolk are sitting*
> *By the salt seashore,*
> *Most industriously knitting*
> *While the wild waves roar,*
> *They're so seriously busy*
> *When their needles flit,*
> *That to watch 'em makes you dizzy*
> *As they knit, knit, knit.*
>
> *At the dances, at the races*
> *At the hearthside, too,*
> *At all sorts of times and places*
> *There's a knitting crew,*
> *And their dainty fingers flicker*
> *As they do their bit,*
> *Moving swifter faster, quicker*
> *As they knit, knit, knit.*

And though some may knit with ardor
For the soldier's sake,
Most are ever knitting harder
While they seek to make
Silken sweaters, light and airy,
For themselves—that's it;
Oh they're patriotic, very
As they knit, knit, knit!

Harrisburg's Red Cross took up a fundraiser suggested by President Wilson's wife. At the chapter's principal entrance, a metal "melting pot" resting on a three-legged frame received donations. The receptacle welcomed "old gold, platinum, silver and fillings from gold teeth, which are of no use to their owners." After three days, the pot held sundry silver, brass and gold items, as well as "Japanese ash trays, spoons, brooches and rings of all kinds."

Disloyal notions pervaded Harrisburg. The press conceded Pennsylvania Dutch fidelity, but misgivings hung over others. An American of lengthy Austrian residence remained hushed and remote at heated war debates. An accused woman forewarned: "In these days of mental stress and unnatural excitement, it is well for everyone to weigh not only their words, but their thoughts as well, and not be too quick in judging others."

Fears arose about a domestic menace. The accused woman under suspicion supposedly had a family member "in a trusted position in the Federal government." Some of the many so-called pro-Teutons in town occupied state offices. Rumor of a German arsonist at a steel plant proved unfounded.

Disloyalty sanctioned retribution. The *Courier* resounded Cincinnati's reintroductions of New England's stocks. Wartime duty, editorialized the *Evening News*, warranted curbs on speech and press. German-born financier Otto H. Kahn called for the "sternest penalty" possible: "He who shirks the full measure of his duty and allegiance in this noblest of causes—be he German-American, Irish-American, or any other hyphenated American, be he I.W.W. [International Workers of the World] or Socialist or whatever the appellation, does not deserve to stand amongst Americans or indeed amongst free men anywhere."

Robert LaFollette came in for special censure. The Wisconsin senator opposed the war declaration and the draft. By calling for peace, he "stands before the nation as one who committed sabotage by trying to throw a monkey wrench into the legislation machinery by which the government sought to avenge German crimes and German insults." His "persistent vilification of the war and conscription made him a pariah in the Senate."

Harrisburg gloried in forming the first branch in the East of the Children of America Loyalty League. Its area overseer, Mrs. George O. Matson, charged youth eighteen and under twenty cents to join. Adult memberships ran from one to five dollars. The organization donated youngsters' fees to the Red Cross.

In the midst of loyalty and security worries, a heavy breeze collapsed Market Street's bond banner, reportedly "with evident pro-German sympathies."

City clergy evinced unimpeachable patriotism. A military chaplain invoked divine aid and recalled George Washington and Abraham Lincoln falling on their knees during crises. A biblical presentation summoned prophecy. War topics blanketed sermons. Congregations conserved food, knitted garments and fulfilled Red Cross obligations. Ministers honored brethren in uniform and considered a prayer day, which was put off because it conflicted with the Liberty loan drive. Dr. Bagnell, mincing no words, doomed pacifists: "You may think it strange…that a Christian minister should recommend death for traitors." He insisted, "We should see to it that we recognize and handle promptly the traitors within our midst."

Divines implicated burlesque as insidious as well. Protesting its evil and degenerate inclination, the Ministerial Association demanded suppression and asked the chamber of commerce "to deal vigorously with any of our citizens who, especially during a period when we are bending every energy to conserve our national resources, are so disloyal, unpatriotic and seditious as to place that before our citizens which inflames these baser passions, lessen [sic] their physical and mental power and unfits them for effective service for the country."

The *Telegraph* condoned the silencing of dissenters. Though disapproving of lynching, it editorialized that the murder of an IWW organizer "would do much toward bringing to a quick conclusion the propaganda of anarchism and treason that has been rampant of late throughout the country." The banning of the National Socialist Party's newsletter won its applause, "for it was far more German than American." The *Telegraph* believed Germanic-language papers should be quashed, too. Curiously, it labeled federal directions to the press "wrong."

City socialists scheduled an assembly at Maennerchor Hall on North Street without aspersions of disloyalty. They planned to organize their ranks and consider future tasks.

The *Telegraph* noted fewer pupils were deciding to take German in Ohio schools. The development came as no surprise. The paper saw a "hard common sense behind it in many cases, no doubt." The *Evening News* punned, "It's unpatriotic to call a village citizen a burgher—now that we're at war with Germany."

The demonization of Germany intensified. Its air power frightened. Defeat of the Allies in France could enable enemy landings in America and bombings of the interior. The *Evening News* warned, "The same 'military necessity' that caused German aviators to fly from Belgium over London and massacre innocent children with high-powered explosive bombs would cause them—once they affected a landing anywhere on the American coast—to murder our women and children too." Reportedly, air raids targeting hospitals in Europe caused the deaths of patients and caretakers. Rumors circulated about an aircraft flying over a Harrisburg-area steel mill.

The nefarious Hun excited the imagination. The state health department investigated allegations of poisonous soap sold by a German vendor. Spokespersons reinforced the enemy's excesses. Dr. Newell Dwight Hillis, a Brooklyn cleric, detailed "German terrorism and frightfulness." Laura de Turczynowicz, a Russian noblewoman, addressed residents "on the outraged Belgium, Poland and French peoples."

Terminology took a patriotic turn. Thomas Addison's "Excerpts from the Devil's Dictionary," an article from the *Telegraph*, pilloried America's adversaries. His characterizations included "Pro-German—a wart developed by the war; dangerous unless speedily removed," "Slacker—one who is willing to 'let George do it'; a plain coward," "Sedition—one of the fine arts practiced by the pro-German press," "Boche—a butcher; disqualified by law for (international) jury duty" and "Kaiserism—a disease requiring certain powerful powders and pellets to eliminate."

Germany gave an incentive to authors. Harrisburgers could peruse Alice Cholmondeley's *Christine*, a look at the German people during the summer of 1914. A.D. McLaren's *Peaceful Penetration* and Professor Archibald Cary Coolidge's *Origins of the Triple Alliance* enlightened readers about the war's backdrop. *The Coming Democracy* by Herman Fernau, a German native, begged his countrymen to cast aside their loyalty to Berlin and place themselves beside the world's democracies.

Affection for France became far-reaching. At Paxtang Park, spectators applauded a wounded French soldier's singing. Owing to "a debt of gratitude," a suggestion went forth to mark a nationwide celebration on Lafayette's birthday. The marquis shined as an essay topic at Central

The beast ravages an ally. *From the* Harrisburg Telegraph. *Courtesy of PennLive.*

High. School administrators noticed a preference for the Latin and French languages instead of the once-popular German. Newspapers advertised lessons in France's tongue, and the YWCA accommodated a large French-language class. Stores sold French-labeled merchandise including flower bulbs, kid gloves and "Joffre Tam[s]," while "Joffre—The Frenchman Loved by Americans" was the theme of a Tech senior's composition. The *Evening News* commended France's military: "It is France at which the Kaiser aims his most savage and smashing blows," and "there stands that glorious Country returning blow for blow—the marvel of an admiring world."

Movies boosted America's ally. The Regent's *Joan the Woman* resurrected a French heroine. At the Colonial, *For France* portrayed a Yankee volunteer in France's air arm. The Victoria booked *Les Misérables*, based on Victor Hugo's novel, showing scenes of the Gaulish countryside. Tin Pan Alley mustered for France. French friendship struck up "Joan of Arc" and "Ye Sons of France Arise."

As fall eclipsed summer, groups assumed war functions. Through cooperation with the National Rifle Association and the War Department, the Harrisburg Rifle Club instructed men on how to handle firearms. The Harrisburgers held a marksman's competition with the Keystone Rifle Club that awarded prizes. The Harrisburg Rifle Club "is doing great work in training young men of this city and community to shoot straight," reported the *Evening News*. The College Periodical League, the Rotary Club and the Robert Disbrow Lloyd Sunshine Society aided encampment libraries. The Commonwealth Club chose to help the Red Cross. The Rotary and the YMHA dined soldiers.

The Order of United American Mechanics favored an assimilation of aliens. It recast itself as the Order of United American Men, and its goals proclaimed advocacy of "morality, justice, education and patriotism" and "proper regulation of emigrants [*sic*] and their education in principles and ideals of Americanism." According to the scholar Adam Goodman, "The war contributed to heightened xenophobia and a growing belief that noncitizens represented a threat to the racial, cultural, economic, and political orders."

In the Chestnut Street Hall, the chamber of commerce met to decide measures. President David E. Tracy distributed directions by the War

German soldiers molest French girls. *From the* Evening News. *Courtesy of PennLive.*

Convention of American Business in Atlantic City that explained the business community's obligations. The chamber invited Newton D. Baker, secretary of war, to speak. Baker revealed that one hundred thousand American troops had arrived in France and, with "a masterpiece of oratory," heralded, "America will win because its ideals are right and because the aim of the German Emperor cannot be right."

More than ever, breadwinners abandoned their families. Deserted kids needed care. The Associated Aids Society complained the war's drives reduced gifts. The society risked a deficit.

The past bestowed icons. Ernest Peixotto published *A Revolutionary Pilgrimage*, filled with images and sites of the American Revolution. Don C. Seitz recalled *Paul Jones and His Exploits in English Seas, 1778–1780*. Thirteen candles burned on a child's birthday cake, symbolizing the original colonies. The *Telegraph* reminded readers of the 104th anniversary of "The Star-Spangled Banner," and Old Glory orchestrated "The Stars and Stripes Will Float" as well as "You're a Grand Flag." A cartoon pictured Uncle Sam with the Statue of Liberty in the background, imploring a young soldier to do his duty and "to make the world safe for democracy."

Emblems symbolized the march to war. The *Evening News* urged, "Wash up the flag," and "Honor your flag by keeping it clean!" Homes displayed doughboys' service banners. Hues epitomized patriotism. Red, white and blue embellished a birthday party and Liberty League badges.

By late summer, the war was affecting lifestyles. Attention revolved around the weighty as the trivial gave way to the consequential. Residents made use of "material and time." They "are saving and working where before they were inclined to wastefulness." Librarian Alice R. Eaton noted a shift to the more eminent volumes, "those dealing with history, travel, description and the like as contrasted with fiction."

Recreation dwindled. The city cancelled Kipona, its Labor Day festival, due to conscription taking participants and to save money. County baseball lost youth to the military and had difficulty fielding teams. Hunting waned with men abroad and ammunition costly.

Harrisburg did celebrate Romper Day, held in Reservoir Park. Children played, and damsels of diverse heritages were decked in dresses of America's allies and danced patriotically.

Services and supplies dropped off. Stores stopped deliveries, and shoppers carried purchases. The *Evening News* commended "patriotic women" for "the elimination of such costly and useless processes…that the energy and manpower of the nation will be conserved for more important matters."

Romper Day dance for the Allies. *From the* Harrisburg Telegraph. *Courtesy of PennLive.*

Military sign-ons reduced the criminal courts' jury pool. Officials feared coal shortages. Motorists needed to ration gas.

The cost of living jumped. Grocers organized to combat inflation. City government promised to check short selling (the failure to value accurately). Yet prices rose on bread, booze, postage, coal and transportation. War taxes contributed. Federal authorities sought revenues from toiletries, medicines, automobiles, soft drinks, chewing gum and motion pictures.

To cope, "Doing My Bit" encouraged families to manage their finances. Economy would result from scrutinized earnings and expenses.

The war compromised female fashions. To conserve materials, designers styled gowns to be slender, short and without sleeves. The "slenderizing silk" complemented food savings but impacted sitting. Half hose spared silk yet bared kneecaps. A rhythmist parodied:

> *Alas it's very, very sad!*
> *My news for fat folks is so bad!*
> *Like pencils they must be by Fall*
> *Or they'll not make their mark at all.*

Another hearkened:

> *Backward, turn backward, oh, time in your flight*
> *And give me a girlie whose skirts are not tight;*

Give me a girl, with charms many or few,
Who does not show her shoetops like
Most girlies do.

Women behaved untraditionally. With men drafted, the School of Commerce and Harrisburg Business College believed women could realize equal employment. Counting nursing, over one hundred lines of work opened up, including sales, railroads, government, printing, elevator operation and chauffeuring. Women clerked for the Pennsylvania Railroad and ran lifts at Bowman's store. The trousered, so-called fair sex hanging wallpaper caught a soldier's eye. The women's supervisor remarked: "I need hands so much I'd a hired 'em in skirts, in tights or without either." He added, "Sex and clothing don't matter just so they got two hands, two feet and a little bit of brains."

High-heeled shoes received scorn. They reduced capability and posture for upright stepping and standstill labor. The *Evening News* tongue-lashed "the women who selfishly and foolishly chose vanity instead of common sense for their parade footgear," saying they "established a bad impression of their own serious purpose." "In the matter of war service," it continued, "even the choice of one's shoe heels, since it involves working efficiency, is NOT one's own business."

Yet wartime rallied women. The state's labor department approved their elevator employment. The Harrisburg Railways considered hiring them. They registered for work with the Dauphin County and a National Defense League committee.

Occupied women drew ridicule. Conceding women's notable exertions once war broke out, a jokester said snidely, "Yes, and did you ever notice that when woman hurls herself into a breach she immediately hurls herself into breeches?" "Look Out for Bullets" headlined the news that the Red Cross Motor Messenger Service planned a ladies' pistol crew. High school students expressed a more respectful tone. One senior essay discussed "Woman's Part in the War."

A curative came to the aid of pressed women. Busy women suffering weakness and anemia "from woman's ills" could revive with Dr. Pierce's Favorite Prescription, promising to invigorate, restore, sooth and strengthen, "a positive remedy for the functional derangements, painful disorders, and chronic weaknesses peculiar to the sex."

The war entangled public education. The military and marriage created teaching vacancies. Administrators retained old maps as teaching tools despite war-related boundary changes. Boys desired in-school martial preparation, a program endorsed by the *Telegraph*. But General Leonard Wood, former army chief of staff and founder of the Gettysburg recruitment camp, advised against it, writing "that pupils [should] be given physical training in the schools and 'get the military training outside.'" Notwithstanding an effort to keep students in school, Central High's Boy's Employment Bureau issued numerous applications to businesses. Nevertheless, student enrollment recorded little variation due to employment.

The rally to arms compelled dutiful parenting. Misbehaving children burdened schools. Properly reared broods aided teachers and alleviated expenses. "So here is a chance," chimed in the *Evening News*, "for patriotic mothers to try a new kind of wartime economy." Likewise, infants required upgraded tending since war increased tot mortality.

Creatures and critters went to war, both as allies and adversaries. Birds helped gardeners by killing insects, particularly butterflies. Pigeon breeders reported their flocks were ready to express messages. Dogs and cats guinea-pigged for gas mask testing. Rats, contagion spreaders and food despoilers, and ants, householders' nemeses, merited extermination. Residents even imagined they saw President Wilson's name scrawled in spiders' webs.

Flies infested Harrisburg. The germ-carrying hordes menaced public health. A fly-swatting campaign had eradicated millions. A second effort, sponsored by the Civic Club, swung into action, stipulating September 29 as "fly measuring day." Newspapers gave support. The *Evening News* declared, "To swat the fly is a duty to the nation these days." Flies bred in the city's filth, fed on foodstuffs and sheltered in residents' homes, the worst time being August. Replacing white light bulbs with blue deterred their influx, and children needed to avoid contact with their contaminative captives. At the counting, a youth came in first, submitting three hundred forty-one-pint pots of dead flies. Altogether, club officials estimated 5,705,000 flies were killed.

Pestilence harried Harrisburgers. Rumors and reports of contagions proliferated. Newspapers recorded outbreaks of smallpox, typhoid, tuberculosis, infantile paralysis, diphtheria and scarlet fever. Over thirty tests confirmed microorganisms in milk. Officials recommended the isolation of friends of a smallpox victim. The school superintendent told mothers their children must be immunized. Hospital employees received shots, and a medical authority thought everyone needed an antityphoid inoculation.

State Health Commissioner Samuel Dixon advanced precautions. He pressed the home front to maintain good health in order to aid "in the national emergency and to take care of the soldiers when they come home." Concerned about contagion, he advised men to put on trousers first and then footwear to steer clear of shoe bottoms carrying disease agents to the pants.

The war rallied the city's economy. Banks' check clearings registered an upsurge. The Lalance and Grosjean Manufacturing Company sought labor to produce clinical and cantonment equipment in a new plant. Facing a "particularly pressing need for enameled utensils," federal officials expressed satisfaction at the firm's response. The Central Iron and Steel Company turned out metal sheets for warships. The Harrisburg Pipe and Pipe Bending Company, operating "at full capacity, three shifts a day," added employees and contracted naval shells, as well as army ordnance. Concerning the company's munitions manufactured for Allied governments, British authorities showered "praise for excellent workmanship and speedy work." Factories hummed on Labor Day, and Harrisburgers identified with the Colonial's *Somewhere in America*, which shows scenes of the Brooklyn Navy Yard.

Harrisburg became a railroad hub. Renowned for their efficiency, lines moved troops, goods and riders. New rules dictated that paying passengers sit while free commuters stand. But the nation's rails congested, delaying deliveries of goods such as fish to city marts.

Labor remained elusive. Want ads spelled out the call:

> *Lathe Operators*
> *Also inspectors and helpers*
> *wanted to work on 4-inch*
> *shells for U.S. Navy…*
> *HARRISUBRG PIPE AND PIPE BENDING CO.*
> *LABORERS—20 wanted at once to work night turn;*
> *35 cents per hour. Apply at U.S. Aviation Building,*
> *Middletown, Pa., Herre Bros., Plumbing and Heating*
> *Contractors*
> *Laborers—Wanted; steady work…Apply Central*
> *Iron and Steel Company*

Boys did farm work, and children collected nuts. Pennsy stopped safety inspections because of understaffing.

Accidents marred industries. A fire broke out close to the Hoffer Flouring Mill, a firm doing government work. At Bethlehem Steel, a worker suffered a "crushed foot." Despite more safeguards, the firm reported an obstructing pipe break and additional injuries. At Central Iron and Steel, a mishap hurt a blast furnace operator. A week before, a conductor's disfigured remains turned up at the Pennsylvania Railroad Station.

The *Telegraph* applauded the State Department of Labor and Industry's "stump for safety." With Pennsylvania contributing a large share of the materials required for war, "it behooves those who are working at home to maintain the men in the lines and in the camps and to take such precautions as will sustain them in health and safety."

The war subdued Labor Day. As some plants ran "full blast" to comply with federal agreements, residents enjoyed excursions and picnics. Retailers and newspapers limited hours or shut down. Officials cancelled the Susquehanna's water festivities. Sober sermons recognized workers for their role in the conflict: Christ Lutheran Church's "The Honor of Labor" and St. John's Reform Church's "The Church and the Labor Question." A pastoral solemnized:

> *Embarked in a maelstrom of broken hearts*
> *America stands by her guns*
> *Turning her back on the peace she loves.*
> *Threatened by treacherous Huns;*
> *But the thought of the hour is the hope that cheers.*
> *When the black pall closes in,*
> *That sorrow and death are bought at a price,*
> *And suffering follows on sin.*
> *Our fathers who settled these fertile shores*
> *Were seeking a sect-free God*
> *And chief of their buildings of rough-hewn logs*
> *Was a place to worship the Lord,*
> *New He repays for this land is called*
> *With the fate of the world at stake*
> *To feed the nations; to shelter the weak*
> *And the arm of the war-god break!*

The municipality's infrastructure and environment underwent upgrades. Harrisburg Railways constructed a subsidiary branch and electric generating station. Building of the Penn-Harris Hotel progressed in spite of labor and material shortages. City authorities anticipated roadway and park maintenance, as well as a sustaining wall for the Susquehanna River's banks.

One commissioner noted the war's priority but believed "the city should have constant attention" since servicemen "are coming back some day and the old home town must not go to seed during their absence."

Some grumbled about alleged apathy. A letter to the *Telegraph* carried complaints about disrespect for soldiers and little citizen sacrifice. The correspondent expressed worry about draft evasions, "pro-Germans" and too few soldier services. In addition, the writer heard "too much wholesale use of profanity and vulgar talk." The Army Recruiting Headquarters scorned public indifference: "The people as a whole are not taking enough interest in this war." The *Telegraph* thought it "startling" that Harrisburgers failed to donate their quota for training camp libraries.

Maybe the discontents despaired over psychosomatic distress and could have comforted themselves with Radway's Ready Relief, the soldiers' restorative, administered successfully "in the treatment of Bowel Complaint, Colds, Rheumatism, Chills, Pains, Aches and Soreness of the limbs" more "than all other remedial agents."

An editorial aired one certainty. Imperial Japan loomed as no threat. America's resource base and military force, along with the vast span between the two nations, "combine to make combat with this country suicidal for the little yellow men who defeated China and Russia."

Chapter 4

MUSTER

November 1917–January 1918

Allied fortunes sustained setbacks in late 1917. The Italians, under assault at the Isonzo River, retreated to the Piave line, and the British offensive in Belgium petered out at Passchendaele. November witnessed the advent of the Bolshevik upheaval in Russia. The Allies, suffering heavy losses, pleaded for American fighting men. The War Department rushed plans.

Harrisburg responded to the summons, although the recruiting office's pet pooch, a collie, "wandered away," deserting the post. Posters plastered the city, and cartoonist Carroll B. Davish's sketches adorned Market Street. The Catholic diocese and the Patriotic Order of the Sons of America urged volunteering, as did soldiers home on furlough. *The Cantonment Manuel*, a recruit's book, eased discomfort about training camp. A Chestnut Street Auditorium gathering heard speeches from the mayor, a Britisher and a Canadian. In early December, the War Department ruled married men could sign up lacking a spouse's consent. But despite the exertions, recruiting lagged.

Harrisburgers came forward. A resident with English parents joined the British military. A child, straying about and hoping to unite with his soldier father in France, turned up at a local fire station. A fifteen-year-old, toting a low-caliber weapon, wanted to enlist. On being turned down, the boy exclaimed, "If youse could see me snipe sparrows with this gun, you'd be glad to give me a chance at the Germans."

By mid-December, a great number had volunteered, exempting the city from draft calls and setting records. Heavy enlistments beat out those in New York City, and by the next year, Harrisburg was leading the country.

Needs still existed. Aviation sought more men, and the navy wanted additional recruits.

Selective service encountered evasions and disqualifications. Samuel LaRue excused himself (his eight petitions for deferment came to naught), maintaining the "Germans c'n wait for me" since "[I] got to get th' corn in now." Linglestown draftee Harry S. Koons suffered the "loss of three toes," claiming his self-inflicted shooting was "accidental." Lawyers insisted registrants accompany dependents to court when requesting deferments. The army granted "absolute exemption" for disabling "flexed fingers, missing trigger fingers, epilepsy, mental diseases, stiffness of the elbow or shoulder, serious hammer toe, or varicose veins." Authorities reported over 50 percent of the first call bodily unfit.

Some selectees failed to report. They winked at bringing back filled-in forms. They changed addresses and withheld residences. In a few cases, men were unknown on the streets they listed. Several gave bogus abodes. A Cowden Street foreigner stated "he was sick in bed and his baby put the questionnaire in the fire to see it burn."

The Dauphin County Jail locked up alleged deserters on the loose. The majority had simply stayed beyond their leaves and sought passage back to camps. Still, the jail detained a number until military authorities retrieved them.

As if to shame draft delinquents, the Victoria ran *The Man Without a Country*. Touted as "a real treat in patriotism" and "a picture that thrills spectators and confounds traitors and slackers," the film portrays a pacifist's enlistment after reading Edward Everett Hale's classic of the same title. The theater's blurb pitched the movie as "easily the most pertinent and timely production of the season!"

Continuous call-ups and frequent farewells ignited emotions. Students, relatives and, in one instance, the Benevolent and Improved Order of the Elks cheered and teared as troops paraded to the Pennsylvania Railroad Station. Sheet music serenaded send-offs. The revived "The Girl I Left Behind Me" evoked parted company. A new release, "Smile and Show Your Dimples," palliated a miss's discomfort:

> *Little girl-ie you look sad,*
> *I'm a-fraid you're feeling bad;*
> *Be-cause he's leav-ing,*
> *But stop your griev-ing: (lit-tle girl,)*
> *He don't want you to feel blue,*

For it's not the thing to do;
It will soon be ov-er;
Then he'll come march-ing back to you.

"Cheer Up, Mother" steeled parents to relinquish their children:

Cheer up, mother, smile and don't be sighing
Dry the teardrop in your eye;
We'll come back with colors flying
After the war clouds roll by.

"America, Here's My Boy" pointed to a mother's willingness to release:

America, I raised a boy for you
America, you'll find him staunch and true
Place a gun upon his shoulder, he is ready to die or do
America, he is my only one, my hope, my pride and joy
But if I had another, he would march beside his brother
America, here's my boy!

Wartime called for prudent liaisons, keeping lonely-heart columnists occupied. The *Evening News*'s Annie Laurie frowned on gifts and photos for soldiers. She discouraged flirtations. The *Harrisburg Telegraph*'s Beatrice Fairfax disapproved of camp visits, elopements and secret nuptials. Both urged loyalty to absent servicemen, and Fairfax favored wedlock following lengthy courtship. In one instance, when parents worried about a returnee's disability, Fairfax stated a woman "will gladly take her chances of standing by a man who is giving himself to his country—and if he comes back crippled or maimed—needing love and devotion, who more proud than the girl who cares for him to stand by the wounded lover who has need of her?"

Newspapers promoted correspondence with departees. Laurie censured writing to the unacquainted and advised happy letters to the known. Parents opposed to corresponding befuddled Fairfax. The *Evening News* editorialized, "There is one insatiable, constant demand from soldiers…the demand for letters and more letters." The *Courier* added:

Every letter that goes to a training camp or overseas should be sealed with
good cheer and stamped with courage. Every message from the home town

should reveal the strength and courage that iles [sic] *behind the lines. No one knows how much they count!*

The *Telegraph*'s cartoon "Ain't It a Grand and Glorious Feelin'?" sketched a soldier, via a letter, receiving news of his baby's birth.

The *Evening News* critiqued unbridled "sentimentality," a female enfeeblement injurious to home front exertions. Openly expressed feelings "are harmful, they are ridiculous—they are un-American," flayed the paper. Reminding readers that both sexes "are IN the war and they are in to win," the editorial exhorted the primary "commandment of a fighter is DON'T WHINE!"

Service flags saluting military men decked the city. The Patriotic Order Sons of America and the Capital Legion, No. 1108, National Protection League made known their members. The Harrisburg Club and the Colonial Country Club posted participants. Central High and Wharton School boasted former students. The municipality's band and an Allison Hill fire station mustered, as did the Fisk Rubber Company.

Churches slated adherents serving, in some cases capped with ceremonies. Pine Street Presbyterian, Park Street United Evangelical, St. John's Reform and Lutheran Church of the Redeemer contributed enlistees. Market Square Presbyterian conducted honor roll disclosures with patriotic airs.

Harrisburg looked after departed soldiers' families. The Red Cross, through its Home Service unit, entertained their kin at the Civic Club; the *Evening News* suggested an invitation for Christmas dinner; and the National War Aid organization, locally known as the Daughters of 1917, explained federal dependent benefits.

The city cared for servicemen. The Pennsylvania Railroad promised their reemployment. In rushed nuptials at the Stevens Memorial Methodist Episcopal Church, the Reverend Clayton Albert Smucker wed Waiva E. Klare and J. Oram Wible before the latter's departure for France. The Red Cross Canteen Committee lavished troops in transit with "hot coffee, pretzels, chewing gum, chocolate, cards and cigarettes."

As Yuletide neared, retailers pitched all kinds of giftware for enlistees. Bowman's carried the spirited and practical "they most need such as good, serviceable sox, sweater coats, gloves, underwear, mufflers, toilet requisites, etc." Diener the Jeweler suggested, "Make it a jewelry Christmas" and itemized "a soldier's watch" along with "trench mirrors," "trench toilet" and "safety razors." Golden Seal Drug Store claimed, "There's no gift like [a] handy little camera to chase away his" longing for home, and Rothert's

A sunken heart. *From the* Harrisburg Telegraph. *Courtesy of PennLive.*

advertised a Victrola as "a friend at the soldier's side—to…sing for him, play for him, day after day!"

At the *Telegraph*'s behest, smoke moneys—contributions to soldiers' cigarettes—burgeoned. Contributions came from an eight-year-old girl, the Captain Howard F. Calder Post veterans, the YMHA's dances and a Harrisburg Academy football scrimmage. A twenty-five-year-old dollar bill entered the pool. Local firms did their bit for smokes. A play earned a ten-dollar donation from jeweler Max Reiter and Company. S.S. Kresse gave cash from song sheet sales of "The Most Beautiful Flag in the World." Plans developed to raise funds by showing the movie *Betty Adopts a Soldier*.

The *Telegraph* made known the doughboys' preference. It ran ads describing soldiers' appreciation, revealing, "One boy pulled out a half-used sack of Bull Durham and caressed it." They would exchange baked sweets for tip-top tobacco and found foreign cigarettes unsatisfying.

Testimonials boosted the smokers' kitty. The GAR sacrificed eleven dollars, asserting, "We as veterans of the Civil War know by experience of the sixties what it meant to be deprived of a smoke." In fact, tobacco, it was said, assisted the North's victory over the South. Guy Empey's book *Over the Top* pictured expiring servicemen requesting smokes to reduce suffering, and the author sold copies to support the tobacco campaign.

Solitary voices spoke out against smokes. Denouncing tobacco industry ads and their editorial support, B.F.M. Sours, a Mechanicsburg resident, charged, "These wicked hyenas care nothing for the men or for the Flag." Under peer pressure to light up, smokers became incapacitated, risking moral and dependable judgment as well as an unrecoverable vulnerability to respiratory disease. Sours concluded, "We may lose in the present war if tobacco cannot be kept from our men" because "it is a deadlier weapon than German steel." The WCTU asked the Red Cross to discontinue cigarette supplies and discourage servicemen smoking, since money is better spent "for the purchase of sweet chocolate, candy and sugar in other forms which both science and experience show to be beneficial to soldiers in giving them warmth, comfort and courage."

More and more the war became homeward bound. The *Telegraph* fashioned a casualty list categorizing "killed," "wounded" and "captured or missing." It ran the regular feature "Letters from the Front." The Rotary Club pledged to return the dead. Private Robert D. Wilson died of disease in camp, resulting in the community's first military burial.

Earl E. Aurand, a resident of Logan Street and a former Pipe Bending Company employee, succumbed of wounds in mid-December, the area's first combat death. His house flew a service emblem of one star with a red-and-white background. Aurand had provided his parents their financial resources. His family eventually received Red Cross aid. The *Telegraph* and a congressman helped his father find employment.

Coincidental with word of Aurand, the *Telegraph* forewarned, "The first of many," advising residents to brace for what the fates may behold. The same issue published, "There's a Green Hill Out in Flanders," a mother's melody memorializing the heartrending loss of a son, versed and chorused with the following sentiments:

> *When they tell the story,*
> *Why should all the glory,*
> *Go to those who fight with sword and gun?*
> *Those they left behind them*
> *Back at home you'll find them*
> *They fight a fight as brave as anyone,*
> *Hist'ry only knows about the others,*
> *Where's our hall of fame for "Soldier Mothers"*
> *There's a Green Hill out in Flanders,*
> *There's a Green Hill up in Maine,*
> *Under one lies a son, neath the sod and the dew—*
> *Sleping [sic] where he fell for the Red, White and Blue*
> *On the other there there's a mother*
> *In a little cottage waiting all in vain;*
> *So here's a tear for a brave heart in Flanders,*
> *And a cheer for a brave heart in Maine.*

Speakers left no uncertainty about the war's ravages and horror. A former U.S. consul recalled a submarine's sinking of the *Lusitania*. A Polish woman spoke of depredations in her publication *When Prussia Came to Poland*. Soldiers spieled forth on combat's terrors in Belgium and France. A British officer revealed realities in *How to Live at the Front*, as did Guy Empey in his volume *Over the Top*.

Cinema and relics imparted the Western Front close-up. The Victoria showed *The Retreat of the Germans at the Battle of the Arras*. William Strowse and

Opposite: Earl E. Aurand, the first Harrisburg soldier to die. *From the* Evening News. *Courtesy of PennLive.*

Above: A reverent reminder of sacrifice. *From the* Harrisburg Telegraph. *Courtesy of PennLive.*

Company on Market Street displayed a helmet taken from a lifeless enemy. The *Evening News* reported, "It is attracting a great deal of attention" and "is the first war trophy of the kind to reach Harrisburg." A city lad mailed Zeppelin fragments from France.

The purity of army camps, menaced by venereal disease, preoccupied the city. The YMCA and the Knights of Columbus raised funds for wholesome activities. Women, railroaders and students gave support, as did newspapers. The *Telegraph* warned of lurking "temptations with which every such cantonment is bound to be surrounded." The *Evening News* reported that "the percentages of soldiers, on both sides in the conflict, who were

The Victoria Theater contributes to the Soldiers' Fund. *From the* Evening News. *Courtesy of PennLive.*

incapacitated because…the evil of prostitution was not suppressed in the vicinity of the camps…were far greater than the percentages that actually fell in battle."

From rostrums, oratory prescribed. Secretary of War Newton D. Baker praised healthy influences, enjoining, "We must…send our boys home with no other scars than those received in honorable warfare." Edward W. Bok, *Ladies' Home Journal* editor, complimented the YMCA's beneficence but told of "a greater evil than the bullets waiting for your boys," quoting General John J. Pershing, who declared, "I don't fear the shells and the bullets of the Boche as much as I fear the women." Edwin E. Sparks, State College president, asked, "If we spend so much time in being bodily clean, why not spend as much in keeping spiritually clear?"

From pulpits, sermons elucidated: the Reform Salem Church's "In the Interest of the YMCA," the St. John's Reform Church's "The YMCA and the War," the Pleasant View Church of God's "Enlist in the YMCA Campaign to Save Our Soldiers," the Otterbein U.B. Church's "Christian Work Among the Soldiers," the Market Street Baptist's "The YMCA Drive and the Boys in Khaki," the Camp Curtin M.E. Church's "The YMCA in the Army Camp" and the Augsburg Lutheran Church's "Solicitude for Our Soldier Boys."

In January, the government printed Smileage Books containing coupons that could be exchanged for tickets to camp amusements, offering "fine, clean, theatrical shows" for enlistees. Sold by post offices and retailers, the books financed the expense of engaging entertainers. Harrisburg's National War Aid and two committees planned to market $5,000 worth of coupons, priced at $1 for twenty coupons and $5 for one hundred. The

Telegraph reflected: "A Smileage Book is a book of tickets.…You buy the book—that's where the 'smileage' comes in—one smile for you and quite a few for the soldier."

The city's WCTU believed sweets would tranquilize the troops. It sent "jellies" to encampments.

Authorities slammed seditious utterances, such as affronts to government officials, doughboys and Old Glory. A former senator and an English officer prowled Pennsylvania, including Harrisburg, and claimed "big crowds" as they publicized pro-German shenanigans. The comic strip *That Son-In-Law of Pa's* warned of enemy propaganda, while residents made known that a German piano tuner from Reading cursed Liberty bonds.

Management at Steelton's Semet-Solvay Company dismissed two employees for ripping a photo of Woodrow Wilson. "One…said the picture was torn down merely as a joke, and that he meant no insult, either to the President or to the flag."

Hearsay haunted Harrisburgers. Rumors "sweeping down upon the city" falsely charged treason in Washington and accused German sympathizers of poisoning tobacco and placing glass bits in chocolate. Finger-pointing alleging Red Cross malfeasance persisted. A public service article advised telephoning verified misinformation to the Bell Company. Bank officers quashed the tattle "that the Government proposes to confiscate the money on deposit."

Fears ran amuck. Recruiting officers, sickened after smoking stogies dropped off by a youth, became suspicious. Consumers believed enemy agents instigated inflated food costs. Speaking at a Board of Trade lunch, British vocalist Harry A. Lauder bared "the discovery of German guns buried in America, of warehouses heaped with food in order that it might spoil and go to waste, of schoolbooks tained [*sic*] with Prussianism and even German school teachers in this country."

The Spy, billed by the Victoria, stoked espionage anxiety. Pitched as a sensational unmasking of enemy operatives in the United States, ads revealed "there were at one time upwards of 10,000 trained agents of the Kaiser in America," reciting their nefarious deeds and subversive schemes. A blurb appended, "The German spy is everywhere," and another cautioned, "There are stormy days ahead for the United States if the enemy spies are not eliminated."

No chastisement was too excessive for disloyalty. The war declaration against Austria-Hungary cast scrutiny on that country's nationals and their possible confinement. A letter to the *Telegraph* criticized suffragist

The Spy aroused espionage fears. *From the* Evening News. *Courtesy of PennLive.*

incarcerations while wondering why "interned Germans are living on the fat of the land, and German spies are either acquitted or receive light sentences and escape prison?" The paper still favored the naming of residents who failed to patronize war bond, Red Cross and soldier fund drives. "Let us know who they are," the editorial pleaded, "so that we may treat them for what they are." It tagged on: "Every German or Austrian in the United States, unless known by years of association to be absolutely loyal, should be treated as a potential spy." The mentality became, "If you're not for us, you're against us."

The city stood on edge. Well aware of Teuton cunning for skullduggery, conspiracy and treason, the *Telegraph* condemned Hun employment in defense plants with the rousing "OUT WITH THEM."

Municipal police prepared for the registration of ethnic foes. Their enrollment took place without incident. The *Courier* endorsed the overdue step with vehemence: "For fear of injuring some innocent persons we have permitted alien enemies to go about their business doing very much as they pleased and the result has been that when our vigilance was relaxed the number of explosions, fires and other outrages have increase[d]." The sheet demanded, "The next spy saught [*sic*] ought to be strung up simply as an example for the rest of them."

In early January, a blaze engulfed tracts of the Harrisburg Pipe and Pipe Bending Company, gutting two large structures situated between Herr and State Streets, adjacent to Cameron and Pennsy yards. With hundreds of plant workers reconstructing, management expected little delay in fulfilling naval shell obligations. A company spokesman rejected speculations of sabotage.

Germanic kultur, stressing individual subservience to the government and territorial expansion by the state, came in for rebuke. It was perceived as treacherous, and Harrisburgers protested its presence. The city disallowed violinist Fritz Kreister's concert. A former Hapsburg soldier, he reportedly sent performance earnings to Austria and "boasted that after the Germans and Austrians had devastated a certain town 'there was not a virgin left in

Playful children execute an alleged spy. *From the* Harrisburg Telegraph. *Courtesy of PennLive.*

Opposite: Market Square
Presbyterian Church. *Courtesy of
Nancy D. Sheets and William Sisson at
the Market Square Presbyterian Church.*

Left: The Reverend George E.
Hawes. *Courtesy of Nancy D. Sheets
and William Sisson at the Market
Square Presbyterian Church.*

the place.'" Kreister eventually cancelled all engagements and entertained
for charities without recompense.

The Market Square Presbyterian Church's Dr. George E. Hawes
impugned Teuton Weltanschauung. Sermonizing on "Some of the Teachings
of German Kultur," he attributed Germany's "fiendish acts" to breeding
and pontificated that the current conflict was more "than a clash between
democracy and autocracy"; rather, "it is a clash between the teachings of
culture and the teachings of Christ."

Schools took pains to suppress inklings of Germanic culture in texts.
Administrators singled out *Gluck Auf* for its accounts of Berlin's regime and
leadership. Tech High pupils removed the kaiser's picture from "writings,"
and language teachers asked their classes if their primers contained any
Teutonized allusions. Erstwhile envoy to Germany James W. Gerard
referenced "German textbooks to show how the German propaganda"
infiltrated the curriculum.

The United Evangelical Church terminated *Die Evangelische Zeitschrift.*
The Germanic journal had given the ministry almost three decades of aid.
Supposedly, suspension followed growing expenses and subscription dips.

Teutonic tags stigmatized their targets. At a WCTU rally, Mrs. John DeGray spoke of a global crusade aimed at "killing Kaiser Bill and Kaiser beer." The *Telegraph* thought shirkers failing to finance the Red Cross deserved Emperor Wilhelm's black cross. When rubella, a contagious bug, shut down Linglestown schools, it was monikered the "German measles."

Caricatures scorned and avenged Prussian transgressions. A fiend approaches a helpless prisoner of war. A German-helmeted beast encounters an Allied tank. The Kaiser drops his sword labeled "autocracy" as a blade inscribed "justice" probes his heart. American aircraft and servicemen cow a sweating Wilhelm in a front-page feature. A pun debased his repute: "The Kaiser is a modern Nero"—admittedly very tough on the Roman.

The despised Hohenzollern rankled youngsters. Two lads scuffled on Capitol Park property by Third and Walnut Streets. When questioned about the reason for the fight, one of the boys blustered, "That mutt, he called me Kaiser Bill." He added, "My name's Bill, all right, but I ain't going to stand for being called a Dutch king." At the Stevens Memorial Methodist Church on South Fourteenth Street, girls accompanied gifts to soldiers with messages jabbing the German sovereign. Mildred Smith of North Fifteenth Street wrote, "Please, when you get a chance at that Kaiser, please shoot him for me." In the same vein, Irene Peregoy of State Street penned, "I wish you would take a good jolt for me at that Kaiser."

Songs spelled out Germany's fate. "It's a Long Way to Berlin but We'll Get There" promises victory followed by laborious effort. "The Stars and Stripes Will Wave Over Germany" foresees that country's surrender. "When We Wind Up the Watch on the Rhine" anticipates a glorious homecoming. "Marching Through Berlin," tuned to "Marching Through Georgia," captures the spirit:

> *America, the land for whom our fathers died to free*
> *Was consecrated by them on the rock of Liberty;*
> *Now at our shores the shadow of the blackest Tyranny,*
> *Phantoms old Macbeth, the Kaiser!*
>
> *CHORUS*
> *Hurrah! Hurrah! We're bound to cross the sea!*
> *Hurrah! Hurrah! Away to Germany.*
> *We've got the boys to take the Stars and Stripes to Victory!*
> *While we go marching through Berlin.*
> *The moans of Belgium thrill us, and the Poilus' heaving sigh,*

They're victims of the Boche's rape and wicked murder eye;
He's blasted homes and innocents and cots where wounded lie!
Vengeance we shout on the Kaiser!

CHORUS
We'll show our by-gone heroes, who've so nobly cleared the way,
We'll fight and die as they have for the grand old U.S.A.!
We'll sing the songs they used to sing—oh how our bands will play!
While we go after the Kaiser!

Naysayers of Germanic erasing held on. Children portrayed characters from *The Katzenjammer Kids*, a Teutonic carryover, for an Orpheum audience. The *Telegraph* wrote of a perverted understanding when "some people have been small enough to object to anything German." Such a view encouraged residents to ignore "that none of the great German composers were born in Prussia; and it is a well-known fact that the Germany of today is not the land of Beethoven, Schumann and Schubert." Harrisburg still feasted on cabbage "sauerkraut." The governor's pooch responded to "Fritz."

An internal threat loomed. Taking precautions, the state withheld licenses from Germans wishing to produce explosives, and draft boards prohibited Austrians from participation. The Harrisburg Reserves, a paramilitary force, held drills and rifle practice.

State, city and military representatives, along with local residents, viewed the Victoria's *The German Curse in Russia*. The film reveals how Teuton "propaganda" set the stage for Russia's disorders, messaging "a strong appeal that all pro-Germans in this Country be imprisoned and that every effort be taken to prevent any from leaving the United States."

A request circulated to organize all men too old for the draft. Called the "United States Guard," the group intended "to protect the utility plants and factories of the country from spies and bomb throwers."

Local socialists expressed unswerving allegiance. Loyal to the core, party members gathering in Maennerchor Hall pledged support for President Wilson's "No Peace Without Victory." Determined to uphold their beliefs, they hoped to increase the dissemination of their sheet, *The Eye Opener*. Anticipating the arrival of utopia, the Hall invited Milwaukee's Alexander Spence, editor of the *Vanguard*, to speak on "The Coming of Socialism."

"Doing My Bit" reminded residents of new responsibilities. Wartime necessitated bond buying, Red Cross work, legislative awareness and austerity. The column asked, "What is it you have left undone that you should do to make your life count in the weight of the nation and so in the power of its arms, the force of its principles and its welfare before the world that is testing it today?" Practicing kitchen economy and aiding military families signaled private duties. For the latter, one should offer "the personal, the intimate, the kindly, friendly help to the individual only a friend can supply." The *Telegraph* saw a consequence from the drives carried out. It believed the city and area had been unified.

Dauphin County's women's tally for war service dissatisfied. Women claimed that once trained, they would seek railroad, post office and government employment. But Red Cross volunteers failed to register, thinking they participated in federal work. Teachers worried registration would subject them to the draft. One official complained, "Harrisburg women are indifferent, almost to the point of being disloyal and unpatriotic."

In late 1917, the government began a new loan campaign to lure those with limited finances, particularly youngsters. Postal officials made available War Savings Certificates that cost $4.12 and matured at $5.00 and Thrift stamps that sold for $0.25. The latter permitted citizens devoid of resources to acquire a certificate over time. Government-provided Thrift cards contained sixteen spaces where stamps could be attached. A filled card was valued at $4.00 and, supplemented by sufficient pennies, could buy a War Savings Certificate.

Harrisburg geared up for sales. Savings associations appeared in workplaces, school buildings, meetinghouses, social centers and private residences. Promoters claimed the letters *WSS* (War Savings Stamps) would become prevalent. Labeled "Baby Bonds," the new issue, hawked as a Christmas gift, caught on.

Despite assistance by department stores, newspapers, children and Boy Scouts, the city slacked. The $28,000 raised fell far below the seven-figure goal. Postal authorities mounted a drive to awaken residents. Dauphin County found itself coated with appealing placards featuring "a plump, handsome baby boy, the individual who is likely to benefit by this saving system."

Poster urging the purchase of Thrift stamps. *From the* Harrisburg Telegraph. *Courtesy of PennLive.*

The *Telegraph* published a letter under the headline "Our War Duty." The writer, G.C.

Heathcote, indicted the community: "The Baby bonds are selling in Harrisburg, but THEY ARE NOT SELLING like moving picture tickets are selling every night at our movie theaters, and until the people of this city and all over this country can be brought face to face with the seriousness of the present day strife, Kaiser Bill has a mighty good chance to win." Heathcote went on: "Why not start a campaign and pledge ourselves in helping our government?"

Ne'er-do-wells jeopardized the city's patriotic reputation. Loungers loafed in barrooms and pool halls, unproductive yet sponging scarce sustenance. Some orated on sidewalks, drawing crowds and blocking window displays. Calls demanded their roundup and roadwork. The *Evening News* made clear, "It is not creditable to the American spirit that in these times when labor is so urgently needed everywhere, that some men are permitted to live off the community."

Gypsies wandered into Harrisburg. Fearing their curse on children, authorities shut down a shanty near Hamilton School. The nomads camped behind the State Arsenal near Woodward Elementary at Eighteenth and Herr Streets and near an Allison Hill primary school on Fourteenth and Market Streets. The *Evening News* fumed: "When money is plentiful and the Nation has nothing else to do but keep the peace, the sight of stupids throwing away their money on palmists, phrenologists, fortune tellers and the like perhaps provokes the public pity, but at a time when no money should be spent foolishly or no man or woman dawdle away their time, the public will have little patience."

"Harrisburg has never slacked!" So buzzed assurance that residents would live up to a peerless past during a Yuletide campaign for Red Cross membership. Officials set the goal at thirty-eight thousand registrants. But the drive fell behind. Households failed to display Cross flags for Christmas. Explanations ran from disinterest in the war's success to disregard for the organization's service. Some shirkers might have been "German sympathizers." The *Telegraph* reproachingly declared, "If you knew the life of an American soldier, lying wounded back of the first line trenches in France, depended absolutely upon an immediate rendition of aid—would you withhold a dollar from the Red Cross—AND KILL THE SOLDIER?" By early January, the campaign had petered out. Harrisburg "fell down." The Red Cross missed the mark. The *Evening News* editorial "The Unattainable" confessed the city "probably was asked to do an unreasonable thing."

The *Telegraph* scolded residents for "a too general indifference" to global war conditions. The paper urged a larger view. Accidents and shortages stemming from the war were misunderstood and contributed to peoples' "inability thus far to adapt themselves to extraordinary conditions." "We must get awake," the sheet reflected.

Wartime demand sped up city industry. The Harrisburg Pipe and Pipe Bending firm hurried naval shell output. The Harrisburg Manufacturing and Boiler Company hired workers, put in machines and expanded plants to expedite coastal artillery emplacements. The Moorhead Knitting Company hastened production and planned a Lyons, France exhibition. Burdened railroads scrambled to provide express companies timely service.

A Commonwealth Trust Company officer's speech to the Alricks Association, which was housed at Nineteenth and Market Streets, told of the banks' contributions. The significance of Liberty bonds and Federal Reserve activity, along with income tax information, highlighted the talk.

The war enhanced Harrisburg's role as a transport route. Indeed, the military valued the location as a supply hub.

A citizen's letter to the *Telegraph* rejected any suggestion of "hard times." He penned, "With careful and painstaking investigation [of] every real news item on conditions throughout the country, we are unerringly led to the only conclusion possible—that business was never better and that prospects of big business in the future are growing bigger all the time."

Accidents accompanied acceleration. In the three months preceding February 1918, newspapers reported fifteen mishaps. All took place at steel plants and rail lines. Steelworkers incurred serious injuries. At Central Iron and Steel, a metal piece hit an employee, another suffered a cracked jaw and a third lost fingers. Misfortune befell the Harrisburg Pipe and Pipe Bending Company. Among its bruised, one received a fractured leg. Railroad mischances turned deadly. Workers experienced broken skulls and smashed ribs. A brakeman toppled between moving freight cars and was sliced in half. A train crash injured riders, taking a Marysville resident's life.

Notwithstanding more building than in 1916, the war soon curtailed construction. Postponements included those of the Valley Railways Company's Walnut Street terminal, an underground cable, new schools and an African American YMCA. Labor and material expenses plus scarcities delayed street repairs and downsized the fire-gutted John Hoffer Flouring Mill Company's restoration.

The Penn-Harris's erection progressed. By late November, the structure was "half way up." The *Telegraph* editorialized about its rushed raising and pressing need: "The growing importance of this city as a military, munition and war supply center makes adequate hotel facilities necessary."

At Middletown, federal authorities enlarged a warehouse and purchased home sites. Harrisburg expressed elation, anticipating a housing heyday and a labor demand.

Railroad clogs delayed deliveries and caused shortages. "Transportation is the war problem," observed the *Evening News*. By late January, the Pennsylvania Railroad was freighting exclusively "fuel, foodstuffs and materials for war purposes."

Harrisburg endured a coal famine. Without heat, businesses and industries experienced slowdowns and shutdowns. Authorities feared widespread hoarding and rash purchases. Customer coal cards limited allotments. The Dauphin County Fuel Administration established marketing standards. Coal dealers overcharging beyond fixed prices faced investigations and fines. Snow held up fuel deliveries, and residents resorted to dredged river coal, bituminous coal and buckwheat (small anthracite bits).

Coal's scarcity blackened the downtown. Federal officials restricted its burning for commercial lighting. The Harrisburg Light and Power Company requested patrons' compliance and threatened disconnected service. In late December, residents abided darkened illumination. Lightless Thursdays and Sundays dimmed sign advertising after eleven o'clock at night. Streetlights remained on, but a gloom hung over the city.

The *Evening News* published coal-saving hints and advised residents to cut them from the paper and place them close to their heaters. Pointers denounced overwarmed homes and suggested not heating unoccupied houses. Furnaces had to be minded: mains and chimneys needed cleansing. Avoid suffocating low flame with excess coal; instead, add fuel slowly. Maintain a "high fire" at all times, but keep some of the flame open for the expending of coal vapors. Be sure grates are ash-free to ensure current into the blaze. Prevent cinders from heaping in the slag shaft, and hose down both.

Severe weather with below-zero temperatures gripped the city. Saving steam heat became a priority. The Harrisburg Light and Power Company urged customers to warm only rooms in use and churches to defer dusk activities. The community nodded. The Olivet Church, the Stevens Memorial Methodist Episcopal Church and the Harris Street United Evangelical Church fell in line. The Harrisburg Reserves and the Boy Scouts cancelled gatherings at the frigid Armory. The *Telegraph* concluded, "We have nothing to do but comply."

Federal decrees curbed industrial and business operations on Mondays, idling thousands of workers. Until exempted, 1,600 employees at Central Iron and Steel and 2,800 at Harrisburg Pipe and Pipe Bending received a holiday. Bowman's, Kaufman's and Dives, Pomeroy and Stewart promised Monday closures, but grocery stores remained open until noon. Banks continued their services. Schools were not impacted by the order.

Locked laundries disordered restaurants' routines and rumpled male array. Unable to arrange soiled napkins' and tablecloths' freshening, eating houses utilized paper substitutes. Collars went unwashed. One laundryman frowned, "A five-day shutdown will have every body [*sic*] turning them over." He added, "Low neck will probably be the style and you know what that would do to us." The *Telegraph* imaged a "collarless" Sabbath tacked on to "meatless" and "wheatless" daytimes, notwithstanding that nearly all gentlemen "would rejoice to see [the collar] relegated to the limbo of discarded styles, along with 'spring bottom pants,' knee trousers, powdered wigs and calfskin boots."

Movie houses, bowling alleys, pool halls and barrooms tried to continue operating. A letter to the *Telegraph*'s editor surmised that virtuous Americans seethed with wrath "that saloons and playhouses, etc., should be permitted to remain open during these five days when our factories and plants (manufactures of war munitions), the very things that would lead us on to victory, should be stopped." The correspondent, signing off as "a citizen," conjured, "Can you imagine the much hated, terrible Wilhelm permitting such a thing?"

The *Evening News* thought coal controls successful for stressing the significance of the "rainy day" concept: save for the future and don't squander "needlessly all that is made." All endure rainy days, and individuals "blind to this fact or indifferent to it, suffer."

The fuel famine modified practices. The *Telegraph* published a single edition on January 21 and shut down early. On "Heatless Mondays," Harrisburg railways operated a smaller trolly fleet. The company eventually listed "skip stops," streets where passengers could no longer board.

In the Fourteenth Ward on a "Fuelless Day," the Harrisburg Light and Power Company's streetlamp had been glowing since the previous day. The chronometer that operated the light lost power, caused by frigidity and snowfall. The most severe wintertime known was hampering services.

Police reported hoarding "coal hogs." One resident sought more after collecting fourteen tons. Another stashed his in receptacles topped with fruit. Criminality corrupted coal distribution. A United Ice and Coal Company delivery man diverted a quarter-ton portion from a home order and peddled it to a different party. Police questioned him.

Fuel deprivation stalked the city. A woman caring for her pneumonia-stricken father dismembered a stepladder to burn. A man broke smallpox isolation to find coal. A mother whose youngster contracted diphtheria needed heat for the child's room. The authorities dispensed coal to the latter, and Mayor Daniel Keister commanded "his department to spare no pains to alleviate suffering." In fact, he prepared to commandeer coal if necessary.

Harrisburgers improvised. A Walnut Street resident stocked sticks but saw the pile consumed in an accidental fire. Heavy snow blocked roads, hindering timber foraging. Officials thought railroads might sell old ties to avoid disposal expenses. Dismantling wooden fencing would beautify properties, claimed the *Courier*. A letter to the *Evening News* asked, "How about the dead wood in Wildwood Park," and added, "Could not that wood which is lying around be gathered up for fuel for the poor people in Harrisburg?" Homeowners used throwaway print to burn "newspaper log[s]." By late January, grocers were selling kerosene for heating.

The *Evening News* queried: How can one keep occupied on a "fuelless Monday"? Reading, calling on shunned chums and penning delayed correspondence came to mind. Of course, "We can do war work."

Living costs jumped 88.5 percent in January. War taxes impacted services. Rail travel, deed filing, financial transactions and amusements experienced hikes. Physicians charged higher fees to meet expenses.

Pricey commodities burdened residents. Butter, oleo, oranges, cabbages, eggs, cigars, milk, chewing tobacco, coal and wrapped bread became more costly. Buckwheat and cornmeal, consumed to boost conservation, were marked higher. Dear ingredients inflated soap. Turkeys imposed "a record figure for the great American bird in this city." Expensive footwear sparked editorial indignation: "It is a miserable situation when business men seize an opportunity like war to gouge the consumers....There has been a suspicion right along that the high price of shoes and other leather products was unwarranted." Some products resisted raises. Pumpkin pies, ice cream and Christmas trees retained rates. The Imperial Tea Company on Chestnut Street advertised nuts and java at prewar pegs.

Locals explored cost remedies. Consumers bought cheaper fowl, sidelining expensive turkeys. They boycotted milk. Bakers thought a co-op would reduce bread prices for the needy. An editorial suggested unwrapped loaves could lower overhead. Posters plastered throughout urged cash and carry, payment at the time of purchase and customers carting acquired goods. Grocers made plans to designate fair charges. Authorities made known a marketing list.

Demand outran provisions. Bottlenecked railroads and hoarding residents sapped sugar and salt. Donald McCormick, the food administrator, set flour prices and discouraged stock stashing. Food pressures mounted. Poor wheat yields, domestic demands and unending foreign needs gave rise to shortfalls. Allied requirements accelerated as cargo vessels succumbed to enemy submarines.

The city rallied to save foodstuffs. Schools and churches distributed cards, pledging conservation. Chamber of commerce members joined the rally. Restaurant and hotel proprietors lined up. Publicity promoted cooperation, and women appeared supportive. But by early December, under 50 percent had signaled promises. McCormick advised "that the latest food regulations are addressed primarily to housekeepers" and "in many families little or no attention has been paid to food saving."

Dr. T. Alex Cairns, speaking on behalf of the federal food administration, told of the ease of food conservation and how refusal aided the enemy. He recommended substitutes for meat, wheat, sugar and lard. He warned: "The great burden of the shortage of food, if we do not conserve, wisely…would fall upon the women and children of the land, for the soldier must be fed first and those at home afterward."

Locals organized. An appointed committee attended output, markets and savings. Along with promoting conservation, officials intended to blunt hoarders and profiteers.

Pledge signees received food cards. Federal authorities requested meatless, wheatless and porkless days as well as sugar and fat conservation. They condemned hoarding. The demand for food stressed railroads and interfered with military traffic. Helping Germany was "much insidious propaganda in the Country against conservation and increased production," they cautioned.

The program lent itself to dispositions. The district Anti-Saloon League applauded prohibition's grain savings. City Catholics acknowledged meatless Tuesdays and observed three meatless "Ember Days." Organizations canceled banquets or revised menus. Children could sacrifice by eating fruit instead of candy. The *Evening News* commanded, "Make the child feel that he, too, and she also are doing their part in the conservation of food for the country."

Residents contemplated food replenishment. Sap-sucking insects brought fruit trees solicitude. The *Evening News* speculated pork could be supplemented if "every patriotic person who has land on which a pig may be raised should give thought to growing that breakfast bacon rasher."

The city officially kicked off meatless and wheatless days in November. Tech boys at lunch observed the new order. Most Harrisburgers complied, but some seemed perplexed, and others became angry. Substitutes like oysters and spaghetti were served in diners. Some customers expressed disbelief of meat's Tuesday prohibition. By abiding, restaurant owners experienced profit losses and implementation problems. Some little diners disregarded a "Wheat Wednesday" proposal—"rather a contemptible thing," scolded the *Evening News*. On request by the Pennsylvania State Hotel Men's Association, some inns carried out "Mealless Fridays." In its dining coaches and eating places, the Pennsylvania Railroad offered war bread containing rye and graham, "said to be very palatable and healthful." Its city restaurant practiced "Wheatless Wednesdays." Wastage stirred rebuke. A citizen claimed he discovered stale bread thrown away by a Chinese restaurant on Market Street. The restaurant's owner fired his chef for the miscue.

As hotels and diners reduced meat purchases, consumers bought at a regular rate. Butchers reported more business and increased Tuesday sales. Residents appeared unmoved by the meatless call. Many "honor the patriotic request of the national food administration more by breaking it than observing it."

Food conservation became an educational matter. The Harrisburg Ladies' Advisory Committee at the Dauphin County Farm Bureau scheduled exhibits and talks. The Pine Street Presbyterian Church's women held demonstrations and offered notions like "How to Save Wheat," "How to Save Meat, Use More Poultry and Fish," "Fast on Candy" and "Save the Sugar, Use Honey and Syrup for Sweetening." The State College's Miss Mary R. Fisher lectured on the "Value and Uses of Grains and Grain Products."

Newspapers performed a public service. Isobel Brands's column offered tips about salvaging leftovers, preparing figs, using gelatin and cooking procedures. "Doing My Bit" warned that superfluous preparations wasted and thought sour milk could produce French cottage cheese. To facilitate wheatless days, the *Evening News* offered, without charge, *The Cornmeal Book*, a publication containing over sixty recipes.

Marketers pitched self-serving savings' themes. Bowman's asked the public for a "cheerful acquiescence." The store pleaded, "Don't waste food," and supported days without meat and wheat. Davenport's diner, calling itself the "Architects of Appetites," hawked lunch alternatives "of equal nourishment and as tasty in flavor." It claimed its wheatless pies exemplified for the country and thought patrons desired more fish. W.B. Rodenhafer retailed "all kinds of sea food" for meat savers and fish consumers. Coca-Cola considered "it a privilege to comply with the Government's request" to conserve sugar by cutting production. Grape-Nuts asserted savings like no rival and assured, "You are conserving when you eat" its product.

Regimentation taught lessons. "Doing My Bit" foresaw "knowledge about the right ways to live" and "better nourishment at less cost." Reducing meat intake and adding fruit, vegetables and fat would balance diets, a subject homemakers ought to consider. Rarebit (Welsh rabbit) afforded nutrition, and nuts contained protein. Morning cocoa consumption would break the coffee addiction. "If we can learn to abhor waste, to save and to be thrifty again," envisioned the *Telegraph*, "it would be one compensation out of dreadful war."

Pest control protected provisions. Cockroach eradication removed the "most disgusting" pilferers. The city waged war on rats, allies of the kaiser that were "doing their 'bit' for him night and day." Combat codes admonished, "Clean up everything!" Rodents colonized in marts, shops and farms and housed in unthreshed and unmarketed crops. But never harm nonpoisonous serpents, falcons and owls. They, like ratters, guard food stocks. Shield fare in secure vessels and exterminate rats with venom, snares and stalking. It was a patriotic obligation for all to awaken the community to the peril, beseeched the *Evening News*.

War gardens warranted urgency. Readiness called for the use of former tracts and new ground. Truck farmers would include women and youths. "Doing My Bit" advised farm machinery's weather proofing and birds' protection. The annual Farm Show provided a heads-up about gardening. Donald McCormick and Shirley Watts anticipated all unused land would hold plots. The International Harvester Company prepared tractor-handling instruction. Walter S. Schell's seed shop exhorted, "Every foot of soil should be made to produce food this year for you and for others" and instructed, "Get busy, plan to grow and 'put up' all the vegetables you can—fill your shelves—if you don't you'll be sorry."

Harrisburg favored the congressionally proposed daylight savings. Welcomed as a "necessity" and a "desirable" war measure, it would encourage recreation, improve public health, conserve fuel and prolong children's play. What's more, "great help would be the additional time home-gardeners would have for the working of their plots in the evenings."

Harrisburgers experienced a water shortage. Securing a pump to refill the reservoir took weeks. Meanwhile, levels dropped due to a Harrisburg Pipe and Pipe Bending's fire and Central Iron and Steel's needs. Residents squandered by running faucets to forestall frozen pipes.

The water shortfall created a crisis. Manufacturers and businesses on war contracts feared interruption. Firemen worried about buildings ablaze. Allison Hill's homes went dry. "Harrisburg waterless" entered the vocabulary. Officials pushed conservation. They wanted pipes cloaked, windows fastened and cellar crannies corked. Mayer Keister proclaimed, "TIMELY DON'T TO SAVE WATER," a list of behaviors residents should avoid to save water. One suggestion was boiling snow. After cleaning his mug in the liquidized snow, he vouched, "Melted snow has the Susquehanna water beat a mile." A large pump finally arrived. The reservoir soon measured highs. Water bans ended, yet conservation continued. Harrisburg had overcome "waterless" days.

Snow blanketed Harrisburg. Clogs impeded movement. Trolleys stilled. Residents trudged. Cold hindered Penn-Harris construction. Rural communities were isolated. Obstructed roads and rails hampered coal and munitions traffic. The *Telegraph* bemoaned, "Good roads are a growing factor in our war preparations and snow blacked [*sic*] highways are the allies of the Kaiser." The city continued to brave the most frigid wintertime recorded. It summoned help. The mayor declared a "Volunteer Snow Removal Day."

Disease disquieted the city. Crammed trolleys transferred germs. Milk specimens revealed *E. coli*. Suburban Enola recorded typhoid fever. Officials

Market Square snowed under. *From the* Harrisburg Telegraph. *Courtesy of PennLive.*

Snowbound streets thwart trolly traffic. *From the* Harrisburg Telegraph. *Courtesy of PennLive.*

Residents trudge to work in paralyzing snow. *From the* Evening News. *Courtesy of PennLive.*

worried about smallpox contamination. Infections broke out before and after Christmas. Precautions were implemented. Middletown boiled water to ward off contagion. Quarantines confined the poxed. A banker and two barristers received inoculations. "Disease is mankind's greatest enemy," bayed a Swift Laboratory ad. The Atlanta, Georgia firm advised writing its medical manager for preparation to fight off its onslaught. Harrisburg needed a pesthouse. The *Telegraph* urged the county and city to build "a modern contagious disease hospital." Unfortunately, labor shortages and material expenses inhibited construction.

In stressing December 6's National Medical Examination Day, the National Association for the Study and Prevention of Tuberculosis explained the reason all required medicinal vigil: "Sixty percent of men called in draft [were] rejected by physicians."

The Red Cross Christmas Seals campaign began in early December. Boy Scouts learned its marketing pitch. Schoolchildren, offered prizes for sales, participated. Pleasant View Church of God's sermon "The White Plague and the Help of the Red Cross Seal" weighed in. Downtown booths aided the push that lasted until January in an effort where the "need is greater than in any previous season."

Prostitution, "one great uncontrolled source of deadly disease," made "the vice problem…primarily one of health." Tarts propositioned johns for flings in bordellos, hovels and autos. Suppressing moral depravity became a "cause of social hygiene," targeting syphilis, a major killer.

Officials shielded soldiers from solicitors, promising to stanch their luring into water holes and evil haunts. The mayor invoked regulations "to restrain the vultures who would fatten at the expense of the soldier's money and manhood." The city kept its word. Culprits faced arrest for furnishing liquor to servicemen. The Fourth Street Church of God's pastor sermonized on "Giving Soldiers Rum." Police raided the "Bucket of Blood" and apprehended Bertha Watkins, "a disorderly house" madam.

Soldiers misbehaved. Two forced entry and stole liquor at George Bolton's store on Ninth and Market Streets. On sentencing, the presiding judge told the men, captured and abashed, "It's a pity that you were locked up in your uniforms."

Harrisburg went after gaming. The *Evening News* wanted unlawful turkey lotteries stopped. The police arrested African American crapshooters.

Swindles and snatches blemished the home front. Bogus agents sought Red Cross and soldiers' contributions. A crook carried off the Cross donation container. War gardeners lost stakes and staffs to sackers seeking fuel.

The Pennsylvania Railroad employs women. *From the* Harrisburg Telegraph. *Courtesy of PennLive.*

Labor shortages initiated employment shifts. Women, once trained, found jobs and status. The Pennsylvania Railroad engaged them for yard and office tasks. The Central Iron and Steel Company hired a woman to shovel refuse. The *Courier* encouraged domestics to exchange the kitchen for the war plant.

Men fumed. When Paxtang quarries employed women, workers walked, formed a committee "and stated their objections to the invasion of women." Quarry operators let the lassies go. At the Postal Telegraph, messenger boys struck as soon as girls received jobs. One exclaimed: "Hully chee, th' women folks is buttin' into everything."

The *Telegraph* recognized the need to employ women. It applauded their contributions and hoped for their postwar engagements. But "coolie" laborers had to stay out. They were racially unassimilable and "unfair competitors," and their admission and repatriation would stir anger harmful to U.S. ties with China and Japan.

Knitting became ubiquitous. The Red Cross invited volunteers and offered instructions. Chairperson Anne McCormick of the Harrisburg chapter wanted men to stitch. They "are wasting their time sitting idly at luncheons," she claimed. "It is a waste of time that is valuable, and it is a patriotic duty to knit for the soldiers."

Residents met the challenge. Homemakers, church members and company employees sewed. Children, including Girl Scouts and young boys, took part, as did the elderly. Disabilities failed to hinder women who were blind, deaf and dumb and wrist-fractured from participation. Patients at the Pennsylvania State Lunatic Hospital joined in.

Elderly German native knits for the Red Cross. *From the* Harrisburg Telegraph. *Courtesy of PennLive.*

Support came from retailers. Soutter's hawked needling tutelage, while Bowman's gave instruction, open to both boys and girls. Marketeers added their two cents. Optometrists and opticians cautioned, "Good eyesight means good knitting—poor eyesight poor knitting." Singer hyped its sewing machine, contending its "work is good and strong, like the soldier boys."

Local stitchers produced quality. The Pennsylvania Cross Division's director complimented the city's chapter: "After five weeks of careful inspection at the warehouse of every knitted garment sent in…we have found your work of such excellence that we authorize your own inspection."

Yarn could be elusive. Knitters needed to tighten balls and prevent slippage. Balled yarn dangled from theater tiers. It dropped on streetcar floors and trailed off on the shoes of passengers to the exits. A motorist zipped down Market Street followed by a runlet of yarn.

By January, health authorities had recognized a national malady. They reported "that thousands of women are breaking down under 'knitting nerves,' and that the spread of this new ailment is becoming very serious."

Wartime affected appearances. Designers militarized belts and boots. Austerity simplified evening dresses. Leather savings eliminated high heels. Authorities pressed economy and home fabrication. One opined, "When the enormous number of men are taken from the various factories to serve in the trenches and in the munition factories this will be a necessity."

Mrs. Victor F. Lecoq sacrificed her head of hair. The chestnut-brown strands helped the Red Cross through proceeds realized from a hairstylist. "I am going to sell my hair for the benefit of our local Chapter," Lecoq announced.

The war militarized toys. Soldier collections and ship replicas retailed in stores readying for Christmas. German-produced playthings lost their American market: "The Stars and Stripes are waving over the land of the Hun, so far as this industry is concerned, and you will believe that if you glance at the wonderful displays in the toy shops of Harrisburg," according to the *Telegraph*.

Thanksgiving inspired widespread but restrained observation. African American clergy objected "to any unnecessary luxuries or social frivolities." President Wilson asked for a unanimity of soul and resolve to help the famished: "There is no better way of arriving at such unity and performing such service to hungry humanity than by neglecting our usual Thanksgiving gorging." Isabel Brands suggested turkeyless makeshifts. The Harrisburg Baking Company rendered thanks for bounty and admonished, "Do not waste bread."

The city celebrated serenely. Football, family get-togethers and furloughed soldiers marked the day. Pastors preached and prayed patriotically. The Salvation Army and Bethesda Mission served the indigent. However, a "vacant chair was a cause of sorrow in many Harrisburg homes."

Harrisburgers commemorated Christmas as was customary. Newspapers discouraged forbearance and urged revelry. Candy was scarce. Christmas trees sold for prewar prices. Mistletoe arrived in time to avert a "kissless" Yule. Trolleys crowded the streets, shoppers shopped and business thrived.

The city took on a wartime ambience. Soldiers milled about, strolling the streets and attending the churches. Factories, where allowed, recessed operations. Residents decorated windows with Red Cross ribbons, but officials prohibited lighting candles because they were a fire hazard. Skating and sleighing mitigated melancholy and longing for absent loved ones.

Harrisburg greeted 1918 quietly, with subdued festivity. Mummers cancelled pageantry. Clergy forsook services. Café patrons ate and drank sparingly. From one joint, patriotic songs issued. "It was a Hooverized New Year's from every standpoint," reported the *Evening News*.

Repose settled over the community. Financial institutions, government offices, shops and stores shut down. Still, factories and munitions works operated. The YMCA conducted athletic contests.

Flag waving resolutions came forward. Isabel Brands advised housewives to conserve, serve, sacrifice, adapt and "not complain."

Anna Hamilton Wood's "1917—New Year—1918" christened the transition:

> *The fresh turned page; the empty slate*
> *Wiped clean of greed, of lust, of hate.*
> *Left for the word decreed by Fate,*
> *For, "Victory!"*
> *A finished year; a stern tale told;*
> *Faith in God's blessings manifold*

With hearts that value more than gold
Democracy!
The chance to LIVE; the chance to DO;
The chance to see the big things thru
With finer courage than we knew
But yesterday!
A year of trial? A year of stress?
Perhaps, and yet a year to bless
By showing us our hidden best.
With honesty!

Franco-American ties deepened. The Pine Street Presbyterian Church's Reverend Lewis Seymore Mudge thanked France for U.S. liberty. Pastors planned to welcome visiting Parisians, a professor and a chaplain. A music devotee sought to schedule a French organist. The Civic Club facilitated the selling of gewgaws produced by poilus.

A "tenderness" existed. Frenchmen appreciated Americans. Doughboys adored French nurses. The *Courier* fretted that mademoiselles might woo U.S. servicemen. The lyrical "When Yankee Doodle Learns to 'Parlez Vous Francais'" breathed the allure:

When Yankee Doodle came to Paris town,
Upon his face he wore a little frown,
To those he'd meet upon the street he couldn't speak a word
To find a Miss that he could kiss it seemed to be absurd.
But if this Yankee should stay there awhile
Upon his face you're bound to see a smile.

CHORUS
When Yankee Doodle learns to Parlez vous Francais
(Parlez vous Francais in the proper way)
He will call each girlie "Ma Cherie."
To every Miss that wants a kiss
He'll say wee, wee on ze be-on ze boule-boulevard,
With a girl, with a curl you can see him promenade.
When Yankee Doodle learns to Parlez vous Francais,
"Oo la la, a sweet papa" he will teach them all to say.

"America to France" poetized the camaraderie:

Take them, O beautiful France,
Close to your generous breast;
Keep them, my dear dead sons,
Honored, beloved, at rest.
Under your glorious flag
Under your red, white, and blue
Near to your gallant boys,
Bury my laddies, too.

Harrisburg answered the calls of distressed peoples. The Red Cross collected moneys for victims of a massive ammunition explosion in Halifax, Canada. Children sacrificed their Christmas savings, and a jailed African American relinquished a Canadian coin. The local National War Aid gave cash to Poles. In late December, residents received a request to help famished Armenians. The Jewish Relief Fund sponsored a dance at Winterdale. Attended by over three hundred donors, the occasion successfully raised proceeds for Jews in the military.

Allied liberation of the Middle East enabled British foreign secretary Arthur Balfour to announce his country's support for a Jewish national home in Palestine. Rabbis sermonized celebrations, and congregations offered financial aid. The *Telegraph* editorialized that "Palestine" as "a home for the Jews" sounded like "a good idea."

Media kept tabs on Russia. The Victoria screened *Rasputin, the Black Monk*, a tale of the Romanoffs' collapse, and *Kerensky and the Russian Revolution*, a portrayal of the dynasty's successor. The *Evening News* cartoon *Deeper and Deeper* depicted Russia's descent into chaos. Dives, Pomeroys and Stewart retailed Isaac F. Marcosson's *The Rebirth of Russia* and Leon Trotsky's *The Bolsheviki and World Peace*, introduced by Lincoln Steffens and ballyhooed as "the world's most sensational book." A health-conscious city noticed a late January report: pestilence raged in Russia.

War or no war, traditional prohibitions necessitated adherence. The Civic Club's board of directors deplored the Victoria's showing of free films on the Sabbath "and hopes that this may not be a precedent for laxity about Sunday entertainments in the future." A lifelong resident considered a movie theater the "House of the Devil."

The First World War fashioned expressions. Harrisburgers became acquainted with "digging in," "doughboy," "Fokker," "Fritz," "Lee-Enfield," "Lewis gun," "poilu" and "no man's land," among others, originating from belligerents and serialized in the United Press's *Trench Dictionary*. The phrase "over the top" (meaning out of the trenches and to the attack) titled a book, headlined a newspaper column and celebrated a Knights of Columbus goal. Shredded Wheat Biscuit boasted, "Going over the top in any field of human endeavor is a matter of physical preparedness"; its product provided "a nourishing, satisfying breakfast, lunch or dinner."

The endless "less" compounds irritated. Coupled with coal, meat and wheat, the modifier suggested that self-denial equated loss. The *Evening News* questioned, "Why not cut the 'less,' which hath an ugly sound and does not at all express the fact that, while we have less, our friends have more?" The paper suggested "Italian coal day—Monday," "British meat day—Tuesday" and "French wheat day—Wednesday."

The idea of establishing a forum to prevent wars gathered momentum. At the First Baptist Church's biblical conference, Dr. A.C. Gaeblein prophesied a league. In its list of book releases, the *Telegraph* made known Theodore Marburg's *League of Nations*.

Postwar publications bore witness to disappointment. Japan's 1931 incursion of Manchuria proved "the League's impotence, its shrinking from Force, the advance enjoyed by the aggressor, the fact of war." When the Japanese invaded the Chinese mainland six years later, the League of Nations did nothing. In 1938, British prime minister Neville Chamberlain confessed, "The League as constituted today is unable to provide collective security for anybody."

In January, the chamber of commerce heard Dr. Iyenage, Eastern and Western News Agency chief, speak about Nippon's role in the global conflict. He promised Tokyo's partnership with the Allies to erase "Prussian autocracy from the face of the globe." He visualized separate spheres of influence: "Just as the United States must be the leader in affairs on the American continent, so Japan must sound the dominant note in the East."

Chapter 5

PERIL

February–April 1918

In the late winter and early spring, the food situation became precarious. Poor harvests and transport shortcomings deprived the Allies. Submarine sinkings and swollen appetites aggravated the crisis. The *Evening News* warned, "The success of the Allied cause depends on America's shipping 75,000,000 bushels of wheat across within the next three months."

Voices pressed for food savings. Editorials urged "eat less" and "let us not grumble." Spokespersons told farmers' wives and Kiwanis members how to husband. At Bowman's, Mrs. J.L. Lamb demonstrated "How to Cook War Meals," and in the Chestnut Street Auditorium, British labor leader W.A. Appleton praised Americans "especially in the matter of conserving food." Officials asked bankers and clergy to save. A letter to the *Harrisburg Telegraph* wanted clubs and churches to "abolish…unnecessary eating" at gatherings. "Doing My Bit" beseeched readers to be a "home soldier."

Advertisements echoed the call. Dives, Pomeroy and Stewart pushed provision economizing, while Hupmobile Sale Corporation and Bowman's pleaded for profligate avoidance. Doutrichs displayed a George Washington image to exhort, "Food will win the war—don't waste it." A Goldsmith's refrigerator promised provender preservation.

Suggestions and signs saturated the city. Making the entire meal with a single serving would save victuals. The *Courier* declared gravy-mopping a plate's residue "will win the war." The paper also thought the names of food slackers should be publicized. Posters, including a message board on Market Street, called for safeguarding vittles. Reservoir Park's notices cautioned about picnic disposal. An official proclaimed, "No one is to waste one scrap of sandwich, bread, butter, sugar or even lemonade." He added, "Nothing for the birdies, as in the days of yore."

Wheat became a priority. Regulations mandated combining it in breads with another cereal at a fifty-fifty ratio. Bakers further restricted white flour in pies and doughnuts. "Victory bread" demand and consumer relish delighted them. A Lemoyne bakery claimed its product met "all the requirements of Uncle Sam without sacrificing the high standards of quality for which Bricker's O-K Bread is famous." Schmidt's Bakery bragged its brand embodied "the bread that's patriotic all the way through and down to the last crumb."

Rules required buying an equivalent white alternative plus wheat flour. By February, stores were selling a fifty-fifty factory mix. According to the *Telegraph*, "Many liked the mixture better, saying that it has more substance and a distinctly pleasant flavor."

Some shopkeepers disobeyed. Officials shut Vendel Mahek's store on South Cameron. The Austrian-born Mahek sold white wheat minus an equal substitute and retailed "to an individual as much flour as he or she cared to buy." The wholesalers Hoffer and Garman on Eighteenth Street suffered a week's closure for retailing excessive quantities of milled wheat to an individual.

Substitutes gained favor. Oatmeal produced cookies and crackers. Barley made breads and biscuits. Spuds, plentiful and celebrated during April's "Potato Week," contributed to the staff of life. Housewives converted parsnips into griddle cakes.

Yet nothing satisfied like cornmeal. Bakers liked its flour. Corn, a grand grain of Native American heritage, "is going to come pretty near wearing a crown this year." Dives, Pomeroy and Stewart anointed the crop the king of America, appraising, "There's more food value in corn than meat, eggs or most other vegetables—and it's the cheapest nourishing food you can buy," adding, "You'll step lively all day after a serving of delicious hot corn muffins at breakfast." Along with bread, it offered recipes for "Hot Tamales," "Beef Scrapple," "Polenta," "Cornmeal and Sausage" and "Cornmeal and Oysters."

The column "Kitchen Economies" suggested saving formulas. Macaroni dishes reduced food costs and provided nutrition. Frequent dumpling eating would habituate households to meals without bread. To conserve white flour, the articles advanced substitute ingredients for pancakes and waffles.

Pastors, patriots and prudes blasted cereal-based booze. The Reform Salem Church sermonized "Prohibition," and the Presbyterian ministry resolved to end "the use of grain foods in the manufacture of beer." The *Telegraph* bemoaned the dissipation and wondered, "How long are we to see our dinner tables robbed?" The paper published letters denouncing the loss and deeming incomprehensible how "this criminal waste can go on in face of the fact that unless we save food we will lose the war."

Customs disappeared. Suppers gave way to bread's loss, and morning meals sacrificed cereal, replaced by fruits—excepting one:

> *My breakfast is not what it was*
> *In days before the war.*
> *They've Hooverized the grape-fruit;*
> *Can't get it any more.*

In late March, the federal food administrator decreed a wheat decrease. Hoover allotted every individual twenty-four ounces per seven days.

Meat makeshifts multiplied. Lamb and veal received recommendations. Protein-rich cheese, fish, greens and beans acquired attention. The *Telegraph* printed a correspondent supporting fish ladders' construction. The Manhattan Restaurant puffed "backing up Uncle Sam…because we served the largest variety of seafood." St. Paul's Parish House sponsored a baked bean dinner.

Doing without. *From the* Evening News. *Courtesy of PennLive.*

Hens' value vaulted. The *Telegraph* editorialized for city-bred poultry. "Doing My Bit" discussed chicken care. The column likewise made known free fowl publications. "Raise poultry if you want to eat" became a catchphrase, each resident obligated to transform his "backyard [into] his munition factory."

Scarce sugar Hooverized sweet tooths. Counter beverages, soft drinks, cookies and candies were shorn of saccharine. Expensive Easter eggs shrank, their chocolate cover thinned. Officials requested a frozen flavored dessert and sherbet production pause.

Residents could consume sweets and be loyal patriots, assuming choices minimized sugar. Authorities approved "gum drops, jellies, jelly beans, marshmallows, lemon drops, stick candy, fruit tablets and chocolate-coated candies with nut and fruit centers." Borden's claimed its "Eagle" condensed milk conserved sweetener. In late April, food administrators restricted sugar transactions to thirty-two ounces per person. However, a prescribed forty-eight additional ounces aided families' canning needs. Investigators uncovered illegalities. Retailers sold sugar against regulations. Weis stores advertised the sweetener's price, a prohibited practice.

Coal's shortage disordered. Manufacturers faced stoppages. The Shimmell Community Center halted socials. The Harrisburg Light and Power Company feared a deprivation of steam heat and city illumination. The *Telegraph* shortened press runs. More coal arrived in late February,

Dark and Cold to Pa   **By Cliff Sterrett**

averting interruptions and supplying households. But quantities dropped below demands, and fuel dealers trembled at cold weather's approach. One coal merchant cheated. G. Frank Milleison of North Third Street short-weighted two orders. Legal actions resulted.

The housing want worsened. Federal curbs, building cuts, labor scarcity and expensive materials worried the chamber of commerce. A worker influx aggravated "the biggest problem now confronting the city." A war-spurred housing market turned to renting. Homeowners let rooms, and realtors leased homes. Many complained of rent extortion. The city's Real Estate Board investigated. A committee probed. The mayor asserted, "Anyone who strives to benefit at the expense of the public during the present war times is a Hun in spirit as well as action."

Harrisburg scrounged for labor. The school district considered evening and summer classes for adult training. Dr. Charles B. Fager led the United States Boy's Working Reserve of the Department of Labor's War Emergency Bureau. Its National Enrollment Week, starting March 18, recruited for farm work. Ministers and "Four Minute Men" spoke of the significance of rural "manpower." The YMCA summoned "Soldiers of the Soil." High school youths received fourteen days of instruction at Pennsylvania State College prior to assignments. The *Telegraph* ran the come-on, "Say, you sixteen-year-old patriot, you can't fight, but you can farm."

The *Evening News* carried a full-page employment ad. Its "MESSAGE to Harrisburg Workers!" revealed jobs for men and women "in all branches of industry" and urged applications in nineteen firms. Factories struggled to retain employees. Middletown refused to hire laborers quitting city plants.

A letter to the *Evening News* favored assigning traveling salesmen to agriculture or industry. Judging their services "useless to retailers," the correspondent envisioned "their salaries as salesmen saved to the consumer, and the burden of their passage and baggage taken from the railroads."

A spirit of urgency enlivened gardening. February plans aimed at twice the previous output. Guidelines prepped tillers. The city promised information. The schools proposed instruction. The Emerson-Brantingham firm explained the tractor's value. The Natural History Society scheduled a speech about vegetables. The Daughters of the American Revolution (DAR) heard a zoologist talk on cultivation.

Publications showered residents. Professor L.H. Bailey's expertise produced *Lessons with Plants*, *Manual of Gardening*, *Principles of Vegetable Gardening*, *Practical Garden Book* and *Farm and Golden Rule Book*. Dives, Pomeroy and Stewart retailed Charles H. Selden's *Everyman's Garden in Wartime*, Eben

E. Rexford's *A-B-C of Vegetable Gardening* and *The Home Garden*, as well as John William Lloyd's *Productive Vegetable Growing*. The United States Department of Agriculture offered, free of charge, its *Farmers' Bulletin No. 255: The Home Vegetable Garden*.

Advice poured forth. Tipsters suggested crop selection, plot size, pest control and disease protection, along with fertilizer use. A letter to the *Telegraph* prewarned about opportune seeding: "A good time to plant is when there is just sufficient water in the soil to keep it moist and when the earth feels warm to the hand."

Newspapers provided planting insights. The *Telegraph* ordered readers a free gardeners' booklet and listed preferred vegetables. In early March, the *Evening News*'s "Doing My Bit" pressed for timely acquisition of gardening provisions. Its farming page reminded tillers, "The seed is the thing in war gardens" and stressed, "If the seeds aren't right the garden will not be right." The sheet ran a series of garden lessons and an informative chart from the International Correspondence Schools' agricultural program.

Residents rallied. The *Telegraph* exhorted, "Food slackers are quite as serious as other kinds of slackers, and all must lend a hand in the raising of food products." The mayor promised teamwork with the chamber of commerce and planned to till his own garden. The city administered a plow service. Pleas addressed women who need not fear loss of attractiveness since "health and beauty are to be found by working in the garden, and in addition to this, the fair gardener will be helping to solve the nation's food problem." Children desiring plots inquired at schools. Girl Scouts also heard the call.

Garden acreage exceeded the previous year. The chamber of commerce sponsored more lots, and the schools acquired more ground. Landowners rented property, and households utilized backyards. The Jennings Manufacturing Company donated space for employees behind its plant. The Harrisburg Benevolent Association granted land to former tillers.

Retailers hawked garden wares. Kaufman's peddled implements. Charles F. Kramer's, S.S. Pomeroy, William Runkle and A.P. Kitchen pushed seeds. Using an image of Uncle Sam sowing, the Holmes Seed Company insisted, "It is a patriotic duty to plant every inch of ground."

Harrisburg waged war against felines. They damaged gardens and killed birds. "Are cats in league with the Kaiser?" wondered the *Telegraph*. Residents hung a bulldog's picture to scare dogs and cats and spread pepper to confront the predators.

A garden ditty, composed to the tempo of "Over There," made plain the exigency:

Johnnie get your hoe, get your hoe, get your hoe;
Mary dig your row, dig your row, dig your row;
Down to business girls and boys,
Learn to know the gardener's joys.
Uncle Sam's in need, pull the weed,
Plant the seed,
While the sunbeams lurk do not shirk
Get to work,
All the lads must spade the ground,
All the girls must hustle round.

CHORUS
Over there, over there;
Send the word, send the word over there,
That the lads are hoeing, the lads are hoeing,
The girls are showing ev'rywhere,
Each a garden to prepare,
Do your bit so that we can all share
With the boys, with the boys, the brave boys,
Who will not come back 'till its over, over there.

A menacing common foe solidified Harrisburg. Anti-German emotion hardened, the Hun brand fully justified. German troops inflicted atrocities. A returned veteran deemed them "beasts." A movie, *The Hearts of the World*, pictured a lecherous Teuton's hands on a helpless French maiden. The Olivet Presbyterian Church screened government-produced films, playing up the "barbarism of the Germans in their destructiveness."

Spokespersons charged Germany had shelved Western values. Wilhelm epitomized the biblical Babylon. His nation supplanted "Nietzsche and Bismarck" for "Goethe and Kant and Hegal [*sic*]." In fact, "The Kaiser's Religion Stands for Religious Autocracy," an *Evening News* article declared.

The city cursed the German monarch. W.F. Bell likened him to a carnivore scheming "to fly at the throats of the rest of civilization and overcome the unsuspecting peoples of the earth." *The Kaiser, the Beast of Berlin*, a motion picture, vilified Wilhelm as the "Jackal of Europe." Youngsters threw mud at his postered image. The *Telegraph* thought the *Syracuse Post-Standard*'s conceived moniker of "William the Frightful" too tame "for the wretch"; instead, it preferred "Butcher Bill, who is going to be gored to death in his own slaughter pen!"

The German emperor demonized. *From the* Evening News. *Courtesy of PennLive.*

The kaiser posed a threat. Dr. Frederick Monsen bared Berlin's conspiracy to take the Panama Canal. George L. Reed analyzed Andre Cheradame's Pan-Germanism publication. The city kept tabs on German residents. Alien registration proceeded smoothly but snaillike. Most of the fatherland's natives had been naturalized. They possessed skills and expressed loyalty.

Yet suspicions prevailed. Harrisburgers blamed German sympathizers for vandalizing a snow shrine celebrating Italian victories. Their alleged food consumption verged on sabotage. Their imputed misinformation jeopardized Red Cross and Liberty loan efforts, leading authorities to say the rumors "are simply a smoke screen behind which are being launched lies that are well designed to strike at the country." Frank G. Fahenstock Jr., Kiwanis Club chief, asked members to unmask the falsehoods with the slogan "Swat the lie."

The German presence annoyed. The *Evening News* snapped, "[Its] influence is bad and [we] are deliberately taking steps to cut it out." The paper reported Cleveland's citizens torching German books in a large fire and quipped about such a "senseless waste" because of a "strong demand for paper rags."

The war hastened the German language's demise. Churches and clubs converted to English's Americanism. M.E. Moeslein observed the Maennerchor Society "dwindling away," retaining a mere twenty German-tongued fellows.

Colloquialisms surrendered their Teutonic taint. Sauerkraut became "pickled cabbage" or "liberty cabbage." German flapjacks gave way to "naturalized pancakes." After a sneeze, "Have a smile!" replaced "gesundheit."

The city proposed to redesignate German-named streets for sons killed in battle. German and Moltke stood out, but hardly any others could be found. Doughboys' surnames could replace Hop, Snow and Cream, handles targeted for jocular jabs. Excepting Hanover, British nomenclature dominated. Harrisburg's German alleyway, enunciated "GAR-muhn," took its name from forebearers. Opposition developed to changing Muench Street's label since it derived from Charles Muench, a Swiss Protestant.

Some sidestepped Germanic erasure. Mr. and Mrs. Frederic C. Martin scheduled a classical recital "of the three B's—Bach, Brahms and Beethoven" at their Riverside residence.

Flag-wavers judged the German tongue insidious. Bishop James Harry Darlington wanted its removal from educational curricula. Pennsylvania's governor also desired its exclusion. The *Evening News* grumbled that the "language of hate is still taught." The Past Presidents' Association of the Patriotic Order Sons of America pressed educators to eliminate the tongue. One person reckoned German a "menace."

The language had its defenders. The *Telegraph* believed one could study German and still be loyal: "Nothing is to be lost thereby and much is to be gained." The paper called Rutgers College "silly" for superseding German with Spanish. Dr. F.E. Dowes urged caution and coolness, arguing, "We are not primarily fighting a language," and tacked on the idea that German "has peculiar value in business and science."

City schools recorded fewer students taking German. Tech boys preferred France's lingo, because when they "enlist they will be better fitted to mingle with the French allies." In addition, the school deleted Teutonic passages from texts. Principal Howard G. Dibble at Central reported, "German is strangling itself to death and it will not be necessary to eliminate it." The previous year, only 9 pupils selected it while 165 picked French. Area districts acted on the language issue. Susquehanna Township High School dropped German in mid-April. Lancaster High discontinued the tongue, as well as Germanic literature in early May.

Harrisburg stood prepared to crush war dissent. Tech fired German teacher H.A. Liebig, a native of Germany but a naturalized citizen who was suspected of Central Powers sympathies. Liebig defended himself, claiming his dismissal was unwarranted. Nevertheless, editorials supported his departure. The *Telegraph* applauded school officials for the outing: "We are not just now engaged in warming serpents in our bosoms." Less serpentine yet just as forceful, the *Evening News* commanded, "The first suspicious utterance or action is a cause for investigation." At Central, Dibble assured the student body of instruction without the threat of enemy partisans. He surveyed the faculty and found all were true patriots.

Left-wing activist Scott Nearing planned a city visit. However, his supposed pro-German views prompted Tech to refuse him at its venue. The *Evening News* approved: "Nearing's experiences in being forced off the faculties of two universities because of his radical views and utterances are not calculated in times like these to persuade thorough-going Americans to open school houses to unrestrained speechmaking." Later charged under the Espionage Act, Nearing risked tarring and feathering in the City of Brotherly Love. Likewise, Mayor Daniel Keister doubted the IWW planned a Harrisburg confab. In any case, William Haywood, its leader and war opponent, would be denied permission to stump.

In April, an Illinois mob lynched the German-born Robert Prager, seemingly for anti-war chatter. The *Telegraph* blamed Congress for vigilantism, arguing it "has been forced upon patriotic Americans." Despite the need to heed constitutional and lawful guidelines, the paper, just the same, pointed out the consequences of unpatriotic propaganda: "Foolish people who utter disloyal sentiments through ignorance or bravado must understand that they are treading on dangerous ground and when they get in trouble they should realize that they have brought it largely upon themselves."

Authorities suspected sedition. Berryhill Street's Harry A. Wenrich, Swatara Street's Jane G. Zea and South Fifteenth Street's G. Russell Fortney allegedly circulated the anti-draft *Kingdom News*, a publication of the International Bible Students of America. Agents seized *The Finished Mystery* from Ida Bowman's North Eighteenth Street residence. The book, written by Pastor Charles Taze Russell, reputedly peddled disloyal expressions.

The Harrisburg Reserves set out to stifle the seditiousness. At a meeting, spokespersons complained about unchallenged statements. Jesse E.B. Cunningham declared, "We have been too liberal, too tolerant with a lot of people who ought to have been strung up to lampposts in this country early in the war." The more restrained E.J. Stackpole called for fair investigations and law observances that would impede "the mob spirit... if it ever showed itself in a blind, unreasoning, unjust way." The *Telegraph* advocated blackballing and casting out dissenters. It stated, "The time is long since here when we can look with tolerance upon lukewarm supporters of the cause....Those who are not intensely for us are against us." The *Telegraph*'s "Do You Know" column remembered how the community dealt with those unsympathetic to the American Revolution: "It gave them twenty-four hours to leave the district."

Films spiked espionage fears. *The Spy and the Eagle's Eye* pictured Americans unearthing German agents. *The Spirit of '17* portrayed spies fomenting labor turmoil. The enemy targeted munitions plants in *The Wasp* and *The Thing We Love*. A simulation fed anxiety. At the Boyd Memorial Building, a mock trial convicted Noble Frank of spying. An alleged spy actually turned up in the city. Authorities apprehended Email Kriegsman on suspicion. The son of an unnaturalized alien, Kriegsman had lived in Germany for many years.

The press howled in a vindictive tone. The *Courier* accused Harrisburg of tolerance: "Its spine has turned to mayonnaise dressing." The sheet added, "There are ten thousand German sympathizers in America who ought to be hung up to the nearest lamp post and shot." The *Telegraph* likewise bellowed for the skipping of due process: "If the government does not act soon and vigorously[,] patriotic citizens may be expected to take the law into their own hands."

Harrisburg mobilized enthusiastically for the third Liberty loan, launched on April 6, the date of the country's entry into the war, with a city goal of $3.5 million. The federal treasury announced an honor flag system to encourage towns to attain allotments. The banner would be awarded once a community satisfied its goal and one-tenth of its residents pledged subscriptions.

Fanfare attended the drive. The actors Douglas Fairbanks and Charles Chaplin stopped by and endorsed the loan. The YMCA conducted a "cross city run" with participants holding bond ads. A billboard on the capitol's grounds listed communities meeting their quotas.

Orators marshaled for loans. Dr. George Edward Reed, an educator, lectured an Ohev Sholom Temple audience, and Rabbi Louis J. Haas

Parade of service flags for kinsmen. *From the* Evening News. *Courtesy of PennLive.*

remembered "The First Liberty Bond Purchaser." Lieutenant Pat O'Brien and Captain E.A. Baker, among others, spoke at the Chestnut Street Auditorium. The same venue heard spokespersons praise the Pennsylvania Railroad's patriotism. In a presentation to the loan's industrial committee, Dr. Bagnell stated bluntly, "The man who can and won't put money into Liberty Bonds is giving aid and comfort to the enemy, whether he intends it or not."

Women entertained loan appeals. A flag-waving gathering paid attention to Madame Schumann-Heink's speechifying and singing. Miss Elizabeth Rachel Wylie, a monetary wiz, addressed women about subscriptions. Wylie presided over the Fortnightly Club, "a group of women interested in spreading financial knowledge among women so they may become increasingly fit to assume the responsibilities thrown upon them by the war."

Businesses and industries galvanized bond buying. New York Life recorded purchases. Theaters donated earnings. Banks facilitated subscriptions. Firestone Tire and Rubber Company invested, as did the Harrisburg Railways. Industrial firms made known bountiful procurements.

Employees supplemented employers' efforts. The Doutrich retailer, the School of Commerce, the Central Iron and Steel Company and the Printing and Publishing House, together with its Central Book Store, registered 100 percent subscriptions. The Harrisburg Railways tabulated purchases. The Pennsylvania Railroad promoted workforce participation via leaflets.

Churches gave the push a helping hand. Services and a Liberty Sunday march backed bonds. The Grace Methodist Church on State Street held a loan worship. At St. John's Reform Church on Fourth and Maclay, Reverend George W. Hartman petitioned for purchases, forewarning a German conquest of America would invalidate its currency and "any one having money would be made paupers." He added, "The only sure way to avert this is to subscribe whole-heartedly to this loan."

The civic-minded contributed. Kiwanis Club members bought bonds at a banquet and promised to aid sales. WCTU volunteers took out subscriptions, and Independent Order of Odd Fellows adherents set a goal of "100 per cent for Liberty."

A takeoff assisted bond publicity. Dressed as the kaiser, a business executive entered a loan team's lunch. While stepping to his seat, "he was bombarded with buns and biscuits, hisses and hoots." Pressured to subscribe or be tossed from the gathering, the fake Wilhelm yielded. "I'll buy vun," he uttered— adding, "Derre no good nowhow."

Warriors affirmed the loan's value. Canadian veterans visited and spoke on its behalf. A French pilot celebrated subscriptions by ringing around the capitol. A doughboy's letter to the *Evening News* itemized how a fifty-dollar loan would equip and ordered, "I'm 'going across'—you 'come across.'"

Touching cries came from those who sacrificed sons. Earl Aurand's mother spoke of the Liberty loan's meaning. She intuitively realized her good-bye meant the last sight of her boy. Sylvester Sullivan's mother told of family members buying bonds and hoped to purchase one herself. She admitted sleepless nights since her lad's death. Calling the German leader a beast, she declared, "I'd like to have a chance at the Kaiser myself."

Youth helped sell and sacrificed for bonds. Girl Scouts pushed sales. Boy Scouts circulated posters, one for homes and individuals, titled "Liberty Bell," and another for retailers embellished with Lady Columbia. Between April 27 and May 4, they solicited the community in a subscription "clean up." The *Evening News* photographed boys who gave away four years' worth of bike savings for a loan. On North Second Street, Mrs. Ira Romberger's children purchased a bond from moneys accumulated in their bank account since 1907. Newspapers posted loan ads. Published singly and jointly, many covered a page.

Enterprises trumpeted iconic boosters. Doutrich's pictured Uncle Sam keeping company with the Liberty Bell and Old Glory. Dives, Pomeroy and Stewart recalled the Revolution's Robert Morris. Various Harrisburg firms recruited the Statue of Liberty, and New Cumberland businesses displayed

Girl Scouts aid Liberty loan campaign. *From the* Evening News. *Courtesy of PennLive.*

an eagle hovering above advancing doughboys. The School of Commerce and corporations hallowed the human sacrifice. They pitched a loan in memory of local war dead.

Bond blurbs recalled German war crimes. On a whole page, the Central Iron and Steel Company intimated, "You can have your share in America's answer to German savagery." Uptown merchants pilloried the kaiser as a "champion brute" out "to conquer worlds with brutishness and barbarism."

Come-ons made clear the need for funds to remain unfettered. Bowman's reminded, "Liberty calls for dollars as well as soldiers." And it warned, "Buy bonds or wear them." "The war…must be won right here at home," prompted the Harrisburg Pipe and Pipe Bending Company. Witmer Bair and Witmer, clothing dealers, questioned, "Of what value is democracy without freedom?"

Uncle Sam's Liberty loan drive nails the kaiser on the noggin. *From the* Evening News. *Courtesy of PennLive.*

President Wilson designated April 26 as Liberty Day to promote bond sales. The holiday gained approval from the chamber of commerce's Merchants' Division, the Harrisburg Retail Grocers' Association and the Keystone Grocers' Association. Mayor Keister's proclamation recognized the occasion. The stores closed at one o'clock in the afternoon. The post office limited hours. Poetic verse pointed up the urgency:

While a mad beast prowls at will,
Whose hands drip blood, whose lustful eye
Appraises to ruin, or kill?
The price? American manhood knows,
As our fathers before us knew,
And the flags of them both shall not return
Till this fearful thing is through!

Music brought "vim and vigor" to the subscription crusade. Troup's marketed John Philip Sousa's "Liberty Loan March." Eighty vocalists organized in five units paraded, airing flag-waving numbers. The Chestnut Street Auditorium staged a recital. A lyric messaged "What Are You Going to Do to Help the Boys":

Your Uncle Sam is calling now on ev'ry one of you.
If you're too old or young to fight there's something else to do;
If you have done a bit before don't let the matter rest,
For Uncle Sam expects that ev'ry man will do his best.

CHORUS
What are you going to do for Uncle Sammy?
What are you going to do to help the boys?
If you mean to stay at home,
While they're fighting o'er the foam.
The least that you can do
Is Buy a Liberty Bond or two.
If you're going to be a sympathetic miser,
The kind that only lends a lot of noise,
You're no better than one who loves the Kaiser—
So what are you going to do to help the boys?
It makes no difference who you are or whence you came or how,
Your Uncle Sammy helped you then and you must help him now.
Your brothers will be fighting for your freedom over there,
And if you love the Stars and Stripes then you must do your share.

"Come across or the Kaiser will," advised the *Telegraph*. But bond sales slowed. The *Evening News* reported, "In this country we are blind to the danger that besets us." The *Courier* editorialized, "Harrisburg is hiding many bond slackers" and agreed with the chamber of commerce about its "smoke out." The *Telegraph* criticized as invalid the excuses of burdening progeny, religious views and offensive soliciting. Steelworkers intimidated an Austrian. They escorted him to a bank, pressuring him to purchase a loan.

Despite conundrums, Harrisburg exceeded its goal by $12,000. "We have gone 'over the top'" magnificently, celebrated the *Telegraph*. The paper perceived a budding "reverence" in the nation: "We are convinced that we are fighting the good fight; that we are on God's side."

Advisory columnists found romance pressured by draft calls, departures and deployments. In spite of the risks, Beatrice Fairfax and Annie Laurie approved nuptials for older couples sacrificial and sincere. The latter concluded, "If you are…willing to give up all other friends and wait…your love is true and if you decide that it is better to marry now I wish you all happiness."

Both frowned on two-timing. Fairfax advised against doing anything with boys at home that would belittle one's beau in France. Laurie's heart went out to soldiers. She scolded a girl desiring to socialize while her love remained abroad: "If you were really in love with your captain you would never consider it a hardship to wait for him and to refuse the attentions of other boys while he is gone." When a correspondent admitted a new attachment in lieu of her draftee, Laurie stiffened: "I think you've shown that you are not really capable of loving any one now, my dear, when your supposed love turned from one to the other quickly."

Fairfax and Laurie responded to letter-writing queries. Fairfax encouraged correspondence with a serviceman in spite of his failure to visit during a furlough. Laurie discouraged chiding those who failed to write back. She also opposed letters to strangers and by juveniles.

America entered the war during an age of racial intolerance and lynching. In Memphis, Tennessee, a mob set an African American on fire in a metal cage; he was accused of murdering a young girl. In Galveston, Texas, Whites lynched Charles Sawyer, suspected of rape. The East St. Louis, Illinois, riots left forty Black people dead, spurring the *Telegraph* to criticize lynch law. In July, the *Courier* claimed an African American flung himself at a girl in Wildwood Park. The Harrisburg Colored Law and Order League investigated and found the allegation false.

Negative images stereotyped Black Americans, who were confined to servile roles. Comic strips poked fun at their speech and appearance. The *Telegraph*'s *Bringing Up Father* by McManus caricatured a fat-lipped, overweight domestic worker. The *Evening News*'s *That Son-In-Law of Pa's* by Wellington satirized a polite and meek man. Sambo references proliferated. An Orpheum Theater

A common American occurrence during the war to make the world safe for democracy. *Author's collection.*

ad illustrated Black children with stereotypical watermelons. It screened the "darktown follies," featuring Rastus in a low comedy musical. Dives, Pomeroy and Stewart advertised a kid's game, Ten Little Niggers.

The Birth of a Nation depicts "a passionate and persuasive avowal of the inferiority of the Negro." Called the greatest movie ever made by a

137

Top: A negative stereotype of a Black woman, typical of press portrayals in segregated Harrisburg. *From the* Evening News. *Courtesy of PennLive.*

Bottom: A negative portrayal of an African American. *From the* Harrisburg Telegraph. *Courtesy of PennLive.*

Foreman: "What's the matter, Sambo, are you sick?"

Sambo: "No sah, boss, I jes don received mah questionnah."

Sambo, a negative stereotype of the Black man. *From the* Evening News. *Courtesy of PennLive.*

Harrisburg resident, it demonstrates a self-righteous South, a "shameful" Reconstruction and an overriding concern about shielding "Southern white womanhood" from Black "beasts." Some Harrisburgers lashed out at the portrayal. A letter to the *Telegraph* asked pointed questions:

> *Why should the black man always be shown in a bad light? Why can not the truth be told? Why is the wrong-doing of the colored man painted so red? Why is it the black man must always appear so black in nature? Why is it so wrong for the black man to join by marriage the two races that the*

white man joined by blood? Did it seem so wrong to a blooded southern white gentleman in the dark days of slavery, when he intermingled his blood with the blood of the negress held a slave and forced to receive his embraces?…God made all men free and equal, what right has man to break the will of God?

The Civic Club's Washington's Birthday observance heard the state librarian tell of Pennsylvania's outstanding forefathers. He concluded *The Birth of the Nation* "is most despicable in its wrong portrayal of Thaddeus Stevens' wonderful work."

Yet race-mixing offended. A local criminal court reproved a White woman and a Mexican man for living together. The judge feared the creation of a "crossbreed."

Despised African Americans suffered discrimination. Color-coded classified ads occasionally called for "Whites only" and Black workers for lower-paying placements. Newspapers identified lawbreakers as "Negro," implying an innate and generic criminality.

In spite of prejudice, segregated Black people gave the war unstinting support. Dr. Charles Crampton, Seventh Ward steward, provided inspirational leadership. He taught Red Cross first aid classes, planned an African American YMCA and chaired the Wickersham Auxiliary's board, a Black church women's organization. Crampton also presided over the People's Form, an educational society established in 1912.

William H. Craighead, YMCA worker, in France. *From the* Harrisburg Telegraph. *Courtesy of PennLive.*

The Form slated patriotic speakers. James Weldon Johnson, an officer of the National Association for the Advancement of Colored People (NAACP) and author of *The Autobiography of an Ex-Colored Man*, anticipated wartime gains for the race. Roscoe Conkling Simmon declared, "Teaching the world democracy my country instructs her own in lessons of liberty." William Edward Burghardt DuBois, the NAACP's *Crisis* editor and war adherent, and William H. Lewis, onetime assistant attorney general, discoursed. Lewis "urged the colored people to remain loyal and reserve all criticism, and cooperate with the government in conducting its various campaigns."

African American ministries rallied. The Briggs Street's African Methodist Episcopal Church heard

African American women of the Red Cross's Wickersham Auxiliary. *From the* Evening News. *Courtesy of PennLive.*

Dr. Crampton and other orators and conducted prayers. Clergy asked congregations to "sacrifice."

Black women responded ardently to war's summons. The Wickersham Auxiliary, created by Mrs. Lew R. Palmer, did Red Cross work. A dance raised funds for soldiers' aid. "Get a divorce and join the army" was the theme of a patriotic parade. A Seventh Ward matron contributed a buck, saying, "Southern slavery was bad enough…but from what I see of this here Kaiser Bill he's suttonly got it all over Simon Lagree."

The *Evening News* published a letter by E.L. Carey Jr., an African American resident of Steelton. Carey commended Black women for "the noble work that they are doing to win the war." He wrote how authoritarianism in the United States held down Black Americans and bid "when this war is over…we hope that Democracy will find a resting place in the hearts of our people; that segregation, jm-crowism [*sic*], disfranchisement, lynching and barbarous murders, based on color, will have a just penalty at the chopping block and such acts be buried headless and recorded in the future history of our Country as a thing of the past."

Black men trooped to the colors. The city honored their dedication. Their enlistments helped the area meet its quota. They received a round of applause at a mass gathering at Tech High. Expressing patriotism, they signed up for the Quartermaster Department's noncombatant Stevedore Regiment. The African-American Perseverance Band serenaded and accompanied draftees marching to the railroad station.

Authorities dealt peremptorily with the disloyal. A young Black man told police, "Germans are coming over to clean you up, and it will be a good thing." A judge told him that "in certain sections they hang people for such utterances." Professor Rothwell Deane, a Bermuda native, made unpatriotic comments about Old Glory and found himself held over for grand jury action.

Vice disquieted the city. The *Courier* wanted bars closed early on Saturdays to reduce lawbreaking. Arrests for selling liquor to soldiers increased. Locals thought military police would curb sales to servicemen passing through the railroad station. Raids broke up gambling dens. Police jailed three men netted at the Crystal Hotel on Market and Aberdeen Streets. The *Evening News* targeted horse racing, dismissing jockey clubs as "non-essential."

Harrisburg became a red-light district. Streetwalkers lured clients to hideaways. Officers pounced on disorderly houses on South Court, Charles and Strawberry Streets, among others. Venereal disease worried officials. The State Department of Health established clinics, including one in the city. The federal and state governments teamed up to control any outbreaks. In the YMCA, Dr. J.W. Ellenberger lectured on "Social Diseases with References to Their Dangers Towards Soldiers and Drafted Men."

By mid-April, vice had spread. Troop camps brought more soldiers to the area. Harrisburg sat beyond the five-mile zone of federal jurisdiction barring brothels near military bases. In compliance with Washington's request, city officials took action against bawdy houses. The situation seemed to have improved because of police raids since the first of the year.

The community was obsessed with immorality. Mayor Keister investigated allegations of "indecent wriggling by a dancer" at an Orpheum performance. The *Evening News* editorialized, "Burlesque of the putrid character…will be the last of its kind here is worthy of a city that prefers to rear its young men in refinement rather than in a brothel." The paper reported new teen dances originating in Springfield, Illinois—the "Death Grab" and "Over the Top"—that, "if permitted to continue, will submarine the perfect morals of the youths." At the Pine Street Presbyterian Church, the Dauphin County Sabbath School Association came up with the slogan "Bim-Wac," an acronym pointing toward a virtuous path: "Clean bodies, minds, words and actions."

The Harrisburg Ministerial Association probed motion pictures. It concluded most movies "appealed to the sex passion or the crime instinct of the audience." The *Evening News* praised the clergy for their service to city parents. In March, a speaker at the Teachers' Institute called idleness the "greatest danger to youth," urging them to substitute war gardens for movie houses.

Little girl knits for doughboys.
From the Harrisburg Telegraph.
Courtesy of PennLive.

The conflict brought forth the unfamiliar. The *Telegraph*'s "War Time Lexicon" introduced *O-C* (commanding officer), *sergeant major*, *liaison officer*, *company runner* and *bandoliers*. Readers became acquainted with *concussion* and *shell shock*. They learned *Na-Poo*, *kicked in* and *pushing up daisies* meant "death." The *Evening News*'s "Names in the News" column covered the battlefield with *pillboxes*, *barrage*, *Rosalie* (French bayonet), *emplacement*, *curtain-fire*, *dugout* and *snipers*. Its column elucidated the political terms *Italia Irridente* and *Francstircurs*, the place names Ukraine and Amiens and the personalities General Ferdinand Foch and Sir Douglas Haig.

Another name hit home. The *Evening News* published a photograph by G.R. Holbert, a South Fourteenth Street resident. Holbert, a sailor, put in duty on the USS *Connor*, designated for Commodore David Connor, a city native born in the eighteenth century.

By the spring, Harrisburg's knitting fixation had snowballed. The Red Cross met wool expenditures and needle needs. The city library's basement housed its sewing circle. Clubs, churches and homes served as venues for bees and teas. Schoolchildren and old folks joined in.

Department stores offered needlers support. Bowman's held a knitting lesson welcoming youngsters. Dives, Pomeroy and Stewart advertised a class.

Entertainment spirited stitching. The Civic Club showed films to knitters. A YWCA program performed a "Knitting Girls" number. Comic strips sketched characters sewing.

The Red Cross begged for socks. A poem evoked:

> *This little khaki stocking*
> *Is not for you to wear,*
> *But for a little trifle*
> *To help the boys o'er there.*

The ditty "Sitting Knitting" personalized the preoccupation:

> *There's dust in all the corners,*
> *There's mending to be done,*
> *There are buttons off and socks all full of holes*
> *Poor hubby's getting thinner,*
> *It's the automat for dinner,*
> *Since wifey started knitting,*
> *He's a lost and weary soul.*
>
> *Chorus*
> *All day long she sits, and knits*
> *For soldiers, and sailors who are fighting o'er the sea*
> *While hubby's shirts are ripping,*
> *She's sitting, and knitting,*
> *Knitting for the boys who're going to*
> *Set our country free*

Winifread Clark's column in the *Evening News* addressed the sewing frenzy. She plugged a helpful book yet revealed a malady. "Knittophobia" is "a new disease…brought on by too much knitting, the doctors say, and it has something to do with nerve centres." Continuous stitching without pause, physical discomfort, anger, curtness, cracked nerves and appetite loss worry loved ones, who call a physician, "and he says you're down with a bad case of knittophobia." Clark hoped for "some kind of humane cure."

The *Courier* reported a remark overheard in a theater on Market Street: "Say, Joe, this girl sittin' next t' me gives me a punch in th' ribs avery [*sic*] now an' then; I'm goin' to talk to her." His friend responded: "Hey, y' better look out—maybe she's knitting."

Chapter 6

FORWARD

May–July 1918

German offensives battered Allied lines between May and July. By late June, the United States had deployed 897,000 soldiers in Europe, including Pennsylvania's Keystone Division. As casualties rose, the Allies cried for more troops. A caricature in a city paper called for three million men.

Harrisburg ranked first for enlistments countrywide and responded to a sign-up drive. City officials, local organizations, veterans, women and theater managers helped. Ten days of programs mingled parades, lectures and community sings.

To enhance festivities, spectators paid a donation to pound pegs into a wooden facsimile of the Kaiser's noggin. "Step up, ladies and gentlemen, and nail the Beast of Berlin for the small sum of ten cents or one thin dime," a hawker shouted. Clergy took exception: Reverend Lewis S. Mudge and Rabbi Louis Haas thought the "stunt" stimulated hateful emotions toward the German populace and "served to incite people of this country to a spirit of lawlessness."

The recruitment push succeeded. May enlistments ran in advance of April as youth scurried to serve. The *Little Mary Mixup* comic strip portrayed children attempting to volunteer. Earlier, a boy of fifteen, disguised in an elder sibling's long pants, had enlisted and received training at Camp Dix until retrieved by his mother. The army encouraged African American sign-ons, needed tank corps men and sought physicians.

The navy used a film as bait. For forty-eight hours, theaters screened *Sea War and Sea Fighters*, accompanied by officials from its Philadelphia station.

Tech High held a large gathering in a push seeking men aged eighteen to thirty-five. The *Evening News* reported many enlistees in the sea service and the naval reserve. The marines came to Harrisburg. Their war stories, told on thoroughfares and in movie houses, sparked enlistments. The corps established an office in Market Street's Central Hotel.

Proper Harrisburg seemed unfazed by a signboard at the railroad station blaring, "Give 'em hell. Join the Army" despite its proximity to the Zion Lutheran Church. Its flag-waving appeal offset its pungent language. One traveler commented, "Say, this town's all right!"

The army advocated pre–training camp information for inductees. The YMCA, the Knights of Columbus, the Jewish Welfare Board and the Harrisburg Reserves provided advice about "why America entered the war, why America must win the war, the character of the American soldier and sex hygiene and clean living."

Relatives and friends crowded rail station send-offs, effusing "cheers and tears" mixed with "smiles." In late July, Harrisburg dispatched nearly three hundred lads.

Harriet Martin Snow poeticized departures:

> *Our Uncle Sam has called us, and it's up to us to go*
> *And help our Allies "over there" to meet the deadly foe.*
> *We'll pledge ourselves to this great cause—go in the fight to win,*
> *Nor stop until the U.S. Band plays "Dixie" in Berlin.*

Compositions told the mood. Doughboys answered an obligation with "Cheer Up Mother (I Am Going to My Country's Call)" and "The Battle Song of Liberty," with the lyrics, "It's the roar and rattle of freedom's battle that's calling us over the sea." Good-byes were the theme of "Long Boy," "Someday They're Coming Home Again," "Sweet Little Buttercup" and the racy "If He Can Fight Like He Can Love, Good Night Germany!":

> *VERSE*
> *Little Mary's beau, said "I've got to go,*
> *I must fight for Uncle Sam"*
> *Standing in the crowd*
> *Many called aloud "Fare thee well my lovin' man"*
> *All the girls said "Ain't he nice and tull,"*
> *Mary answered "yes, and that's not all."*

CHORUS
"If he can fight like he can love,
Oh, what a soldier boy he'll be!
If he's just half as good in a trench.
As he was in the park on a bench.
Then ev'ry Hun, had better run
And find a great big linden tree.
'Cause he's a bear in any Morris chair
And if he fights like he can love
Why, then it's good night Germany!"

Lovers promised and pined for faithfulness. "Au Revoir, Not Good-Bye" lyricized a girl's willingness to wait. "Your Lips Are No Man's Land but Mine" epitomized a soldier's expectation of fidelity:

I'm coming back some day when the fray is over my darling
I know you'll be true, dear
So I'll never be blue, dear
Across the foam in No Man's Land I'll soon be fighting
But I know your lips are no man's land but mine.

The YMCA pursued volunteers and funds, planning a July 4 recruitment push. A demand in France summoned "auto drivers, store-house workers and construction men." The Christ Lutheran Church's sermon the "YMCA at Home and Abroad" lent support. The *Evening News* murmured, "Not enough Americans in Harrisburg and nearby have hearkened to the appeal to serve the boys in France under…the Y.M.C.A." It asked, "If unwilling to help fight the war, are you also unwilling to help the fighters fight?" Once General John Pershing emphasized the need for more moneys, the community prolonged its "Y" fund campaign.

As the wounded overflowed French clinics, the need for nurses became apparent. The city mobilized to enroll twenty-five of them. The *Evening News* editorialized the need, and appeals were addressed to the Harrisburg Hospital staff. By late June, the drive had exceeded its goal with thirty-four pledged to serve abroad. The *Telegraph* execrated the elderly for hiring nurses and claimed "thousands of such are being held in America, many right here in Harrisburg, by selfish persons whose families should look after them in such a fearful crisis as this." At the instigation of the Women's Committee of National Defense in late July, the city strove to meet a new goal of forty recruits.

The Junior Red Cross needed money for knitting supplies. In a takeoff of the tag game, children exchanged markers for cash from those touched as "it" on city sidewalks. Public, private and parochial schools participated, and "Tag Day" garnered over $4,000. Top collectors received prizes. Webster Elementary placed first. Its pupils celebrated by parading about Harrisburg's Allison Hill section, saluting Old Glory and singing "America," as well as "God Save Our Men."

Harrisburgers rallied for Red Cross funding. Mayor Daniel Keister endorsed President Wilson's call to action. Officials hoped to gather $150,000 between May 20 and 27. The police department donated over $98, some seized from a convicted crook. The Cross prohibited pressure, stating, "All contributions must be gifts of love." Nevertheless, four police officers risked dismissal for failing to subscribe.

Much to-do aided the drive. A downtown theater showed *The Spirit of the Red Cross*, posters covered the city, newspaper cartoons and comic strips referenced the Cross and poets versified. For example, the local cleric James Henry Darlington penned "The Cross of Neuve Chapelle," reflecting a nurse's attention for a mortally wounded warrior:

> *The Christ on the Cross looks down*
> *On the dying at Neuve Chapelle*
> *Is there blood on his martyr crown*
> *As the Christ on the Cross looks down:*
> *Is it anger which makes him frown*
> *At the deaths from shot and shell?*
> *The Christ on the Cross looks down*
> *On the dying at Neuve Chapelle.*

Edmund Vance Cooke added:

> *After the hot assault, or hard heroic stand*
> *Hark, some one calls to you from no man's land*
> *Just a friend of yours and mine, a suffering soldier-man;*
> *No, you cannot reach him—but the Red Cross can.*

Churches weighed in. Pine Street Presbyterian pastor Mudge preached "The Gospel of the Hand," an entreaty for Red Cross assistance. Sunday sermons on May 19 typified the appeal: "The Sacred Order of Mercy—the Red Cross" at the Market Square Presbyterian Church; "The Scarlet

Sign, a Red Cross Plea" at the Pine Street Presbyterian Church; "Red Cross Service and Christian Duty" at the Redeemer Lutheran Church; "The Red Cross Beatitude—Blessed Are the Merciful" at the Fourth Reform Church; and "Red Cross—Holy Communion" at the Lutheran church. Rabbi Haas talked about "Angels of Mercy" in the Ohev Sholom Temple.

Retailers arranged window displays. William B. Schleisner Stores exhibited presidents' pictures, war souvenirs, placards and a Civil War print. C. Ross Boas Jewelry Store showed battlefield relics.

Corporations brought their influence to bear. The Harrisburg Pipe and Pipe Bending Company, the Central Construction Corporation and Uptown Merchants ran full-page press ads. The Central Iron and Steel Company exploited local enthusiasm for athletics, sponsoring a baseball game for the Red Cross. Other concerns chipped in. The Harrisburg Trust Company wanted an extra dividend to stockholders sacrificing for the Cross. The Merchant National Bank donated $500. The Silk Mill and the Bell Telephone also contributed.

Children and women parade for the Red Cross. *From the* Harrisburg Telegraph. *Courtesy of PennLive.*

Ordinary people threw in their bit for the Cross. Women paraded, wearing white gloves as suggested by Dives, Pomeroy and Stewart. Officials cautioned ladies about footgear. "Use no high heel," they said. "High heels cause the casualties in women's parades." A seventy-eight-year-old marched the procession's length. Mrs. Elizabeth Sullivan, whose son died in action, presented five dollars.

Youngsters found ways to assist. They performed music and recited poetry at a community get-together. They scheduled a make-believe circus. Camp Fire Girls paraded and hosted a "Hit the Kaiser" contest at St. Paul's Episcopal Church. Harrisburg Academy students lent the Cross promotional attention. A Civil War veteran came across. Moved by the Reverend Mudge's sermon "The Scarlet Sign," the octogenarian surrendered his pension pay. African Americans roused for the Cross. At St. Paul's Baptist Church, the assembled accumulated over one hundred dollars.

The city opened a grassroots appeal to market War Savings Stamps (WSS). The drive began with a May 11 gathering and continued two days later. Workers conducted door-to-door solicitations, established stalls at avenue crossroads and pushed $20 sales. They aspired for $3 million in promises.

Churches and schools participated. For example, St. Matthews Lutheran planned to donate. Harrisburg Tech students competed for stamp purchases. Children marched in a promotional parade interrupted by rain.

Public figures pushed the campaign. Mayor Keister, in conjunction with the White House and the commonwealth, announced "June 28 as War Savings Day." He trusted the "people of Harrisburg will respond to an extent that will more than reach the quota which has been set as our share and our particular part in this particular effort for furnishing the sinews of the war against the Hun."

Residents came out. Employees at Dives, Pomeroy and Stewart's and Bowman's department stores organized to sell stamps. The John Heathcote Agency in the Telegraph Building sold $112,000 in value. Metropolitan Life Insurance salesmen obtained the company's medallion for dispensing. The Pennsylvania Railroad's International Association of Machinists and the Local Union No. 520, Journeymen Plumbers each chipped in $200.

Fraternal organizations lined up. Lodge No. 107 of the Loyal Order of Moose bought $1,000 in stamps. The Elks and Rotary formed units to promote sales. Postmaster Frank C. Sites asked members to approach their fellows for donations. The Kiwanis wanted members to march.

An African American gave up his military pension to buy stamps through 1918. The Spanish-American War veteran had seen action with the Tenth

United States Regulars. The man's "wages are not big, but he knows what war is, and he is still doing his bit."

Boy Scouts came up with a gimmick. Using chalk, they scribbled "4.18," the price of a WSS, "on street corners, fences, telegraph poles and every other available place." They planned to vend stamps on city boulevards.

The press carried the crusade forward. The *Telegraph* praised pupils for their patriotic parading and stamp purchases. The paper merited stamps over bonds since they are "purchased in very large number of cases out of savings, whereas in many instances Liberty Bonds are purchased from money in the bank or the sale of other property."

Letters to the *Telegraph*'s editor suggested stamp schemes. Correspondents advanced signs in club rooms and on business fronts. Retailers could place flags on "letter heads," "wrapping paper" and "cash slips." Others wanted cards in trolleys and billboards on lots. One person thought kites, a balloon and an aircraft dropping posters could be utilized. A photo of a laughing infant lettered "Buy me a baby bond" was considered. Finally, a writer recommended, "If some of the people…would go out and ring doorbells or stomp around at a corner and beat a drum to get people to crowd up, it would make our fair city's total pledges run away up." The *Evening News* seized on youth props. It pictured ownership of "baby bonds" by a four-month-old and a nine-year-old.

Cartoons flag-waved the stamp push. *Pave His Way*, including a road sign pointing "to Berlin," reflected an American soldier advancing over paving blocks reading "thrift stamps," "W.S.S." and "war saving stamps." *Keep the Old Fuse Burning* illustrated a hand lighting an explosive directed at the kaiser; its shirt sleeve read, "Thrift stamp pledges." *The Great American Home* showed a houseowner welcoming kids selling stamps. Another displayed a boy vending lemonade saying to a customer, "Change in thrift stamps, mister."

Comic strips echoed cartoons. *Snoodles* by Hungerford portrayed children being spanked for cutting up a thrift stamp book and a drugstore sign urging the stamps' purchase. *Bringing Up Father* by McManus exhibited posted encouragement to procure. Pictured under the phrase "Buy thrift stamps here," Allman's *Doings of the Duffs* had a character declare, "Give me enough to equal the fare from here to Berlin!" The artist also drew a character hanging a banner in a window prompting, "Buy thrift stamps." In a series, Wellington's *That Son-in-Law of Pa's*, Pa found employment for his son-in-law so he could afford stamps, fired a maid to release money for purchases and watched his son-in-law parade about with an emblem saying, "Buy war saving stamps and help your Uncle Sam."

Newspaper ads complemented cartoons and comics. In a statement below a drawing of children saluting Old Glory, Dives, Pomeroy and Stewart elucidated, "Thrift Stamps and War Savings Stamps make better citizens of whoever owns them—and they are within everyone's resources." Bowman's directed, "Mr. Small Saver buy a thrift stamp for 25¢," "Mr. Big Saver do your bit with 'two bits' more—and then some. Every little bit helps to hit the Hun." "Help lick the Kaiser buy War Saving Stamps," exclaimed the Excelsier Cycle Company.

A poem phrased an obligation:

W.S.S. the Pledge
What is this pledge they would bid me sign?
A promise true with this heart of mine
To stand by the land which has sheltered me;
To loan of my substance, endlessly;
To uphold my flag with a steady hand;
When days look darkest, to understand.

What is this pledge they would bid me sign?
A binding contract with Father Time
To rid the sea of its hidden death;
To choke into silence the cannon's breath;
To help in drying the whole world's tears;
To free little children of anguished fears.

What is this pledge they would bid me sign?
A step in the stairway of things divine;
A lesson in going without to-day
To save in the bigger and broader way;
A chance to remember the dear lads gone
And lift up their burdens to "carry on."

The Kaiser, the Beast of Berlin returned to Harrisburg. The *Evening News* hyped, "Never in the history of the screen has any production swept the United States with the same effect." The paper claimed it would help bring WSS "over the top."

Despite the flurry of the scurry, stamp sales lagged. Instructions urged campaign volunteers to push purchases beyond the customary in order for Dauphin County to outshine Philadelphia, its competitor. The mayor designated July 20 "Baby Bond Day." To celebrate an American victory at the Aisne-Marne, he wanted each Harrisburger to acquire stamps.

Residents heeded America's allies. A cartoon admonished, "Time for all to help." Allied banners fronted the Telegraph Building. The Penn-Harris Hotel installed flagstaffs to fly the emblems of visiting comrades.

Belgium's plight moved the city. *The Belgian*, booked by the Victoria, pictured that country's lot. The Ridge Avenue Methodist Church raised money to clothe Belgium's babies. The J.H. Troup Music House sold "My Belgian Rose," a song promising American mindfulness:

> *Rose of Belgium, drooping so low*
> *Lift up your head for we love you so*
> *Robbed of your sunshine you're fading away*
> *But you'll live to bloom on a happier day*
> *America is calling you*
> *Speaking in words divine*
> *My home shall be thy home*
> *And all my treasures thine—*
>
> *America will bring back your bloom holding you to her breast*
> *No harm shall befall you*
> *And you'll find peace and rest.*

Officials considered celebrating Belgium's independence day with speeches and music.

Foreign spokespersons gave voice to the Allied call. A Chinese man spoke of his country's contribution. A Briton acquainted an audience about happenings "over there." An Italian's oratory urging local aliens to support war policies stirred listeners.

The *Evening News* noted Britishers' thoughtfulness. Along with observing July 4, they established Sammy's Blighty League, welcoming doughboys into their homes and hoping to commiserate with their mothers. The paper predicted "that from now on we Americans are going to be better neighbors and closer friends with our Anglo-Saxon cousins."

Italy heartened Harrisburg. The films *On the Isonzo* and *The Warrior* testified to the country's courage. Italian residents paraded patriotically with the mayor to commemorate Italy's entrance into the conflict. The *Telegraph* lavished praise: "We in the United States began only to understand the heroic character and the fighting qualities of the Italian people." The

Evening News beheld "a new era of sympathetic feeling here between the two countries" and applauded Rome's area descendants' wartime assistance. Italian flags bedecked the community. In an ad, the Dauphin Deposit Trust Company expressed gratitude: "We remember today with appreciation the part that our ally Italy has taken in the war for freedom." It added, "For three long years she has held back the Hun." "Names in the News" educated readers, explaining "the Alpini" referred to the Alpine's Italian infantry. Isobel Brands's "Kitchen Economies" promoted Italy's cuisine as nutritious, inexpensive and easily prepared.

Harrisburgers took to France. Lieutenant George Flanchaire, an ace, performed aerial acrobatics over the city. The Blue Devils, an elite combat unit, stopped by, paraded and pushed the Red Cross. One of the Frenchmen drank coffee at the Rustic Restaurant on South Third Street and conversed with Miss Marguerite Guiffant, a native of his hometown. The *Evening News* commented, "Harrisburg's good fortune in being given an opportunity to entertain, hear and see the famous 'Blue Devils of France' cannot be overestimated."

France's emissaries came to the city. Tech High hosted representatives of the French Mission to the United States. Pierre de Loeschnigg, a Parisian native, accompanied them through the school. A French army chaplain told of his country's sacrifice: "Not one family in France has not lost at least one member, since the war began." *Le Matin*'s editor spoke to the chamber of commerce of Gaulish resolution: "We will fight to the last life, to the last beating of our hearts, until the clouds disappear and the sun of victory, not your victory, but the victory of the ideal for which we are fighting, is shining once again."

Fashion responded to the ally. C.B. Rodney on North Third Street carried the "Liberty Belle," footwear "with full French heels." Dives, Pomeroy and Stewart marketed the "Blue Devil Tam," an azure silk cap of France. Bowman's bragged about revealing the newest nuance, the "Blue Devil," a "shade that has been made famous by the fighters of France."

Comic strips intimated fraternization. *That Son-in-Law of Pa's* labeled characters "Fleurette" and "Alphonse," French given names. In the *Doings of the Duffs*, an officer of France appeared. *Somebody Is Always Taking the Joy Out of Life* pictured a woman's warning about the allure of mademoiselles: "Those French girls over there are winning their way into the hearts of American soldiers."

Language books smoothed teamwork. American servicemen and Red Cross volunteers found Jean Leeman's *French in a Nutshell* and William

French Blue Devils visit the city. *From the* Harrisburg Telegraph. *Courtesy of PennLive.*

Robert Patterson's *Colloquial French* useful. Indeed, "Names in the News," a column, broadened vocabularies. The *Evening News* serial introduced residents to France's *chauvinism, sabotage, liaison, marmite, escadrille, sap, Zouave, mitrailleuse, echelon, Croix de Guerre, enfilading fire, grenade, proletorial, abatis, soixante-quinze* and *salient.*

Music cemented ties. Troup's on South Market Square retailed the Victor Record "Lafayette (We Hear You Calling)" that summoned obligation:

> *Out of the ages from history's pages*
> *There comes a silent plea*
> *Yet we can hear it Lafayette's spirit*
> *Calling from over the sea*
> *For there's a debt unpaid*
> *To France who needs our aid.*

Poetry warmed the relationship. "No Sammee!" originated from the doughboys' nickname:

> *Just then in the dusk come a pair of kids*
> *And one with a voice like a katydid's*
> *Come runnin' with arms stretched out at me*
> *And sort of chirrupin' "No Sammee!"*
> *You know in the lingo the kids use here*

That means "Our friends. " Well, isn't it queer?…
When she snuggled close to my neck—and held —
There was somethin' inside of me swelled and swelled,
Till I almost busted
"Say," says Sid,
"Don't it get your goat when you catch a kid?
Would you think we'd be fightin' for kids like these
And for others that none of us ever sees,
Or maybe ain't born yet!"

Films reinforced Franco-American camaraderie. *Smashing Through*, a French war reel, screened clips of the U.S. Navy. *Heroic France*, an up-to-date portrayal of America's ally, showed battlefield realities and urged military readiness.

Harrisburg went all out for Bastille Day, a celebration of French independence. At Mayor Keister's behest, chamber of commerce chief Andrew S. Patterson formed a council. It scheduled band performances, flag flyings and clergy cooperation. The local observance concurred with a countrywide "Committee on Allied Tribute to France."

Thanks for past French support during the American Revolution became customary. When France's 1789 upheaval had broken out, sentiments embraced the French people. The Bastille's fall had inspired regular attention. Harrisburg nearly missed being named Louisburg, and Dauphin's designation for the county derived from the Bourbon monarch's progeny. The *Evening News* approved reciprocity. "Even as France observed our Independence Day so we in the United States should observe her Bastille Day." It vowed, "Harrisburg will do its duty."

Dives, Pomeroy and Stewart exploited the occasion to hawk flags. It advertised the ally's silk banner as inexpensive and argued, "Every American home owes a debt of gratitude to France, and it is only fitting that American homes be decorated with Tri-Color next Sunday, in celebration of Bastille Day."

French flags adorned Harrisburg. Residents made Bastille Day "a momentous event in the history of the city." Reservoir Park held ceremonies. Harrisburg Railways Company provided efficient transit for lines leading to the site. Notables spoke, including a French officer. Musicians performed, and citizens sang. Local Italians took part.

Ministers bestowed wholehearted blessings. Their sermons sanctified. The Market Street Baptist Church themed "The Fall of the Bastille," as did the Fourth Street Church of God's "The Bible and the Bastille," the

St. Matthews's Lutheran Church's "Bastille Day and Its Meaning to French People," Zion Lutheran Church's "God's Hand in History (French Revolution)" and Saint Paul's Methodist Church's "French Independence Day." At the Pine Street Presbyterian Church, the Reverend Mudge resounded the global impact of the Bastille's collapse, claiming it "paved the way for religious freedom in America as well."

Edmund Vance Cooke's "Ye Friends of France," to the tune of "La Marseillaise," gave meaning to the festivity:

> *Ye friends of France, allied in battle,*
> *Now sound again your clarian* [sic] *call;*
> *Men shall not be as Kaiser's cattle,*
> *But freedom shall be shared by all.*

A pumped Mayor Keister cabled French president Raymond Poincaré: "The citizens of Harrisburg, Pennsylvania, extend greetings to you; and through you to our beloved allies, the brave people of France, on this, the anniversary of the Fall of the Bastille," solemnizing, "God speed the triumph of our righteous cause!"

President Wilson heralded May 30 as "A Day of Humiliation, Prayer and Fasting." He prompted Americans to gather and ask God to "give victory to our armies as they fight for freedom."

The *Telegraph* discerned a "new significance" for Memorial Day. The city and region recruited thousands of lads "ready to sacrifice themselves for the nation." In fact, six had already given their lives: Harrisburgers Earl E. Aurand, Sylvester P. Sullivan, H.D. Buckwatter and Frank E. Zeigler; Camp Hill resident Charles L. Phillips; and Steelton native Andrew Askin.

The *Telegraph* thought Memorial Day provided an opportunity for tree-planting dedications to the military. The gestures would serve "as living memorials to our soldiers." Trees had been placed previously, following the paper's recommendation.

Harrisburg prepared to celebrate. Dives, Pomeroy and Stewart and groceries promised closings. Reservoir Park shut its golfing course to shield picnickers. But despite the festivities, the Red Cross scheduled Memorial Day work.

The marketplace commercialized the ceremonies. Collin's Style Shop announced a Memorial Day clothing sale. Keeney's Cozy Corner furnished florals: "This is the day we pay tribute in flowers to the memory of the loved ones who have gone to the other shore." J.H. Troup Music House believed its recordings and Fisher and Cleckner supposed its shoes timely for the occasion. Bowman's propped sketches of the Statue of Liberty and Uncle Sam to remind residents of what "should be a day of solemnity." Doutrich's proclaimed that "over there," America's "long range guns are paving the way to victory."

The *Evening News* highlighted Hershey Park's flag waving. Draws included bands, concerts and a showing of *The Kaiser, the Beast of Berlin*. Harrisburgers paraded. Three patriotic marches tread city streets. One featured Roman Catholic congregations.

Ministers solemnized the day. The Memorial Lutheran Church's "The Unceasing Cry of Spilt Blood," the Fourth Street Church of God's "The Debt of Memory to Our Worthy Dead" and St. Paul's Baptist's "True Patriotism, If I Perish, I Perish" heeded the call. Market Square Presbyterian and Pine Street Presbyterian conducted a combined ritual. St. Stephen's Episcopal ministered on May 30. The Fourth Street Church of God counted $2.50 expended for Memorial Day flowers.

The *Evening News*'s "The New Wreath" pictured, among Old Glory and stars, Uncle Sam placing a garland on a tombstone reading "OUR HEROES." This issue also included a photograph showing U.S. burials abroad.

Five thousand residents jammed Reservoir Park for June 14's Flag Day. A parade of Kiwanis, Harrisburg Reserves and Home Defense League from the city's center preceded ceremonies under Elks supervision. Bowman's marketed banners.

Flags "dotted" Harrisburg for a turnout of speeches, rites and songs. Spokesmen addressed the emblem's history and importance. A church choir performed. Musicians rendered the "Red, White and Blue" and "The Star-Spangled Banner."

Public-spirited citizens brooked little tolerance for Old Glory's disrespect. Police arrested a bystander on Market Street for refusing to remove his hat during the national anthem. At Reservoir Park, three men suffered physical assault for failure to doff their caps.

The *Evening News* elucidated the banner's significance: "Our Flag—is the flag of hope and promise, the emblem which adds strength to the arm and courage to the heart of liberty's fighters."

Verse verified tribute:

> *OUR FLAG*
> *The hour of its birth was a wonder-hour*
> *For God's hand drew the plan.*

The angels offered their wings for white;
The blue of the firmament spoke for "might,"
And its blood red bars were a holy sight,
The living force of man.

The hours of its testing were shadow-hours
As, tattered by shot and shell,
It faced the blaze that the cannon yields
Defiled by the smoke of the carnage fields
Cheered by the lips which grim death seals.
Undaunted, it passed war's hell.

The hour of its proving, its mighty-hour.
Has come to your flag and mine.
Wrapped in the folds lies the fate of a world
With blackest of evils against it hurled!
But God's was the hand which its lengths unfurled.
The "call" was in tones divine!

The hour of its triumph, its victory-hour
Is showing the light of dawn!
And the Flag of Flags to the end of time
Shall carry a meaning and name sublime
As obliterator of lawless crime
For multitudes yet unborn!

The *Courier* pressed the city to "whoop it up" for July 4. "Harrisburg calls you, Mr. and Mrs. Citizen," the paper declared, "to take your part in this patriotic jubilee in order that you may demonstrate your love of country, love of liberty and love for your neighbor, whatever nation gave him birth."

Motivated by President Wilson to include naturalized Americans, the mayor established a committee to organize Independence Day festivities. Help came from the YMCA and the chamber of commerce. The *Telegraph* editorialized, "Celebrations of this sort…are bringing together the people of this country in solid alignment against the Prussia autocracy." Edward Moeslein chaired a group signing on foreign-born participants.

With the motto, "Everybody in it," July 4 "will stand in history as the first reception tendered by native-born citizens of the United States to the foreign-born residents among us, whom it is hoped by this and other means to so wholly Americanize, that they will hereafter recognize the Stars and Stripes as their only flag."

Outlying communities took part. Steelton and Penbrook paraded. The mayor welcomed rural areas to participate on learning of their concern about being labeled "slackers."

Retailers drummed for the Fourth. Doutrichs displayed a Spirit of '76 image and J.H. Troup a Statue of Liberty likeness. Bowman's readied Allied flags. Astrich's recommended white apparel for marching.

Supplication graced the holiday. The *Telegraph* reminded readers of Washington and Lincoln seeking divine guidance and asserted "surely there never was a time when we as a people and as a nation needed the help of God more than at this moment." The Rotary Club agreed. It voted for a community prayer of two minutes. Preachers ministered hour-long services.

City establishments closed for the Fourth. The parade shut down bars and clubs. The war plants suspended operations. The *Evening News* decided against a holiday issue. The Red Cross stopped services so volunteers could marshal. Venues throughout Harrisburg carried out programs. Sports, speeches and soldiers' drills occupied the Island. Ethnic dances and band music headlined at Reservoir Park.

Officials wanted to crown July 4 with Harrisburg's most magnificent parade. They expected twenty thousand participants. Fraternities, fire houses, clubhouses, associations, manufacturers, retailers, Red Cross volunteers, Girl and Boy Scouts, as well as unnaturalized residents, received invitations. The *Telegraph* imagined the procession "will be known as the Great Parade, just as the present war is known as the Great War."

The march required funds. Committee persons entered factory floors and department stores, canvasing and hoping to meet the $10,000 goal. They acquired $3,794 by June 26. A letter to the *Evening News* questioned the expenditure. The correspondent thought the money could be better spent elsewhere since the "nation, the Red Cross and starving Belgian children are pleading for every cent we can spare for aid."

On the Fourth, twenty-two thousand paraded. Organizations mobilized members. Girls carried a Liberty Bell. Flags adorned march lines. Sixty bands struck up, including the nation's oldest, the Repasz out of Williamsport, formed in 1831. Twenty-seven military vehicles took part in the pageant. Boy Scouts assisted. They manned ice-water posts. They aided police with traffic, attending to youngsters and women at crossings, keeping cars out of paraders' paths and enforcing parking regulations. As marchers neared the Hope Engine House on North Second Street, a

Fourth of July parade. *From the* Harrisburg Telegraph. *Courtesy of PennLive.*

bell sounded from the station's dome, a Civil War trophy seized by federal forces in Virginia.

Disregard for the national anthem affronted. A spectator refused to doff his hat and had his loyalty questioned. A marcher used his flag to strike the offender's headgear, which landed among paraders and was stomped on, to the delight of bystanders. At Reservoir Park, a man declined to stand. He was manhandled to Market Street as the audience shouted, "Treat him rougher!"

Newspapers lavished praise. For example, the *Telegraph* opined that the "celebration was a great success and worth every ounce of effort and every penny expended," because "native and foreign-born good humoredly rubbed shoulders…and each went home with a better opinion and a clearer understanding of the other." It noted the unity of native and alien and believed the nation's "melting pot appears to have been super-heated" by the German menace.

The *Telegraph* quipped about the march: "If the Kaiser could have seen yesterday's parade, he'd have known for certain that some of his spies lied to him about pro-Germanism in the United States.…Perhaps we are wrong, but something tells us there are a lot of sore corns in Harrisburg to-day."

A stunt, called a "little thriller," was spotlighted at the festivities. "Bill" Strother, nicknamed the "Human Spider," shinned up the side of the Penn-Harris Hotel, made a headstand at roof's rim and positioned Old Glory atop a banner's staff.

Federal authorities prohibited pyrotechnics. The military needed gunpowder. The city observed the Fourth without buildings ablaze and hospital admissions. The *Telegraph* applauded the fireworks ban and thought that, after similar celebrations, the "country will have abandoned as completely its former folly as it has the building of bonfires on election night."

The school district voted to exclude German. Yet a minority on the panel thought students should decide themselves. Moreover, the ban ignited a firestorm. The *Telegraph* argued the army needed German speakers and the demand would intensify in postwar business. The paper cautioned, "We must not permit our common sense and good judgement to be warped or misled by our wartime emotions." J. Horace McFarland agreed and thought the ban "appears to be neither wise nor patriotic." He criticized Pittsburghers for Teutonic music's elimination and feared Martin Luther's banishment. Speaking in Fahnestock Hall, Mrs. Tade-Hartsuss Kuhns defended German study, arguing that her country's "success was due to the fact that her countrymen are good linguists." She favored consideration of Germany's past and regime "so that the world may learn of the false lies with which Germany has been saturating history."

Nevertheless, German-language opponents prevailed. In the Tech High auditorium, Professor C.H. Tyne criticized its instruction during wartime. He also wanted attention to Germany's notables done away with. The national American Defense Society crusaded "to have disloyal school teachers punished and to abolish the teaching of the German language." Likewise, it favored suppression of the Teutonic press in the United States. The local Elks lodge resolved to prohibit Germanic speaking in its clubhouse and keep enemy foreigners out. A cartoon celebrated the "German Language" as "Another Dead One."

German values and institutions came under exacting examination. At the Neighborhood Club on North Sixth Street, the Reverend J. Bradley Markward stigmatized philosopher Friedrich Wilhelm Nietzsche as the "Prophet of the Mailed Fist" for his "theory of the Super-man." The Dauphin County Historical Society met at its South Front Street headquarters to talk over "Some Phrases in the Evolution of Prussian Frightfulness." New York's Rabbi Stephen Wise made a contrast: "Germany is a government of militarism, by militarism and for militarism, while the United States is as our forefathers said a government of the people by the people and for the people." In the Civic Club, the Reverend George Preston Mains told the Daughters of 1812 of Berlin's war aims. He believed indoctrination convinced Germany "that the German people are a super-people with an

German becomes another dead language. *From the* Evening News. *Courtesy of PennLive.*

absolute right to rule the world." The country's academies, universities and churches, he claimed, have imbued this outlook.

Propagandized messages condemned repeatedly Berlin's way of war. On May 7, the *Telegraph* printed, "Three years ago to-day beastly Germans sent the *Lusitania*, with her load of men, women and babies to the bottom of the Atlantic." At the Colonial Theater, the motion picture *Lest We Forget*, a "semi-documentary," reenacted the liner's sinking. At the Chestnut Street Hall, the chamber of commerce scheduled films and slides to "show the horrors of the German methods of warfare." Evangelist Robert E. Johnson left no doubts about the foe. At the Olivet Presbyterian Church, he alleged the "German people have become demons since the outbreak of the war."

The Kaiser's flaying continued without letup. A riddle targeted him:

> *There once was a Hun called Attila*
> *Whose instincts were like a gorilla*
> *He destroyed what he slew,*
> *But, between me and you,*
> *The Kaiser is worse than Attila*

Somebody Is Always Taking the Joy Out of Life by Briggs portrayed characters cursing Wilhelm for discomforts and sacrifices. On South Third Street, White boys playing war put a Black youth taking the German leader's part in a barrel and bombarded it with ash, trash and brickbats. The youngster emerged and screeched, "I ain't gwan to play Kaiser anymore."

Patriots avoided the enemy's fare. Consequently, boycotts of "sauerkraut, hamburg steak and German cheese" caused the Hotel Columbus to discontinue serving them. Waiters offered Harrisburg steak instead. Walnut Street's Bergstresser House reported a customer's spurning of "German mustard" and exclaiming, "I'll use ketchup!" A prohibitionist warned of German brew: "It is an ally of the kaiser and the devil."

Spokespersons confirmed sauerkraut's innocence and import. As it was an inheritance from the Netherlands instead of Germany, federal food administrators declared its neutrality validated: "Those who make free use of it will be performing a patriotic service by stimulating a greater use of cabbage and thus saving staple foods needed abroad." The Armour and Company's R.J.H. DeLoach proclaimed sauerkraut "a good American product" in spite of its label and argued, "[The] more kraut we eat the more we will have of other foods to send abroad." Fearing waste and cutbacks, Herbert Hoover regretted commotion over the dish.

The *Telegraph* rallied for sauerkraut. Vaunting its fidelity, the paper argued, "It is pro-ally and pro-American and above all else pro-Pennsylvania." A Berks County poet added:

> *Sauerkraut is good,*
> *Sauerkraut is fine,*

I think I ought to know it,
For I eats it all the time.

Lynchings marred the nation's war for democracy "with unabated fury." Sixty-three African Americans, including five women, and four White men perished at the hands of mobs in 1918. Lynchers escaped prosecution and conviction. City newspapers addressed the rampages. The *Evening News* advised that the lynchings of unnaturalized Germans undermined the war effort. The *Telegraph* blamed local officials, saying mobs "are not always maliciously disregardful of the law" since "they are driven by desperation to inflict summary punishment upon those who [*sic*] offenses are overlooked by those whose duty it is to suppress crime."

Appeals pleaded for mob rule's end. The African American Knights of Pythias sent resolutions to President Wilson. The *Telegraph* championed the overtures, asserting, "Colored men do not mean that crime should be protected"; however, "they do believe all men should be protected in their rights and that the guilt or innocence of the accused should be left entirely in the hands of a jury of his peers." Wilson called for lynchings' cessation. He characterized the vigilantism as patterned after Germany's "lawless passion," an emulation that "disregarded sacred obligations of law and made lynchers of her armies." E. Luther Cunningham thanked the *Telegraph* for supporting the Pythias's plea. He alerted the paper to a petition submitted to the U.S. Congress, a document from the National Colored Liberty Congress pressing for the halt of mob lawlessness.

In a letter to the *Telegraph* signed "A True American," a correspondent complained of racial discrimination in Harrisburg. A Market Street store's clerk had denied his desired purchase of a drink, saying "that he was not permitted to serve people of my color." The letter went on: "If the conflict in which we are engaged is for the betterment of humanity in general… does it seem reasonable that such conditions should exist here at home?…It's reasonable to think…prejudice should be removed from our own eye, before attempting to remove the beam of oppression of the Hun from the eyes of the civilized world."

Delinquent troublemaking increased during the war. Schools reported misbehavior. Young men brawled in city streets. In an antic, a youth positioned dynamite sticks at the entrance of a Hershey Chocolate Company building. Teenaged girls, aged fifteen to eighteen, solicited soldiers. Wearing "white skirts and pink sweaters," they strolled city streets until sunrise. Hearsay disclosed that the Pennsylvania Railroad Station served as their haunt.

Police corralled the "pink sweater girls." They arrested and scolded eight. They asked parents "to keep them off the streets." Authorities apprehended George Dikeman of Berryhill Street for aiding solicitations. They also arrested Tony Murphy of Cowden Street and Grace Burke for keeping a juvenile for unchaste intentions.

Soldiers became victims of scams. Sharpers diverted money sent to military camps into their own pockets.

Vigilance hung over outsiders. A patrolman pinched Evileno Veago for possessing "concealed deadly weapons." His hearing followed.

Enlisted men transgressed. Police seized two from Middletown's air unit who bought booze, became tipsy and hijacked a car. Authorities pursued a sergeant who purchased merchandise at a jewelry store with a worthless check. A soldier procured alcohol from Louis Barber, whom police detained.

Harrisburg pounced on prostitution. Tillie Dale of North Seventh Street and Emma Eichelberger of Wallace Street went to trial for operating brothels. Cops swooped on Mrs. Thomas Fannasy's house on Washington Street. They raided Stella Collier's Cowden Street address for a second time. As they departed, enlisted men approached the residence.

The city dealt with an outbreak of necking. Fuel-saving lightless nights encouraged the behavior. Lovers huddled in the "secluded nooks of Wildwood, and River Front and Island Park." Police chased one hundred out of the latter. Many young girls had soldier companions. Some opposed interference with the spooners since the same level of activity occurred half a century before. Nevertheless, Mayor Keister dispatched patrols to end the goings-on since he had gotten reports of immoderate revelry "in the 'lovin' game.'"

Apparel's sacrifice came under consideration. Despite a frugality concern, H. Marks and Sons, a Fourth and Market Streets haberdashery, pitched new attire to avoid a "shabby" look that nullified "efficiency." Yet the real patriots, the *Telegraph* suggested, would refrain from embellished dress since "economy is the word of the hour and the advice goes out to wear little clothing."

The war changed women's attire. Mary Ruth Fisher advised clothes saving and nightgown non-buying. Federal authorities reported the unavailability of steel stays. The comic strip *Polly and Her Pals* exhibited women tailored in waistcoats. Skirts retained their length in spite of lower-heeled footwear.

Wool and cotton conservation entertained a risky slogan, "Wear fewer clothes." City misses already dressed unbecomingly, and many would be jailed if they went further. *Polly and Her Pals* pictured Pa startled by a woman sporting a low-cut, cavernous blouse, asking, "You gonna wear that open-faced frock in public?" He added, "I'm for economizing on clothes"; still, "Hoover knows they's a limit."

Coal savings shifted into high gear. With shortages likely, the chamber of commerce's Manufacturing Council examined the problem. A steelworks reported scarcities. Officials pressed residents to reduce lighting and can with gas or oil. The Colonial Country Club fired timber. Fort Hunter decided to shut doors if coal's use was prohibited. Some thought of extending daylight savings through the wintertime to enhance the electric flow.

Economizing cut services. The Harrisburg Railways Company inaugurated skip stops, totaling ninety-five in January and more in July. The city ordered lights dimmed. Lightless nights applied to weekdays except Fridays. Persons complained about commercial beams burning. Most Harrisburgers complied, utilizing candles and kerosene. Seventy-eight of eighty-one municipal clusters shut off three of five streetlamps. Critics worried about traffic and crime. Violators risked punishment. Ten experienced reprimand. To dissuade evening business, the Dauphin County Fuel Administration restricted nighttime elevator rides. The "First Stop Third Floor" rule required businessmen to climb to their second-level headquarters.

The war induced methodical housewifery. "Doing My Bit" instructed, "It isn't only a wise economic movement to systematize housework and so save time, but it is a patriotic duty as well." The column proposed expedients for meals, marketing and labor. Every aspect of housekeeping should be arranged. With a servant scarcity, homemakers needed to reduce laundry's burden. The selection of an appropriate ironing board would help.

Sacrifices impacted residents. They paid more for ice due to costly deliveries. Appealing to consumer patriotism, the Alspure Ice Stores pleaded for cash and carry. Intending thrift, retailers charged more and reduced service. S.S. Pomeroy, a grocer, promised punctual deliveries "where necessary although the government has asked everyone to help save by cutting down." *Doings of the Van Loons* sketched Ma complying: "There now you see I am only doing a good turn for our country by not having any bundles delivered!" The city was rezoned for more efficient milk transport.

A sugar shortage loomed. Candy contained less of the sweetener. Sherbets and ices experienced bans. Ice cream sold in only three flavors. Restaurants and hotels faced cuts. Grocers limited shoppers to thirty-two ounces. To prevent hoarding, authorities required canners to fill certificates warranting allotments. By July 11, six hundred Harrisburgers had applied.

Problems ensued. Applicants failed to follow procedures, submitting incomplete and unidentified forms. Some residents breached the maximum by making purchases at different stores. A local official closed the ACME on Second and Chestnut Streets for sales violations. Stopgaps materialized to cope. The *Evening News* favored breeding bees. In an ad, Postum promised its brew saved the sweetener. Despite the fuss, sugar existed in abundance. Dealers reported more than needed the next month.

Residents did without the customary. The Bell Telephone Company ceased telling time and giving wake-up calls to patrons. These services burdened operators and metal equipment, the latter hard to acquire since the government commanded the supply. "Copper, lead and some of the other materials essential to a telephone plant," according to Bell, "are among the necessaries that have been commandeered." The Civic Club tabooed platinum presents.

The war continued to increase female employment. Industrial courses appeared at the YWCA. Corporations hired women chemists. Central Iron and Steel engaged Ethel Peace as a "trenographer," a first. The *Evening News* identified an authentic "Liberty belle," a miss engaged in munitions production.

Women offset transportation's labor loss. Three hundred took the place of railroaders. The *Telegraph* reported they performed well and Pennsy's "Philadelphic division is now falling into line and will soon have a big army of women." Cliff Sterrett's *Polly and Her Pals* illustrated Aunt Maggie's pride as a full-time conductress.

The absence of men opened other avenues. A crowd gathered to watch a woman, a soldier's spouse, paint a barber's pole at Third and Market Streets. The Bowman's shop and the Metropolitan Hotel took on girls to operate elevators. Patrene Duncan, the head operator, remarked: "This is better than standing behind a counter in a store all day."

Women hired for hazardous duty caught the eye of cartoonist Sterrett. His *Polly and Her Pals* alluded to "lady cops." Ladies did field and farm work. They toiled in war gardens. Sterrett pictured Polly catching attention in a plot. Doggerel commended the sowing lass showing sass:

> *I cannot join the Army, for the Army told me so,*
> *And lots of men are heavier an' wiser,*
> *But I'm ready for all comers with a garden rake, an' hoe,*
> *And I'm raisin' peas an' beans to beat the Kaiser!*
> *The Navy doesn't want me messin' up a pretty deck,*
> *They've chased me out of each recruitin' station,*

But me an' Herbie Hoover's gonta win the war, by heck,
An' I've got the finest garden in the Nation!

Outdoor toil alarmed women about their appearance. One gardener thought the sun might inflict freckles. But an ad claimed home front advantages for the youthful image and contended the gray-haired "have found a way out by using Q-bon Hair Color Restorer."

Women risked disfavor for avoiding their bit. Annette Bradshaw's feature column "Her Problem" pictured three companions, with one idler captioned: "She doesn't knit and she doesn't make sweets for the soldiers, and yet she wonders why she isn't quite popular in that college group." One writer thought the inactive should be drafted and believed "it would do all of us a whole lot of good."

The conflict prompted speculation about women's status. In a letter to the *Telegraph*'s editor, a male Red Cross worker reminded readers how female volunteers treated the needy impartially. He seemed to suggest their example entitled them to some semblance of "equality."

Harrisburg scrambled to secure labor. Businessmen needed clerical help. Firms with federal contracts required skilled workers. Shortages impacted services. The retention of servants, store employees and restaurant waiters worried employers. The city lacked playground personnel. The Scouts sought masters. The labor loss threatened the ice supply.

Workplace demands concocted stopgaps. Residents, schoolboys and prisoners farmed. Old men swept streets. Railroads recalled retirees. Establishments hired the unconscripted.

The federal government addressed the labor crisis. Officials ordered draft boards to threaten the deferred in "non-essential occupations" with conscription. They could avoid the military if they obtained a "man's job." The nonessential included waiters, servants, clerks and "ushers and other attendants engaged in and in connection with games, sports and amusements, excepting actual performers." Barbers on Pullman trains made the list.

Somebody Is Always Taking the Joy Out of Life by Briggs humorized the dilemma. A loafing man, handed a circular that reads, "Work or fight," seeks employment in want ads and finds a job cutting grass. He exclaims, "D—n the Kaiser."

Firms' ads prevailed on workers to stay in place. Avoid the temptation of somewhere else because Harrisburg offers job openings, said one. Another implored, "Look before you leap." It carried photographs of houses and touted little "need to seek better living conditions, finer homes or schools, more diversified amusements." Enhanced by an Uncle Sam image, a late-July pitch emphasized the employer's responsibility to treat employees justly and added, "The rolling stone gathers no moss." The Central Iron and Steel Company summoned those touched by "work or fight" to "come with us and help lick the Kaiser." Draft boards enforced "work or fight." Locals complied. Men got to work. Idlers suffered arrest.

A *Telegraph* editorial encouraged vacations despite the labor shortfall. Yet it warned inflation made travel expensive and sighed, "Is it any wonder we 'cuss' the Kaiser?" Ten days later, the paper reported Harrisburgers forsook the shore, mountains and car travel to remain home and do their bit.

Population growth spurred a housing demand. But construction lags limited accommodations. Migrants found few dwellings and encountered exorbitant rents. A committee probed complaints, and the mayor warned profiteers. An officer criticized landlords for excessive charges and tenant evictions during fuel shortfalls. He mandated their heaters must function economically.

How to furnish homeplaces became "more and more a grave question." A *Telegraph* series exposed housing conditions. A manufacturer feared labor loss. Some workers lodged outside Harrisburg, which required a commute. City slums menaced public health. The crisis discouraged industrial expansion and cost employment opportunities. A realtor judged, "The situation is critical." Calls went out for governmental assistance. Chamber of commerce representatives visited Washington. Popular opinion favored state and municipal help.

Harrisburg bustled with the hubble-bubble of manufacturing and distribution. The city produced steel for ships, munitions, gun carriages and railroads. It made machinery that aided ammunition output. The government contracted area-fashioned silk, construction lumber and gunstock wood. Locally turned-out pretzels, cigars and mattress bed sacks comforted doughboys. City paper production contributed to military recordkeeping. Area shippers transported apples and highway-making substances.

The *Iron Trade Review* recognized Harrisburger Francis J. Hall's work in Washington. Hall, Central Iron and Steel's vice president, won praise as a "right-hand" man: "When the extent of the country's effort to establish adequate shipping to meet wartimes is considered the great importance of the services by Mr. Hall may be accurately measured."

Harrisburgers took to the hoe. The city counted 2,500 war gardens, 140 more than in 1917. Ads encouraged planting. The *Telegraph* publicized available ground in Bellevue Park. The Harrisburg Rubber Company cut hoses' costs. "Doing My Bit" offered the novice tips: "When to cultivate….

How much to cultivate. How often to cultivate.…And how deep to cultivate the precious soil." The column urged sidestepping slopes to prevent moisture's run-off.

An editorial rebuked the wrongheaded. Noticing some decided against unprofitable gardening, the piece reminded residents that the nation's food issue "is not one of price, but of production." Daylight savings time gave laggards opportunity to turn over the soil.

In truth, green thumbers benefited. Working a hoe demonstrated more love of country than swinging a golf club. It furthered physical exercise, produced foodstuffs and helped family budgets. "The average size war garden," claimed the *Evening News*, "can be persuaded to pay the average family's income tax."

Cultivated plots required protection. Mulching shielded plants. For critter and ailment management, formulas called for lead arsenate, copper sulfate, soap suds and lime. *Snoodles* by Hungerford pictured a boy spraying pests. A quip instructed, "Don't spend all your time talking about swatting the Huns 'over there'—use up a portion each day battling with the bugs in your war garden." The four-legged trespassed. *Doings of the Duffs* by Allman illustrated a character's warning about a dog.

Thievery plagued gardeners. Vigilance crews watched out for pilferers. Authorities offered a twenty-five-dollar reward for arrests. "Such thefts," stated the *Evening News*, "are regarded as far more serious than ordinary sneak stealing, because they opposed the work of patriotism now going on in the gardens."

A North Street cultivator showed off. His Green and Seneca Streets plot yielded potatoes weighing close to a pound each.

Wartime hobbled most construction. The military's Middletown projects received priority. Officials put off school, bridge, rail and recreational improvements. A need existed for upgraded roads. Housing starts stalled, but the Penn-Harris neared completion.

The war did spur some infrastructural developments. Crews upgraded roadways between Harrisburg and outlying military installations. Swollen railways necessitated an additional bridge. Motorists felt a pinch. Increased demands and shipping problems diminished oil and rubber. Gasoline savings and tire protections became obligations. Firestone Tire hyped, "Patriotism and common sense" rallied around smart and inexpensive automobile employment. The *Evening News* preached each "owner should conserve and preserve tires in the same patriotic manner as he buys Liberty Bonds, War Savings Stamps or follows the suggestions of food conservation as outlined by Hoover."

The Penn-Harris Hotel close to completion. *From the* Harrisburg Telegraph. *Courtesy of PennLive.*

The Harrisburg Motor Dealers' Association initiated Council of National Defense suggestions. Saving manpower and materials received attention. Garages stopped Sunday services beyond six o'clock in the evening and terminated comprehensive demonstrations for customers. Their steps earned acclaim since efforts to restrain Sabbath driving meant the sacrifice of mechanics' profits.

The city kept eyes peeled for replenishment's wastage and provender's misuse. Lieutenant Flachaire's landing in a wheat field resulted in crop loss and locals' chagrin. The *Evening News* blasted the rich for food extravagance, editorializing, "The offenders ought to be ashamed of themselves and be made to pay the penalty for their criminal habits." "Doing My Bit" demanded: "Are you saving every scrape of meat, every ounce of fat, every grain of wheat and the other cereals, making the fullest use of every part of vegetables you can?" Police killed wandering dogs to save food. In a similar vein, *That Son-In-Law of Pa's* had a character remark, "Yep, feedin's beef to a perfec'ly useless animal, is waste!"

The press promised belt-tightening. Gathering at the YMCA, the Newspaper Publishers' Association resolved to save paper. Conservatorial concerns converted trash. Instead of tossing, residents learned metals, papers, cloths, "rubber of all kinds…old batteries, hair switches and hair combings" could be useful. They were also reminded to accumulate bottles for canning.

Disturbing conditions blighted the city. Cars and motorcycles sped noisily through streets, disquieting sleepers and angering workers. Dead dogs and cats were strewn about avenues and neighborhoods, threatening pestilence. Clean-ups collected at least three and as many as fifteen carcasses each day. Industrial accidents injured employees and delayed production. The *Evening News* applauded "those brave souls who every day toil in powder mills and munition factories. [A] danger is ever present and death lurks near them."

Contagions preoccupied the municipality. Dr. Leonard Keene Hirshberg's *Evening News* column addressed combating wartime afflictions. In May and June, authorities considered a new hospital. The next month, the health office recorded 1,130 transmittable occurrences between January and mid-year. Bacteria in ice cream remained a worry. United Ice and Coal Company offered advice: avoid placing victuals on windowsills and verandahs since "germs, dirt and dust are always flying about and are apt to settle on the food." It assured customers that "Alspure Ice is made from water that has been filtered, boiled, reboiled, skimmed and again filtered."

Harrisburg acted. Its ashmen picked up rubbish to deter tuberculosis. The Civic Club held a fly-swatting competition. "Doing My Bit" assisted, asking, "Do you kill every fly you see?" It insisted, "Don't let one fly escape." The column called for rodent elimination. A druggist joined in, peddling ingredients for Pesky Devils' Quietus, an insecticide.

Fears mounted of venereal disease transfer. The state opened a North Second Street clinic to cope with the scourge. It worried about the impact on servicemen. Authorities placed "notices in public toilet rooms warning the public of the dangers of the diseases and the necessity for prompt and proper treatment." Doctors received "rules and regulations" concerning those infected.

Maladies multiplied despite precautions. Draftees became sick. Smallpox cases sprouted in the city and at Middletown. Fortunately, the pox ebbed, and Harrisburg shut down its pesthouse in late June.

Meanwhile, a mystifying sickness broke out suddenly in Europe. Spain, Russia and Scandinavia suffered. In Northern Ireland, Belfast munitions employees became ill. Officials in Dublin, Ireland, forbade mass assemblies and public parades.

Chapter 7

HOMESTRETCH

August–October 1918

The war shifted to in the Allies' favor. Americans, supporting French troops, held off the Germans at Château-Thierry and battled the enemy in the Argonne. They breached the Hindenburg line and took countless prisoners. By August, Germany's leadership had realized the conflict was lost.

City draftees and enlistees continued to step up. Conscripts received pre-enlistment information. Police, to the mayor's alarm, registered with the local board. A father forfeited his deferment to avenge the death of a younger sibling. Enlistments rose. African American draftees paraded before departure. Sadness attended farewells.

Shirking slackened selective service. Authorities detained a disorderly draft evader. Men deserted. Police arrested one deserter with a stolen car and jailed others from the South. Two locals lied about their matrimonial status and faced perjury indictments. A soldier wounded himself. Another died by suicide in his Greenwood Street home. The *Harrisburg Telegraph* published a cartoon showing a character seeking draft excuses.

Locals cast suspicions on a pigeon. The blue carrier homed daily at locksmith Samuel Gray's on South Court Street. It had undoubtedly deserted its training camp and escaped Gray's efforts to collar it.

Harrisburg reached out to soldiers. The Red Cross Pennsy canteen intensified services. For those in transit, the YMCA provided bathing and entertainment. Newspapers encouraged motorists to offer rides, and jitney owners complied. Servicemen participated in organized baseball and enjoyed a free Victoria movie. A private residence on Berryhill Street welcomed soldiers, and a *Telegraph* comic strip illustrated their invitation to dinner. The Civic Club tended amusements, dances and eats while the city library donated books. The club's weekend attractions triggered poetic attention:

Come over to the Civic Club
And have a little fun,
Before you leave for Europe
To defeat the treacherous Hun.

There's dancing and there's music
And a lot of other things'
The "cooky jar" is always there
In charge of Mrs. Jennings.

Sugar biscuits, ginger snaps.
Raisin buns and tarts,
(Just like Mother use to make)
To please the "Sammies" hearts.

Come over to the Hostess House
When feeling fine or sad,
We'll give you just a taste of home,
For each one is "our lad."

Still, service personnel misbehaved. Authorities ordered military police to the city. They arrested bootleggers selling booze to soldiers. Uniformed men drank and got drunk. They also committed crimes: one attacked a hotel employee while another robbed a druggist. The military considered closing saloons.

Police attempted to curb the streetwalker's lure. They apprehended four in August, one near Broad and Cowden Streets and another at Cowden Street's "notorious No. 18" haunt. That month and into September, they raided disorderly houses on Marion, North Seventh and Cherry Streets.

In August, the Rotary Club viewed the federal film *Fit to Fight* in the YMCA, a screening intended to inform enlistees and draftees about the threats of booze consumption and social unchastity. Worthy, as well as vivid and educational, the vehicle served forthcoming pre-enlistment audiences. One observer called its contents "the most startling exposition of the frightful results of dissipation and the dangers which attend the association of men with immoral women that has ever been put into lecture or picture form."

Wartime challenged conventions. Beatrice Fairfax's column asked, "Are you looking after your daughter?" She lamented the lack of discipline and the risk to a wayward's innocence without chaperoning. She criticized vamping with soldiers and reminded parents, "The female of species is more deadly than the male." Fairfax believed "Sammy would be content to go his way if the girl did not so often block it with her smiling attentions." An editorial pressed for the protection of maidenhood and servicemen. The soldiers' attire fascinates those twelve to sixteen, so "it's brutally unfair to her and to the lads who wear the uniform that you do not guard her better."

Moral as well as physical well-being became uppermost. Edward F. Allen's 1918 book narrated *Keeping Our Fighters Fit for War and After*. The presidentially prescribed Commission on Training Camp Activities (CTCA) tried to safeguard soldiers and neighborhoods near encampments and their residents—specifically youthful women—living in those areas from the "traditional 'vices' of soldiers—venereal disease and promiscuous sexual relations." Troubled mainly by booze and sex, "the CTCA labored to replace 'the less savory attractions of the saloon and whorehouse with more wholesome pasttimes.'"

The Edgar Lewis Production Company filmed *The Troop Train* in Harrisburg. Promoted as a "great patriotic propaganda" feature and based on a *Saturday Evening Post* yarn, the movie intended to demonstrate American love of country and animosity for things German. The storyline portrayed a heroic citizen who discovers saboteurs' schemes to destroy a troop train. He slays the enemy, but a biased jury condemns him to death. Patriots eventually rescue him. City theaters told of the filming and encouraged residents to participate. Between 1,500 and 2,000 showed. The production company shot at Fort Hunter and on the capitol grounds with the cooperation of local and state authorities. Its director selected Harrisburg "because of the beautiful scenery and the opportunities it presented." The Victoria booked the motion picture.

Indeed, movies animated Harrisburgers, screening their true feelings. Patriotism received cheers. Viewers applauded the sight of American servicemen. As the enemy retreated, youths flag-waved whoops like "Sock 'em!" "Go to it Yanks!" and "Treat 'em rough!" The city's bellicosity increased daily.

As instructors and diversions, motion pictures and their stars helped morale. Leading man Douglas Fairbanks "did more to relieve the strained minds of the American public and let them relax a bit from the necessarily [*sic*] rigors of life in wartimes" than any other. War pictures garnered new patrons. Residents who never went to the theater became moviegoers. Sitting beside regulars, they rooted for Allied victory.

The Orpheum billed *Hearts of the World*. Produced by D.W. Griffith, the film storied a French idyll disquieted by war and German occupation. Griffith pictured Prussian brutality, Allied attack and villager liberation— another version of the enemy atrocities genre. The *Telegraph* argued, "No one who is a red-blooded American citizen can view the unfolding of this story…and not vow vengeance on the Hun hordes and their barbarity." Yet the *New Republic* deplored the movie's impact: "Here we have an art of pure emotion which can go beneath thought, beneath belief, beneath ideals, down to the brute fact of emotional psychology, and make a man or a woman who has hated war, all war, even this war, feel the surge of group emotion, group loyalty and group hate."

The *Telegraph* upbraided an audience for remaining seated during the playing of "The Marsellaise," the French national anthem.

The war's mounting intensity heightened prayer's value. A "War Angelus," proposed by New York's Rotary Club, won endorsement by its Harrisburg chapter and called for supplication one minute every day at eleven o'clock. The program's advent on October 7 opened with factory whistles blowing and church bells ringing. Mayor Keister wanted the entreaty to call for American victory.

The Red Cross practiced a silent moment of its own, inaugurated on October 23. Volunteers offered a sixty-second daily prayer for servicemen abroad.

The lyrics of "A Soldier's Rosary" comforted the maternal:

> *A mother's last words to ev'ry soldier*
> *"Kneel down at night and say your prayers"*
> *But he's so weary, thro' days so dreary*
> *After all his trials and cares*
> *Don't worry mother, he serves his Maker*
> *When he serves his country's needs*
> *No matter where each act is a pray'r*
> *And they form the links upon a soldier's beads.*

Cleveland native W.E. Cochran beseeched for Germany's punition and ruin:

O' God, I pray of Three
Let those things come to be
To punish Germany

Through all the coming years
Let her heart break—with fears
And shedding endless tears.

Let all her hopes be vain,
Let her hear the curse of Cain
For the millions she has slain.

Let her bear the awful blame
And let her hated name
Be whispered low,—with shame.

Let her hear the steady beat
Of Five Million Allied feet
On Berlin's doomed street.

And until our sword is pressed
Upon her naked breast
O God, don't let us rest.

God is not mocked. Whatsoever a Nation soweth, that shall it also reap.
Germany as a Nation must be destroyed.

Calling the labor shortage the nation's major predicament, the *Telegraph* pressed women to occupy positions vacated by draftees. A full-page ad bid, "Women must enlist for the second line of defense—the mills and the factories, the farm and the store, the bank and the office—just as readily as their brothers have volunteered of that more dangerous work on the battlefields of Europe."

Many women answered the summons, replacing men in unaccustomed roles. In addition to stinting as elevator operators and railroad employees, they drove buses and trucks. One woman kept a quarry company's books. Another clerked at a hotel. Lady mechanics, wearing overalls, caught residents' attention.

Newspapers portrayed employment novelties. An *Evening News*'s sketch, "The Girl He Left Behind Him," pictured a woman doing farm work. Another drawing showed a girl running an elevator. One of its comic strips referred to a policewoman. The *Telegraph*'s funnies carried a character mentioning the opposite sex laboring at a hotel. The paper likewise published a photo of female mechanics.

The State Industrial Board devised dress regulations for women's factory labor. "Shop Clothing," a list of rules from the state to protect industrial workers, cautioned against adorning with "jewelry…loose ribbons and ornaments." Women were advised to "leave their high-heeled shoes at home." Footwear should have a comfortable fit with reduced bottoms. The coda told machine tenders to wear headgear to prevent hair from catching in an apparatus's operating cogwheels.

Fitness pitches pestered ladies with monotonous messages. An ad for Lydia E. Pinkham's "Vegetable Compound," a drugstore remedy, reminded the ill, "To do your duty during these trying times your health should be your first consideration." For those working, Dr. Pierce's "Prescription" promised "results in most of the delicate derangements and weaknesses of women." To withstand the pressures of service and employment, doses of "Nuxated Iron" ensured blood that provided "life, vim and vitality."

Clothing conservation put a squeeze on design. Dives, Pomeroy and Stewart advertised female shoes limited to eight inches in height, following federal guidelines. Shortened and close-fitting petticoats prompted the quip, "Our girls are conserving below, above and on both sides, to say nothing of the arms." The comic strip *That Son-In-Law of Pa's* stated, "All clothes are to be lower, higher, tighter and thinner!" *Polly and Her Pals* had Pa asking, "How'd all you wimmin come to adopt paper clothes?" A woman responded: "By order of the Cloth Conservation Committee."

Harrisburg's wartime trades earned prominence. Steel factories turned out munitions, weapons, ship and truck parts as well as construction materials. Tin manufacturers contributed utensils and builders' plates. The city produced primary products. Potatoes provisioned military camps. Wheat fed hungry Europeans. Apple butter satisfied soldiers' taste buds.

By early September, Harrisburg had become a major distributor. Among other goods, its railways carried munitions and grains. The municipality figured in still another import. For two months, Harrisburg's telegraphic transmissions ranked behind those of only five other cities nationwide.

The War Industries Board designated the city its main office for subregion no. 5 of the Philadelphia District for its Resources and Conversion Section.

Keeping fit during wartime. *From the* Harrisburg Telegraph. *Courtesy of PennLive.*

Located at the chamber of commerce and chaired by D.E. Tracy of the Harrisburg Pipe and Pipe Bending Company, the board informed Washington about local industry's home front activities.

Accidents continued to mar the area's economy. Injuries and deaths afflicted steel shops and rail yards in particular.

Total war demanded workplace harmony for support of fighting forces abroad. Ads implored industrialists to be dutiful and fair to labor. Correspondingly, pleas requested workers be reasonable, steadfast and diligent. A cartoon exemplified cooperation, picturing a soldier and a laborer shaking hands. The *Telegraph* editorialized an anti-strike message. In late October, Central Iron and Steel granted its workforce concessions.

Labor Day march across Market Square. *From the* Evening News. *Courtesy of PennLive.*

Burdened rails triggered consideration of deepening the Susquehanna. In a speech to the Rotary Club, Major William B. Gray, judging Harrisburg the "best transportation center in [the] East," saw "no reason why the Susquehanna river should not be made navigable for freight and passenger traffic at a very reasonable cost." This idea had been pondered in the past, and the State Water Supply Commission, the Rotary and participants in a meeting at A.W. Myers' State Street home showed solicitude. Gray spelled out the watercourse's situation:

> *The Susquehanna river as a means of transportation occupies an unique and extremely strong position. It not only traverses a rich farming country, but it embraces the anthracite coal region, the central manufacturing district of the state, and valuable deposits of brick shale, brick and potter's clay, limestone, cement rock, building and concrete stone quarries, also great steel and iron and other industries are located on its banks. These would furnish the business and the destination would be the entire Atlantic ports through which the Susquehanna would be brought in touch with foreign commerce.*

Excepting military projects, the war delayed and limited construction. Builders had Middletown and Marsh Run depots up and ready before November. But contractors put off work on a Second Baptist Church. After postponements, Mary Sachs women's clothing shop opened in early September. The school district did erect the Thomas A. Edison secondary on Nineteenth Street and the Susquehanna Open Air building at Fifth and

Seneca. The Pennsylvania Railroad's new freight depot received finishing touches. Furthermore, after many postponements, the Penn-Harris Hotel announced a January First opening.

The conflict continued to forestall upkeep. Labor and material shortages prevented street repair and paving.

Postwar building drew attention. Returning soldiers seeking jobs could be employed on public projects. The city planned a communicable sickness facility. The Rotary endorsed a loan for roads.

Through the summer and into the fall, paucities became more acute. The *Evening News* suggested raising lambs to cut the price of wool. Donald McCormick wanted the Harrisburg Country Club and the Colonial Country Club to allow sheep grazing on their golf links. A coal scarcity loomed. The housing shortfall continued, a threat to the acquisition of federal contracts. Labor remained sparse. An ad asked workers to remain at their positions. A cartoon alluded to the difficulty of finding help. A table at the railroad station sought laborers and hoped to prevent their departures. Tech students harvested fruit in a neighboring county. The chamber of commerce complained about "a waste of manpower" when painters daubed a Liggett and Myers Tobacco Company plug on the Senate Hotel's wall.

African Americans gave the war fulsome support. Many of Harrisburg's Black men enlisted. Their churches, adorned with service banners, brought home "the patriotism and loyalty of our negro citizens." The Baptist church's brethren performed a flag-waving pageant featuring the icons "Uncle Sam, the Goddess of Liberty and Miss Liberty."

But racial incidents discomforted the community. In Steelton, Blacks residents assaulted a policeman about to arrest the sister of one of the assailants. Also in Steelton, a grocer shot and killed an African American, reportedly in self-defense. In an ensuing riot, four persons suffered injuries.

In mid-September, the *Courier* disturbed White readers. The sheet reported a Black male lured a White woman. Of the sixty-seven persons lynched nationwide in 1918, according to the NAACP, fourteen had been accused of aggressing White women.

Black men endured negative images. Cartoons and comic strips poked fun at their speech, appearance and intelligence. They were demeaned as "Sambo." One artist used the offensive "nigger." In early October, Dickinson College upheld racial segregation. It expelled two African Americans, telling them to apply elsewhere because incoming Southerners "might make it unpleasant for you." The college defended its decision. Troubles, it argued, originated from the Students' Army Training Corps in that "the men must live together in the intimacy of common barracks, lavatories, mess hall, etc." Race mixing violated federally mandated separation in military encampments.

Dickinson came in for criticism. A *Telegraph* editorial called the college's action "a regrettable thing." One of its reporters discovered most public opinion backed the expellees and exclaimed, "At this time unity is what the country must have to beat the world's enemy." A letter to the editor held prejudice responsible for "the antiquated idea of race superiority," recalling President Lincoln's condemnation of slaveholders' racism and reminding readers of Aryan arrogance. It added, "The position of this college becomes more and more perilous as the world approaches its goal of universal brotherhood and good will towards all."

The *Telegraph*'s position won applause. In commendation, a correspondent asserted, "The colored American's right for moral gain is not half so popular as exploiting his wrongs for material gain but in the end it counts for so much more in human progress and 'making the world safe for democracy.'" The NAACP and the Waiters' Association likewise welcomed the paper's stand. Ironically, the same *Telegraph* edition receiving acclaim printed the ad "WANTED—White woman, or girl, for general housework."

Harrisburg cursed slacking. When the city failed to meet its War Savings Stamp allotment, the *Telegraph* bemoaned, "In all other forms of war work this community has excelled." Some failed to help the fourth Liberty loan. At its headquarters, staff checked on local laborers' bond purchases. Buyers condemned nonsubscribers and thought "it [an] outrage steps are not taken to compel those who hold back to aid [the] nation in war."

Shirking accusations led to a defamation suit. Leroy A. Martz, a Penbrook resident, sued Jacob C. Reich, also of Penbrook, for $5,000. He claimed Reich "called him a 'slacker' and emphasized the alleged slanderous remarks with plenty of profanity for trimmings."

Flies became prey. An officer promised Middletown soldiers a furlough for each fifty swatted. He observed, "The boys are attacking the pests with a fierceness that compares well with the offensive spirit shown by the Yanks overseas." Harrisburg's Civic Club supervised a second swatting competition running until the end of September. Seventh and North Streets' Harry Sigmund came in first, submitting 296 pints of battered bugs to officials at the Patriot-News Building.

The Harrisburg Library on Front and Walnut Streets carried out patriotic-spirited services. In addition to its basement housing the Red Cross's headquarters and storage center, librarian Alice Eaton made available federal information about military drill and food safety. She spearheaded book collections for army camps and lent the Civic Club literature for its weekend entertainments.

Eaton energized the United War Work campaign. She acquired and exhibited its placards and assured all borrowed books contained a chit explaining the push's necessity. Its campaign committee selected her to chair a spokesperson's bureau.

The librarian kept tabs on home front reading. Wartime novels attained appeal. Patrons sought volumes about Normandy and Picardy provinces. According to a report, "There is hardly a day passed without some requests for books which describe the Marne region of France." Young boys found heroic accounts of Nathan Hale, O.H. Perry, Davy Crockett and U.S. Grant to their liking.

The library carried on, announcing a circulation of 109,015 books between October 1917 and September 1918.

Harrisburg turned out for the fourth Liberty loan, programmed identically to the third. The loan's committee directed teams to solicit industries and households, setting a $6,133,640 goal with the motto: "Double [the] last subscription." The Gilbert Hardware Store on Market Street served as headquarters.

Fanfare accompanied the drive. A musical march merged with a choral ensemble in Reservoir Park. Mayor Keister proclaimed "Unconditional Surrender Day," calling on "citizens to buy bonds and stun the Kaiser."

Boosters bustled for bonds. Sloganeers whooped: "Glorious Fourth" and "Double the third." Flyover aircraft dropped leaflets. The "Alien Squad," a multinational military unit, appeared at the Market Street headquarters. Italian soldiers and French legionnaires visited to give their assistance. Actor Douglas Fairbanks, on a loan quest, stopped and spoke at the rail station. Bulgarians and a German woman made purchases, professing their loyalty. A mother whose son was killed in action invested, shaming those who did not.

Visuals aided the push. Flags of "four cross bars" decked windows. Posters clothed the downtown, one urging, "Come on!" The YWCA displayed its Blue Triangle image in support. The *Evening News* appropriated the Statue of Liberty, illustrating the idea that "victories are no excuse for letting up on buying bonds."

Spokesmen alluded to history to wheedle subscriptions. Donald McCormack reminded residents what befell Babylon's King Belshazzar, who dallied against an adversary at the threshold. He warned waiting could have dreadful results. McCormack rued, "Harrisburg with Dauphin county has given 5,600 men to face the barbarian on the field of battle before it decided that it would not lend its dollars to support them." Dr. Frank Crane recalled how the country's conflicts of 1776, 1812, 1846 and 1898 fought "to liberate the common man" and gave a lecture titled "American Democracy Is the Antidote for Germany [*sic*] Autocracy."

Clergy provided momentum. Sermons highlighted bonds at the Fourth Street Church of God and the Pleasant View Church of God. At the Grace Methodist Episcopal Church, the Reverend Dr. Robert Bagnell sponsored a Liberty loan gathering. The Messiah Lutheran Church's pastor Henry W.A. Hanson told Central High students "Why We Should Buy Liberty Bonds." In a letter, Bishop Philip R. McDevitt asked priests to inform the faithful about the fourth loan.

Fraternal orders subscribed. The Knights of Columbus purchased $500 worth. The Kiwanis exceeded a goal of $25,000. The Cornplanters Tribe of Red Men pitched in $300. The school district contributed. Central High's chapel housed a large assembly in support of the loan. Administrators granted a $22,600 investment.

Youth participated. Hundreds of Boy Scouts shouted, "Buy more bonds!" At the loan's Market Street office, Girl Scouts sold subscriptions, knitting between sales. Over 150 elementary and high school students authored competitive compositions for prizes about the fourth loan. One observer remarked, "It certainly was astonishing the grasp even the 10 and 11-year-old pupils had on their subject."

City newspapers gave bond marketing wholehearted endorsement. Cartoons and comic strips promoted and praised purchasing. Local and national concerns advertised on behalf of the loan, quoting public figures like evangelist Billy Sunday, Senator Henry Cabot Lodge and labor leader Samuel Gompers as pitchmen. Editorials warned, "Don't be deceived" about the war's imminent end and pleaded, "End the scourge of Hunnism with a mighty surge of PATRIOTISM NOW!"

Poetry lent a hand. A.K. Strouse, a Tech student, penned:

> *The Liberty Loan is a trick of our own*
> *To pay for the War as we go;*
> *The Kaiser, the miser will never be wiser*
> *We'll bury him deeply below.*

A Dives, Pomeroy and Stewart ad explained one's obligation:

We'll hear no more of "Hunnist blight"
Or of unhappy Belgium's plight,
If we'll just lend the way they fight—
Good night!

The *Evening News* revealed that Dauphin County rested in a Federal Reserve district given the right to name a ship for its counties' contributions to the fourth Liberty loan. The paper suggested the designation Dauphin since the county received its name from a Frenchman, the son of ally Louis XVI, who aided Americans in their revolution. Such a christening seemed timely "when all Dauphin Countians are throbbing with affection and admiration for France."

The area squelched inklings of disloyalty. The distribution of a calendar reading "peace and good will" by Dr. John J. Mullowney, a Quaker, met censure: "Harrisburg people have too many sons on the other side to be deceived by German peace stuff at this time." Lancaster residents threatened to tar and feather the Zion German Lutheran Church's minister for gatherings allegedly partial to America's enemies. The chapel's board removed him from his post, and the police, fearful of disorder, enjoined his immediate departure from the community. Principal Arthur E. Brown of the Harrisburg Academy gainsaid a rumor his institution hired an instructor relieved from a Maryland college because of Germanic proclivities.

Routine protocol became obligatory. When a German, John Vitenbaugh, failed to go hatless during a rendering of "The Star-Spangled Banner," a federal marshal placed him under arrest. The state Department of Instruction ruled Mennonites' children must salute the flag at school. Superintendent Dr. Nathan C. Schaeller told their families it "is not a religious matter but something of plain every day [*sic*] patriotism." The *Telegraph* agreed, spouting that youngsters must be trained to hail Old Glory and saying any "parent who teaches his child otherwise is not a good citizen." (In 1943, the U.S. Supreme Court would rule in *West Virginia State Board of Education v. Barnette* that the "action of the local authorities in compelling the flag salute and pledge transcends constitutional limitations on their power and invades the sphere of intellect and spirit which it is the purpose of the First Amendment to our Constitution to reserve from all official control.")

Corporate management stepped in line. The state auditor general reported most of a particular class of companies excised "German" from their forms of address.

Literature proclaimed patriotism. Jacketed with an image of Uncle Sam beating a mutt identified as "yellow dog," Henry Irving Dodge's *The Yellow Dog* debased Americans loyal to Germany.

Good Germans inspired regard. Dr. Maximilian Grossman spoke on behalf of the federal Committee on Public Information (CPI) at the Zion Lutheran Church on South Fourth Street and won accolades such as "scholar," "clear-thinking" and "loyal." The sixty-eight-year-old Conrad Hoffsommer of South Seventeenth Street passed away uttering, "I hope I shall ive [*sic*] to see the day when the Kaiser is defeated."

The campaign against the Teutonic tongue continued. Schools substituting French for German enhanced Allied relations. The *Courier* wanted the enemy's vernacular banished, demanding, "Who, in the name of all that is fair and lovely wants to twist his jaw, mastering this stig-tossled, beastly, language which in course of time will be extinct as the dodo?" Judging Germanic studies a "distinct menace" as well as the "most insidious form of treason," the paper described Berlin's lingo as "a harsh, unwieldly language that sounds exactly as brutal as the people who speak it [and] should be wiped from the earth." A cartoon titled *Absent, with Teacher's Consent* ordered, "Outside, Heinie, outside!!"

Yet national emergencies Americanized Germans. U.S. soldiers deployed in Europe bearing Germanic surnames served with unquestioned loyalty. The American Revolution naturalized sauerkraut, eaten as descendants danced to the tune of "Yankee Doodle." The need to consume 1918's bumper crop of cabbage overshadowed fussing about nomenclature. The *Telegraph* reassured, "It is the patriotic duty of Americans to make use of it because of its food value."

Bumper crop of cabbage. *From the* Harrisburg Telegraph. *Courtesy of PennLive.*

Germany's war crimes sparked a boycott. After learning of a British officer's murder with an enemy-made shaving blade, the Front Market Motor Supply Company asked, "Shall we go on buying German razors?" It promised "never knowingly to purchase any raw materials or manufactured articles, regardless of quality, workmanship or price, made in Germany or by German sympathizers." The *Telegraph* editorialized to steer clear of Teuton toys: "Is any American so cold of heart that he

Allied Lie

Allied propaganda.
From Look Magazine's *A Contribution to the Cause of Peace. Author's collection.*

would willingly place in the hands of his daughter a doll made possibly by one of the fiends who chopped off the hands of Belgian babies?" It added: "Or who would want his son to play with an utematic [*sic*] toy devised by that same devilish ingenuity that invented poison gas and the fame [*sic*] thrower?"

The city flayed leniency for Germany. The *Telegraph* repudiated compromises, negotiations as well as terms and advocated "an immense war indemnity." The *Evening News* demanded the blotting out of Prussianism so the German people could reclaim their credence. Both papers favored unconditional surrender.

Caricature reduced the adversity to animality. *Snoodles* by Hungerford identified garden insects, body lice and canines as German. *Evening News* cartoons portrayed *The Beast Seeks His Lair*, a representation of Germany, and counterposed a snake tagged "Hohenzollernism" with a woman typifying "Civilization."

Color symbolism defined the conflict. A city man portended Germany's black eagle subdued by America's snowy erne "in a white cause." Indeed, Dr. Leon Keene Hirshberg argued color differences reflected national moods and behaviors. In "Secrets of Health and Happiness," his *Evening News* column, he declared black, derived from Scriptures, poems and clinicians,

Left: Belgium fights off the fiend. *From the* Evening News. *Courtesy of PennLive.*

Right: The creature skedaddles to its den. *From the* Evening News. *Courtesy of PennLive.*

"produces a dogged, dull, obstinate state." Germany's flag embellished its mark and character. On the contrary, Allied red, white and blue banners exalted, evoking agreeable feelings. He believed red promoted healthiness while white and blue produced a plea for a favorable disposition, since "they hold the attention better."

From early August until late September, the *Telegraph* serialized "The Kaiser as I Knew Him for Fourteen Years," an insider's look. Dr. Arthur N. Davis, who treated the German leader medically, waived professional confidentiality and bared all. His perceptions divulged Wilhelm's attitudes, aims and machinations. Davis forecasted Hohenzollern doom, anticipated Teutonic democracy and thought Germany's worldwide welcome conceivable. He revealed, "No doubt that if Germany had succeeded in her efforts to gain control of the major part of Europe she would have soon looked toward the Western Hemisphere and the Far East." At one point, he wrote, the kaiser had interjected: "Davis, America—must—be—punished for—her—action!"

Imperial Germany provoked. Native Americans of the Onondaga Nation dreamed of scalping Emperor Wilhelm when Berlin detained and imprisoned seventeen of their brothers. They severed all ties with Germany

German-named child maligned by peers. *From the* Harrisburg Telegraph. *Courtesy of PennLive.*

and, according to onetime Harrisburg resident and tribal adviser Edward H. Gohl, planned a war declaration.

Espionage fears, fed by the cinema, placed the city on edge. The deluge of movies featuring enemy spies booked in theaters included *The Kaiser's Shadow*, *No Man's Land*, *Joan of Plattsburg*, *The Crucible of Life*, *Till I Come Back to You*, *In Pursuit of Polly* and *The House of Hate*. When the city's John Cannon allegedly claimed to be a German agent, a group of stalwarts chased him down and seized him. He later said he ran away out of fear and denied spying.

Western Front combat inflicted heavy losses on Harrisburgers. In August, seventeen-year-old Frank Hawk died. The Camp Curtin Memorial Methodist Church commemorated his memory. In September, the Paxton Presbyterian Church remembered Lieutenant James Galt Elder. The same month, the *Telegraph* reported the death of North Third Street's Charles Edward Weitmeyer. The paper listed football player "Ed" Fettrow of South Fifteenth Street killed in October. A shell fragment wounded former police offer Lieutenant George J. Shoemaker, who resided with his spouse, Marie, and daughters Katherine and Edith on Fulton Street. At month's end, six city soldiers appeared on the casualty tabulation.

At least 5,600 Harrisburg-area servicemen faced the enemy in battle. The city planned the rehabilitation of those wounded. H.B. McCormick led the chamber of commerce's Manufacturing Council, which aimed to find industrial employment for the disabled. Mayor Daniel Keister gave support as vice chairman of a Red Cross Committee for veterans' aid. He proposed a placement office and employment count.

The city set out to honor its soldiers. The *Telegraph* printed a letter advocating commemorative trees for each man who served. A sapling-lined entry to Reservoir Park at Market Street came under discussion. Officials decided only those killed in action would be memorialized with plantings on avenues or at schools. They also considered a large plaque that would show the "name, address and rank of service of every city and county boy."

Lieutenant George J. Shoemaker, former policeman wounded in France. *From the* Evening News. *Courtesy of* PennLive.

The *Telegraph* favored a bridge at State Street across the Susquehanna, arguing, "How much more fitting such a memorial would be than a more or less ornamented marble column, with its useless collonades and carved approaches."

The war altered superstitions. The numeral 13 forfeited its ominousness. Rather, soldiers at the front sloganed, "Beware of No. 3!" They declined a third furlough, "fearing it would be their last." To boot, they embraced the "black cat as a mascot and luck-bringer."

Soldiers away craved tidings from the homestead. On August 24, the *Telegraph* began "War Weekly," local happenings summarized for out-of-town servicemen. The supplement could be easily scissored and posted as a typical letter. The paper's Circulation Department offered to send soldiers its daily: $5.00 for a year; $2.50 for six months and $1.25 for three months. Needing only the recipient's name, unit or vessel, it promised, "We will do the rest."

War trophies fascinated Harrisburgers. Soldiers mailed German helmets home. One sent an enemy's handkerchief. The mayor desired bagged field guns for display on the capitol grounds. A train carrying German ordnance stopped in the city and received press attention.

The trooper's nickname spawned dispute. The army chief of staff requested an end to "Sammies." The American soldiers became laughingstocks. Their allies wondered why they carried a tag implying "perfumed, beribboned [*sic*] weakling," an imputation of "effeminancy" undeserved. Europeans labeled them "Yanks," considered "a good mouthful of masculine admiration." "Sammies" received a death sentence, "Doughboy" seemed cashiered and Southerners disliked "Yanks." But the latter originated before the Civil War, traced to the American Revolution that brought North and South into existence.

Harrisburgers cold-shouldered soldiers passing through. The Red Cross canteen welcomed detrained westerners, yet as they strolled city avenues, "there is not a cheer and hardly a handclap."

Lovelorn columnists upheld propriety to shield young women catering to servicemen. Beatrice Fairfax and Annie Laurie urged formal introductions. Laurie distrusted wedlock after short, fleeting encounters. Fairfax disapproved of flirtatious and informal contacts: "Acquaintances made in this way…are not to be recommended to young girls." She reminded readers, "Conventions have been instituted for the protection of women and they would do better to abide by them."

Both columnists sought to contain readers' impulses. They cautioned teenage girls about relationships, marriage, work overseas and kissing. Laurie told girls to think about "other things." Fairfax suggested war tasks at home. The two respected parental consent for nuptial ties. Laurie approved of goodbye kisses but not for boys corresponding with other girls. Fairfax commended a correspondent's objection to unwanted advanced: "Your conduct was quite proper.…A great many young men make it a point to treat girls with this lack of respect."

Both columnists favored letters overlooking soldiers' impropriety. Despite a flirtatious contact with a soldier, Fairfax approved of a girl's correspondence. To another, she supported writing to a serviceman who drank on furlough. She and Laurie wanted girls to pen even if soldiers failed to reciprocate.

Laurie warned of the perils of teenage girls riding in cars with strange soldiers. Two teens motoring with strange soldiers received her rebuke. "Never," she cautioned, "place yourselves in such a position." She drew their attention to "impersonal" conversation, book reading and Europe's war.

Letters requested guidance about gifts. Laurie discouraged expensive items that encumber: "I should advise you not to spend a great deal of money for anything without being very sure he will really need your gift."

The war brought about mixes. Laurie told of a girl drawn to a French officer but without her father's consent to marry. She thought well of an association with an Italian. Fairfax trusted amour would surmount faith variance. "The tremendous world war in which we are engaged seems to have given everyone more of the spirit of religion," she reasoned. "Real religion means brotherhood, not bitterness."

Misses worried their beaus might return disabled. Fairfax doubted one's caring. To a soldier, she expressed disdain for his intended when he revealed her attitude: "If a girl marries a man before he goes to war, and this man should die, or come home maimed, she would be in a fine fix."

The columnists condemned faithlessness. Laurie frowned on a teenager stringing along a soldier lover, a deployed correspondent and a home front companion. She concluded, "I think that you are thinking too much about the boys for a girl of your age, and if I were you I should stop it." Fairfax denounced a two-timer for violating her engagement by dating a serviceman. She complained, "So many girls act this way."

Lawlessness seemed boundless. Fisticuffs and free-for-alls erupted on city avenues, much of it attributed to inebriated workers from Marsh Run, Middletown and war plants. Ruffians roamed parks, exploiting the policing void. The *Telegraph* cheered officials making an "effort to squelch the rowdies who have taken advantage of the absence of many of the men at the front to override the authorities here and there."

Harrisburg discontinued the sale of intoxicants. Less drink resulted in fewer crimes and reduced arrests. Surprisingly, after the ban, women more than men became tipsy. The *Evening News* on October 25 reported, "The last twenty-four hours five women have been arrested for being drunk and disorderly on the streets."

Chapter 8

EPIDEMIC

October 1918

O n September 20, Washington forewarned of the advancing Spanish influenza. Threatening the Great Lakes Naval Training Station, the contagion spread across Lake Michigan's northern shoreline, impacting Chicago and Canada. It shut a state school in West Chester, Pennsylvania.

Soldiers became victims. Fort Dix in New Jersey suffered deaths. Camp Colt recorded five fatalities. By the end of the month, the scourge had reached Middletown.

The state education department alerted teachers. What seemed to be flu infections appeared in the eastern counties and along the commonwealth's borders. Still, the superintendent doubted the alien ailment's presence.

Authorities blamed Germany for the flu. U-boats supposedly landed men on the Atlantic coast, "and it would be quite easy for these agents to turn loose the germs in theaters and other places where large numbers of people are assembled."

As flu deaths climbed at an alarming rate, President Wilson issued regulations for self-protection:

1. *Avoid needless crowding—influenza is a crowd disease.*
2. *Smother your coughs and sneezes—others do not want the germs which you would throw away.*
3. *Your nose, not your mouth, was made to breathe through—get the habit.*
4. *Remember the three Cs—a clean mouth, clean skin and clean clothes.*
5. *Try to keep cool when you walk and warm when you ride and sleep.*

6. *Open the windows—always at home at night; at the office when practicable.*
7. *Food will win the war if you will give it a chance—help choosing and chewing your food well.*
8. *Your fate may be in your own hands—wash your hands before eating.*
9. *Don't let the waste product of digestion accumulate—drink a glass or two of water on getting up.*
10. *Don't use a napkin, towel, spoon, fork, glass or cup which has been used by another person and not washed.*
11. *Avoid tight clothes, tight shoes, tight gloves—seek to make nature your ally not your prisoner.*
12. *When the air is pure, breathe all of it you can—breathe deeply.*

The pestilence swelled. It struck over twenty-five states, reached epidemic proportions in New England and infected more than twenty-nine thousand soldiers in encampments. The Harrisburg Hospital reported the city's first flu case on September 26.

Dr. Leonard Keene Hirshberg's *Evening News* column readied locals for the influenza. Its signs are "congested eyes, sore throat, headache, muscle pains and a slight fever for two or three days," he wrote. Its microbic origin remained mysterious, he added, but its cures are "isolation, rest in bed for three days, sunlight, brisk massage and a plain, simple, nutritious ration."

Edward Vance Cooke's "The Latest Wheeze" jingled the epidemic's outbreak:

When your head is blazing, burning
And your brain is turning
Into butter-milk from churning,
    It's the Flu.
When your joints are creaking, cracking,
As if all the fiends were racking,
All the devils were attacking,
    It's the Flu.

CHORUS
It's the Flu, Flu, Flu!
Which has you, you, you
It has caught you and it's got you,
And it sticks like glue.

Left: Flu kills Sebastian Bowers, local soldier. *From the* Evening News. *Courtesy of PennLive.*

Right: A city man, Robert A. Boll, succumbs to the flu in the service. *From the* Harrisburg Telegraph. *Courtesy of PennLive.*

It's the very latest fashion;
It's the doctor's pet and passion,
So sneeze a bit,
And wheeze a bit;—
Ka-chew! chew! chew!

As the disease spread, city health officer Dr. John M.J. Raunick's headquarters functioned on the Sabbath. He advised repeated antiseptic doses to sanitize the proboscis and the windpipe. He likewise cautioned about sternutation: "If those who fell into the clutches of these afflications [*sic*] would be careful about their sneezing, would cover their nose and mouth every time they feel a tickling sensation fortelling [*sic*] a sneeze, and would catch the germs with their kerchief, there would be many less victims." The *Harrisburg Telegraph* assured residents, "Dr. Raunick is trying his best to make the 'flu' fly."

The flu disordered the community. Residents fell ill. Hospitals became overburdened. They limited visitations. People died. Undertakers ruled funerals private, restricted to kin.

The city came to a standstill. Quarantines quieted dance halls, saloons, theaters, libraries and churches. Schools closed. Football ceased. Stores shut down at six thirty on Saturdays.

The contagion disrupted schedules. The chamber of commerce canceled a speaker. The Harrisburg Reserves postponed drills. Call-offs impacted the Ladies' Society of the Lutheran Zion Church; the Capital Legion, No. 1108, the Keystone Chapter; United Daughters of 1812; the YWCA's gym courses; the Author's Club; the Civic Club; the Sunshine Society; the Keystone Lodge, No. 1070, of the International Association of Machinists; the Kiwanis; the Friendship and Co-operation Club of Railroad Men; and youngsters' Halloween romps.

Church closures cut off clergymen from their flocks. The *Evening News* decided against publishing a page of church services on October 5 due to flu-related cancellations. Reverend Edwin A. Pyles, Harrisburg Ministerial Association leader and Fifth Street Methodist Church pastor, asked city faithful to pray at home.

Dr. George Edward Hawes spread the gospel from posts on a board fronting his Market Square Presbyterian Church. Realizing those who feared the flu craved "spiritual" reassurance, he posted Psalm 91: "Be not afraid for the pestilence that walketh in darkness, nor for the destruction that wasteth at noonday. It shall not come nigh thee." Psalm 57, good for the Angelus, followed: "Be merciful unto me, O God; for my soul taketh refuge in thee; yea, in the shadow of Thy wings will I take refuge, until these calamities be overpast." He later posted a verse from Samuel II:

> *And David built there an altar unto the Lord and offered burnt offerings and peace offerings. So the Lord was entreated for the land, and the plague was stayed from Israel.*

The Camp Curtin Memorial Church's pastor John H. Mortimer messaged his congregation:

> *Churches closed, but God lives and religion is a reality. Keep heart! Pray! Have your church in mind! Observe every precaution advised by the Board of Health! Help everywhere you can!*

By late October, many ministers had disfavored chapel shutterings. One advocated openings for brief, daily services "devoted entirely to prayer." He feared closings incited public "panic." Regretting that the Lord's house received equal treatment to movie houses and barrooms, another informed, "The church stands as an institution to itself," and added, "I believe prayer, worship and devotion would have been a great help in meeting this trouble." Still, another saw no danger in gathering for short periods since trolleys and stores were crowded regularly. Many complaints about closures came from the African American community.

On October 30, Dr. Hawes imparted the following:

Was there ever a time when there were such universal wars and epidemics; such deep sorrows and so many broken hearts? May it be that God is chastening us, as nations and individuals [because] of our worldliness, and thus trying to bring us to our knees in humility and penitence? We may fight against men and win; but to fight against God is to lose. Our churches have been closed for some time, but they will be opened again. Will you be among the worshipers? Think on these things.

Music became a flu victim. The Capital City Lyceum Course's "Plymouth Singing Party" and the Wednesday Club postponed their programs. Songstress Louise Homes put off her local tour. A Fourth Street Church of God choir member died. Movie theater organists, fearful of lengthy closings, departed the city and found employment elsewhere. Music instructors and their students came down with the bug. Music shops experienced a drop in sales.

Edna Groff Diehl bewailed the restraint:

The moon that long October night,
Rose cheerless over city light.
The street crowd surged—but where to go?
The bar? the concert? movies? No!
Old Influenza's locked the door
To Pleasure Land. Oh, what a bore!

The affliction curbed services. Sick calls came from trolley drivers, construction workers, mailmen, police officers, plumbers, milk deliverers and railroaders. The Pennsy Station stopped selling candies and magazines. The local court suspended hearings. The *Telegraph* apologized for print errors, citing hired-hand scarcity. The county register of wills passed away.

Many households did without laundry help. Washerwomen feared catching the disease when touching contaminated tubs. As a consequence, commercial laundries flourished.

The flu loaded the war-clogged Bell Company's telephone lines. Its managers and health officials pleaded with the public to dial only pressing calls. The company reported telephone operators out sick and a depleted workforce of 90 performing the duty of 150, declaring, "This is one time that Harrisburgers can be patriotic without speaking a word."

Taking care of the dead fell behind. Coffins became unavailable. Undertakers put off funerals. Overworked gravediggers labored until dark with few ready to relieve them. The East Harrisburg Cemetery scheduled over thirty interments for the week of October 24 but booked no more until further excavations. Cadavers piled up. One resident dug his wife's burial pit.

One utility's business thrived. The telegraph office sent a steady stream of death dispatches.

The epidemic hampered wartime endeavors, distracting patriotic organizations. Quarantines hobbled the Red Cross. Nevertheless, its staff created a committee to combat the bug. It summoned nurses, made hospital bedding and produced patients' garb. The Cross also helped the victimized families of servicemen. But its Jewish auxiliary canceled a meeting, and the drive for Belgian relief stopped accepting donations.

The influenza undermined the bond push. Promotors restricted mass meetings, with some held outside. They worried about the quota. The *Evening News* editorial "Germs and Bonds" asserted, "If we have half the 'pep' of the lads over seas, we ll [*sic*] will do even better on this loan drive than if the Spanish 'flu' had not tried to put a spoke in the wheels."

Industries ailed. Some had military contracts. Employee losses slowed operations at the Central Iron and Steel Company, the Harrisburg Cigar Company and the Elliott-Fisher Company.

Railroads ran off timetables. Freight traffic slowed. Area conscripts delayed camp partings.

Authorities enforced an anti-spitting ordinance. Offenders faced fines and arrests. A letter to the *Telegraph*'s editor corroborated: "It is important that one should think about this dirty habit at all times." The writer wanted "cards" reading, "Don't spit on sidewalk, it spreads disease," distributed mainly to kids, who would give them to spitters, adding, "It will educate the children along sanitary lines and help stamp out the influenza epidemic." Mayor Daniel Keister exclaimed: "It isn't that the city needs or wants the $1 fine; this spitting on the sidewalks must be broken up and we mean to do it."

Top: Emergency influenza hospital in neighboring Steelton. *From the* Evening News. *Courtesy of PennLive.*

Bottom: Emergency clinic at the city's open-air school. *From the* Evening News. *Courtesy of PennLive.*

The epidemic overwhelmed hospitals. The municipality sought more facilities. As officials recorded four thousand flu cases, the city utilized the open-air school at Fifth and Seneca Streets, an institution for tubercular pupils, as an emergency hospital. Custodians made available the Harrisburg Country Club, the Masonic Temple and the Fort Hunter dwelling. Pastors offered the First Baptist Church and the Memorial Lutheran Church. African

American cases received care at St. Paul's Baptist Church at the initiative of preacher E. Luther Cunningham and physician Charles H. Crampton. The emergency clinic at the Riverside residence of George Saltzman began treating victims on October 10. The city set up tents for hospitalizations and called for nurse volunteers.

Health officials suggested preventives. To reduce crowding, trolleys should carry only the seated, and their windows must remain open. Streetcars should be fumigated "at the end of the line."

Industries could cooperate. Changing employee shifts would lower passenger loads during busy hours.

A reader's letter to the *Evening News* wanted the post office aired, demanding, "Open [doors] wide and ventilate and help the suffering public."

Warnings went out about casual osculation. Dr. Raunick cautioned: "Kissing is another prolific method of infection, and this practice should be stopped except in cases where it is absolutely indispensable to happiness." The *Evening News* reported advice given to California women, asking them "to Hooverize on their kisses" by pecking through hankies. In advocating "Kerchief Kisses," it asserted, "There is no doubt…that many of the less serious epidemics, which spread rapidly, have been caused by promiscuous kissing by women among themselves and children."

Harrisburgers kept their heads. Customers assented to closures. Retailers resigned themselves to losses. One observer expressed "praise of the coolness of the city's people."

Dr. Raunick moved expeditiously against quarantine violators as some tavern owners ignored the shutdown. Penalties ranged from a one-hundred-dollar fine to a month's incarceration or both. When Peter Kohlmann's saloon sold alcohol from its back entrance at 1304–6 North Seventh Street, he faced prosecution.

Notwithstanding precautions, the influenza plagued Harrisburgers. The disease took Edward H. Ripper of Kittatinny Street, "the first local man to succumb," on September 28. Four days later, Nicolas Negro became a victim. Within twenty-four hours, a death occurred at Middletown. By October 4, the city reported one thousand infected.

Flu cases surged. By October 6, Harrisburg had 2,000 ailing. The next day, the *Evening News* told of an additional 323 taken ill within twenty-four hours. The paper gave notice of 4,000 on October 9.

The scourge landed many at death's door. The Harrisburg Hospital recorded four fatalities on October 11, another four on October 12, seven on October 14 and four more on October 15.

Two doctors, L.M. Shumaker and W.A. Streeter, perish while battling the flu. *From the* Evening News. *Courtesy of PennLive.*

The epidemic shattered families. Eleven children lost their mother. In a five-day period, a man's mother, wife and father-in-law passed. The demise of Samuel Olsen of Liberty Street orphaned his five offspring. The Red Cross attended poverty-stricken youth.

One flu patient went raving mad. She leaped out of her bedchamber window, falling to her death.

On October 19, the city listed eight thousand flu-afflicted. Mortality claimed 5 percent. Employers grieved for employees taken. Bowman's memorialized O.J. Kelly: "In its heavy toll of death exacted by the grim epidemic this store mourns the loss of one of its most valued associates." On October 21, the retailer included the following in an ad titled "Two Vacant Chairs": "Two of our store family were summoned Saturday by Him whose commands are supreme—Miss Hildegarde Fox and Miss Marie Young." It avowed, "For years they had enjoyed the esteem of those with whom they worked, and to those bereaved we extend our sympathy." A letter to the *Telegraph* lamented:

> *The management and employes of the City Star Laundry hereby express their sympathy to the relatives of Katie Feeser, Annie Holby and Marie Strunge, who died during the present epidemic....We ask the relatives to put their trust in God, knowing that He does all things for the best.*

The influenza martyred caregivers. A doctor died before his child's birth. More physicians passed on, including Dr. Hyman R. Wiener. Elsie

Blurring the flu with a flue. *From the* Harrisburg Telegraph. *Courtesy of PennLive.*

M. Wilver, a teenage nursing trainee, departed, and Anna Gaughan sacrificed her life.

By October's last weeks, newspapers detected the plague's ebbing. The *Evening News* declared the "flu epidemic is dying." The *Telegraph* perceived a rapid decline. The *Courier* quoted officials who announced a slow mastering of the pestilence.

But residents still expired. As late as October 26, James G. Mies, register of wills, remained occupied.

The flu tabulated a ghastly loss of life. On October 24, Pennsylvania counted 20,000 dead. The *Telegraph* revealed the commonwealth's reckoning and reported, on October 30, 1,788 state deaths within twenty-four hours. The Harrisburg vicinity recorded 528 victims. Of these, 440 resided within the municipality.

The mayor sought to comfort the flu-stricken. He requested youth join hands with police to quiet the streets. Racket disturbed patients. In particular, he singled out automobile and motorcycle drivers. Their "cut-outs" (speedy departures) made "the air hideous with miniature artillery explosions." The Boy Scouts helped. They distributed posters prepared by law enforcement discouraging needless noise. City Commissioner Charles W. Burtnell, also Motor Division of the National Defense chief, appealed

to motorists for the utilization of their vehicles to carry caregivers to the residences of the inflicted.

Face covers became common, produced by the YWCA and distributed by the Red Cross. Residents received word to make their own if without and demanded caregivers wear masks while minding the infected. The *Evening News* insisted that "masks must be kept clean, must be put on outside the sick room, must not be handled after they are tied on and must be boiled thirty minutes and thoroughly dried every time they are taken off."

Pharmaceuticals hawked flu preventives and cures. Safeguards included Gorgas's antiseptic spray, Chasco-Vin's tonic, Gude's Pepto-Mangan blood fortifier, Munyon's Cold and Grippe Remedies, Lifebuoy's germicidal soap, Hill's Cascara Quinine Bromide and Borden's Malted Milk's food digester. Coleps and Laxative Bromo Quinine pitched regularity, the latter promising to "keep the system in condition to throw off attacks of colds, grip and influenza." Among the restoratives, Kondon's Catarrhal Jelly and Dr. Jones Liniment, called Beaver Oil, offered "relief."

The Dauphin County Council of National Defense alerted Harrisburg to alleged profiteering by doctors, pharmacists and morticians. Investigators issued notices to a physician and a funeral director. A Penbrook resident wrote the *Telegraph*, praising doctors but denouncing undertakers and druggists for "deliberately profiteering": "We see a lot of people who proclaim patriotism, but they spell it p-r-o-f-i-t."

United War Work meeting held outside; influenza precludes inside gathering. *From the Harrisburg Telegraph. Courtesy of PennLive.*

From Illinois, Zionist Wilbur Voliva promoted his flu remedy. Consume onions, he ordered. They deter bacterial infection and discourage human contact. He promised, "If you eat onions, people will keep away from you, and that is important in checking the influenza epidemic."

Cartoonists strove to lighten the bug's burden. Sterrett, Briggs and Hungerford satirized the sneeze as a flu-catching telltale. Two comics played with words. Sterrett swapped the phrase "Spanish fandango" for "Spanish influenza," and Hungerford drew a child using "flue" for "flu." An artist in the *Evening News* sketched a youngster who was punched because he said another had "Spanish influence."

The flu bug brought people out of doors. Walkers teemed on the riverfront and roadways. YWCA high schoolers tramped the countryside. Nuptials for Annie M. Strite and Raymond R. Kleinfelter transpired in the open air. United War Work officials conferred on the capitol grounds. Oak Troop Girl Scouts met outside the dwelling of Reverend Smucker on Thirteenth and Vernon Streets. When the disease killed Westminster Presbyterian Church's pastor Edwin C. Curtis, his remains reposed by a living room window, enabling mourners to see the corpse as they filed by outside.

In late October, a *Telegraph* editorial pointed the finger of blame for the raging flu, stating the sickness and death began in run-down neighborhoods. The paper likened slums to "a snake that winds its slimy path from the gutter to the palace, spreading its poison as it goes….We, all of us, are now paying for the crime of bad housing."

In the midst of a flu surge, the United War Work Campaign prepared a November 11 kickoff. Organizers sought a local collection of $180,000 to contribute to the national goal of $170.5 million. The funds raised for military personnel would go to the Salvation Army, the YMCA, the Jewish Welfare Board, the YWCA, the American Library Association, the National Catholic War Council of the Knights of Columbus and the War Camp Community Service. Sixty-four squads planned to comb the area for fifty-seven thousand donors.

Chapter 9

PEACE

November 1918

The war rushed to its conclusion. Between September 26 and November 11, American troops participated in the Meuse-Argonne offensive. They took over 16,000 captives, seized numerous guns and brought Sedan's railroad within artillery range. Doughboys suffered over 117,000 casualties. In early October, Germany sought peace. The Kaiser soon abdicated and absconded to Holland on November 9. Forty-eight hours afterward, the Allies announced an armistice.

Despite the glad tidings, the United War Work Campaign swung into action on November 1. Lasting for eighteen days, the fundraiser solicited Harrisburg and advertised what soldier services donations of five, ten and twenty-five dollars would support. With truce rumors about, promoters reminded donors of an ongoing need:

> *PEACE!! Does not mean the immediate return of our Boys;*
> *PEACE!! Does not mean the return at once to PEACE conditions;*
> *PEACE!! Does not mean that our sons have ceased to need our care.*
> *PEACE!! Means that the SEVEN SOLDIERS' WELFARE ORGANIZATIONS have*
> *today undertaken a greater task; their need for funds is multiplied.*

The city mustered behind the drive. Victory Boy and Victory Girl clubs sprang into action, the boys promising to "earn and give." They received awards for their efforts. Collegians helped, expressing "the spirit of the football team." Boy Scouts got involved. Industries and retailers displayed posters and took out ads. One placard pleaded, "See him through. Help us to help the boys." The Harrisburg Pipe and Pipe Bending Company bought a full-page advertisement. Bowman's invoked General Pershing's concern "for the boys over there," and Kaufman's pressed, "Be a million per cent. American Now….Give to the War Work Fund in seven-fold measure."

Financial institutions stepped up. The Harrisburg Trust Company disclosed a special dividend, hoping stockholders would give the bonus to the United War Work Campaign. The Central Trust Company, the First National, the Merchants National and the Commonwealth Trust Company each subscribed $1,000.

The push secured sacred sustenance. The YMCA scheduled a Prayer Week for its realization. Pastor Mudge plugged, "Give to the seven great war organizations till the last dollar and get into the church and take a part in its great work." Reverend Bagnell touted the United War Work's labors in the combat theater.

Campaign managers sought to accelerate their efforts. They sponsored a November 10 program on capitol grounds, which highlighted speeches, music and uniformed soldiers. The event took place without solicitations because of its Sabbath scheduling.

An unending communication link helped the undertaking. It urged homemakers to telephone, "I was asked to remind you and six other women and to ask you to be kind enough to call up seven of your friends and ask them to do the same."

Edmund Vance Cooke poeticized patronage:

Seven Sisters of Service
Come with their open hands;
Christian and Jew and Gentile, too,
From the far-off battle lands.
Have you felt the fire of a righteous ire
Through muscle and bone and nerve?
Then hasten your share for the "Over There,"
Where the Seven Sisters serve.

The *Harrisburg Telegraph* editorialized the feeling expressed in a current lyric "that applies particularly to the War Work campaign:"

One for all,
And all for one;
And God be with us all.

A letter to the *Telegraph* refreshed for readers that "a Rhine monster tried to sow the world with dragon's teeth to sink his monster fangs in the jaws of democracy." America defended the democratic way of life and "refused to permit the Hun to crucify civilization on the cross of autocracy." The correspondent asked, "Can there be anything but shame on the wealth that does not fund a cause so great as the United War Campaign?"

The fundraiser attained wartime goals. It went "over the top" by $9,183.74. Moreover, the coalition among Protestants, Catholics and Jews forged national unity.

As the epidemic abated, Harrisburg prepared to lift flu bans. The Market Square Presbyterian Church messaged Psalm 103: "Bless the Lord, O my Soul, and forget not all his benefits; who forgiveth all thine iniquities, who health all thy diseases; who redeemeth thy life from destruction; who crowneth thee with loving kindnesses and tender mercies." Management aired and disinfected the Majestic Theater. Administrators freshened the public schools.

Dr. Benjamin Royer's health office hesitated to end the ban and hunted for help to retain closures, knowing liquor interest opposed the policy. Royer asked for women's assistance. He argued "certain interests, who are putting dollars above human life, are bringing pressure to bear."

The *Telegraph* warned: "Danger not yet passed." The city's open-air hospital counted thirty-five patients and called for nurses' aides. It added, "The situation is pressing." The Harrisburg Country Club welcomed exhausted care providers for rest and recreation.

Cliff Sterrett's *Polly and Her Pals* drew attention to protective masks. A character christened them "flu aprons or bacteria bibs." In another installment, Polly warned about putting holes in Pa's mask since "a million microbes can march through the eye of a needle."

The influenza's orphaned children required resources. Red Cross allocations increased. By November 4, they stood at $1,560.84. The next day, authorities discontinued the ban. They planned to close the open-air hospital.

Reopenings snowballed. Theaters greeted patrons. The Hostess House again entertained and feted soldiers. The Harrisburg Reserves returned to drills. The courts rescheduled sessions. The Harrisburg Academy resumed classes. Soda fountains experienced a busy rush. The retailers wanted to cater to customers until nine o'clock. The Globe assured the public its building, "with many wide, open areas—high ceilings and many windows, is a well-ventilated and sanitary store for every person to shop in."

The flu closed the Harrisburg Library for more than a month. It renewed services on November 5. Staff withheld fines on overdue books if returned within a short period. Twenty-four hours later, Miss Helen Alleman restored the school libraries program for ten institutions, nine primary and one secondary. In spite of war and flu, 17,964 or 20 percent of the city area's populace registered to borrow books.

Church bells summoned the faithful. The Zion Lutheran Church's Ladies' Society held a postponed sauerkraut meal. The Market Square Presbyterian Church, the Pine Street Presbyterian Church, the Camp Curtin Methodist Church, the Olivet Presbyterian Church, the Second Reform Church, the Epworth M.E. Church and the Fifth Street Methodist Church once more offered prayer and ministrations. Dr. Hawes borrowed wording from the Book of Psalms to give blessing to the ban's lifting: "I was glad when they said unto me, let us go up into the house of the Lord." The Augsburg Lutheran Church memorialized those taken by the epidemic.

Several wondered if the suspension of services sapped turnout. Two ministers thought not. They believed churchgoers persevered and actually augmented attendance. A third person believed the influenza's lapsing and the war's ending intensified Harrisburgers' spiritual lives.

Associations took up suspended affairs. The Harrisburg Maccabees; the East Harrisburg WCTU; the Sunflower Troop, No. 1, Girl Scouts; the Ladies' Order of Owls; and the A. Wilson Norris Auxiliary went back to work.

Guests enjoyed a deferred social. Miss Zella L. Rebuck gave a Halloween celebration at her North Fourth Street residence.

Officials worried about a 12:00 a.m. bar reopening. They anticipated a "flying wedge" on water holes. If pell-mell erupts, "this city will witness a disgraceful orgy of drunkenness and disorder." Authorities should delay saloon openings until dawn to shield the community, the *Evening News* advised. The paper reported the customary gang of revelers when bar doors gave access.

The Bell Telephone Company of Pennsylvania thanked Harrisburgers for their self-denial during the influenza. Aware telephoning needed relegation to emergencies, residents acquiesced to "personal discomfort and sacrifice." The company added, "The nature and fulness of the response evidenced a most impressive public sympathy and spirit of helpfulness."

The *Telegraph* quipped, "Most of the 'flu' appears to have flown." With few hospitalizations and numerous discharges, the epidemic seemed on the wane. Nonetheless, the temporary clinic in Steelton still serviced patients.

As state officials cautioned about the contagion's recurrence, pharmacists pitched preventives. For Dr. Pierce's Golden Medical Discovery, Dr. M. Cook added:

> *The cool fighter always wins and so there is no need to become panic-stricken. Avoid fears and crowds. Exercise in the fresh air and practice the three Cs: A Clean Mouth, a Clean Skin and Clean Bowels.*

The Mustarine rub-on presented a pneumonia curb. Gorgas Iron, Quinine and Strychnine and Ton all promoted post-flu robustness.

In mid-November, the influenza looked unrelenting statewide. The press blared of its raging and swelling. Lancaster County experienced an outburst. Dauphin County's Almshouse reported five persons had taken ill. Officials discussed reimposing the ban.

The pestilence orphaned 50,000 and killed 42,096 commonwealth residents. More locals perished from the disease than died in the war.

On November 7, the *Evening News* headlined "Huns Quit!" claiming an armistice ended the fighting. The paper's daily "Good Evening" greeting wisecracked, "Here's your hat, Bill! What's your hurry?" The unexpected report surprised the city. Before celebrating, Mayor Daniel Keister waited for verification. The news turned out to be false, spread by an untrustworthy press service. The *Telegraph* berated the *Evening News* for "another war fake" and a "yellow journal hoax."

The untrue tidings proved harmful. Celebrants exploded a pipe bomb, killing a boy and hurting onlookers. A mob beat and shot a factory foreman "mistaken for a foreigner who is said to have torn up an American and an Italian flag."

The actual armistice's confirmation reached Harrisburg on November 11. The city went wild. The mayor requested store closings. Saloons shut their doors. Schools dismissed their students. The post office stopped its deliveries.

Officials promised a more formal celebration later, but the news set off twenty-four hours of revelry. Whistles, horns, bells, drums, pounded pans, discharged firearms, yelling, truck cut-outs and crying women aroused a frenzy. Employees deserted work. Crowds gathered, many on Market Square. By three thirty, forty-thousand people swarmed the streets. Bands played the national anthem. Homes and businesses displayed Old Glory. Individuals carried the flag. Governor Martin Brumbaugh spoke. Residents paraded. Celebrants strewed the streets with paper.

The war ends. *From the* Harrisburg Telegraph. *Courtesy of PennLive.*

This page: Armistice festivities ran for twenty-four hours. *From the* Harrisburg Telegraph. *Courtesy of PennLive.*

Heavy drinking precipitated uncalled-for antics. A rum inebriant went nude. A burlap bag covered his member, and a taxi whisked him elsewhere. An angry gang assaulted an alleged pro-German, denounced for denigrating the U.S. banner. The police carried him off after he fell from a sock to his puss. When a fight broke out in the Martin Hotel's bar on Market Street, a patrolman unholstered his pistol to restore order.

Newspapers credited divine intervention for peacetime's advent. According to the *Evening News*, Americans "could never have reached these hallowed days without the guidance and superior help of an Almighty God." Calling the armistice "the greatest news in the history of the world" and commemorating humanity's vanquishing of barbarianism, the *Telegraph* reprinted the April 10, 1865 news of Appomattox: "War Is Ended…God Has Granted Victory."

Four days later, Kreider Hesiery Mill workers in Lebanon, Pennsylvania, attacked a female employee. A brawl nearly ensued. The girl, "a descendant of pure German blood," supposedly regretted the kaiser's collapse.

Music facilitated celebrations. The C.M. Sigler's on Second Street marketed the appropriate numbers "Liberty Bell (Its Time to Ring Again)" and "Bring Back the Kaiser to Me." A Thirteenth and Market Streets venue held "Victory Dances" throughout the week. The J.H. Troup Music House on the square foresaw earnings amid rejoicing:

> *Now—if ever—your home needs music, music of mirth and gladness, of patriotism, gratitude and thanksgiving. And music you may have. We are splendidly ready to serve you.*

In fact, retailers exploited winning for profit. Some used the Supreme Being as a prop. Kaufman's urged patrons to "give thanks and praise to the Almighty." The Wonder Store sanctified "Allied and American heroism, with the help of Almighty God, and with the Holy Spirit and strength of a whole world of Freemen back of it has Conquered—The Prussian Beast and his whelp lie dead or caged." Others pitched with the triumph. Astrich's offered a Tuesday "Victory Sale." William Strouse ran a "Victory Overcoat Campaign."

A cartoon manipulated color symbolism to celebrate. Captioned "The Greatest News in the History of the World," it juxtaposed a light angel and a dark skeleton.

The armistice busied the Bell. It serviced seventy-five thousand telephone communications on November 11. Many callers contacted newspapers.

The revelry prompted postponements. The United War Work committee shelved a scheduled get-together. The Boyd Memorial Hall put off its "open house" of entertainment for twenty-four hours.

Mary Harriet Morley's "The Allies' Glory" enraptured liberty's realization:

The battle cry of freedom,
I hear in distant land
The woeful cry of children
Silenced by Allied hand.

The devastating influence
Wrought with crime intent
The Hun, the evil monster,
The Allied hand has rent.

The Allies cry for freedom,
The freedom God has meant
To tear from German evil graps [sic]
The tyrant's wail silenced.

The Allies gain the victory,
The Armistice is signed;
Their hats off to Woodrow Wilson
A greater President hard to find.

They wave their flag for Pershing,
For Foch, their leaders grand,
The Stars and Stripes will ever be
Recognized in Foreign Land.

Clergy solemnized the celebration. The Reverend Hawes made available the Market Square Presbyterian Church for prayer throughout the day. The Ministerial Association's chief, Pastor E.A. Pyles, proposed a "big public thanksgiving service in recognition of the favor of the Almighty in the cessation of hostilities." City observances paid special attention to the kaiser's overthrow. In giving gratefulness for the triumph, Pine Street Presbyterian's program opened with the singing of "Praise God from Whom All Blessings Flow" and the reading of Psalm 33 for its commemoration "of international thanksgiving." The next day, the Reverend L.S. Mudge spoke on "How Victory Was Won." The Chisok Amuna Synagogue on Sixth and Forster Streets also celebrated.

Forthcoming Sunday sermons hailed the war's end. Topics included "The Perils of Peace" at Grace Methodist, "The Cessation of Hostilities" at Trinity Lutheran in Camp Hill, "America and the World's Rebuilding" at Messiah Lutheran, "The Victorious Soldier" at Green Street Church of God, "The Lesson of the Great War" at St. Stephen's, "The Lord's Victory and Ours" at Market Square Presbyterian and "Lessons of Wartime," as well as "Responsibilities of Peace Time," at Capital Street Presbyterian.

The date of a formal celebration parade became an issue. Officials targeted Thanksgiving, but preachers feared conflict with church services. The mayor agreed, favoring the victory processions some other day. The *Telegraph* believed residents "are tired of parades" and "have had enough of marching." To conserve cash, it wanted to "roll two funds into one, and have a gigantic welcome-home for the men in khaki."

African Americans hoped the war's outcome would enhance their station. In a letter to the *Telegraph*'s editor, a Steelton native reminded the city of the "colored" man's sacrifices in previous conflicts. He prayed for a democratic temper and a nation free of racial conflict to greet returning veterans. He trusted "that our people shall be given their full rights and privileges as American citizens, and that all forms of race discrimination will have disappeared," including "that men will be measured rather by their ability to do than by their color." The correspondent borrowed from W.E.B. Du Bois: "There shall dawn a day when it shall not be asked of the artist, is he black, but can he draw."

The *Telegraph*'s classifieds contained color qualifications the same day the paper carried the Steelton resident's plea. The *Evening News* puffed stereotypical images. In early November, its comic strip *Doings of the Duffs* by Allman demeaned African Americans. Later, the paper ran C.M. Sigler's ad for "The Pickaninny's Paradise," a ditty offensive to Black children.

The *Telegraph* received a letter taking exception to its printing of an ad showing Black troops expressing their "broken language." The writer, identified as Knocker, argued similar jargon "is used in all the races, both black and white, and we do not care to hear any more or read such papers that print such articles."

The Nigger, a movie from a like-named play, made the rounds. Portraying a racist governor who bears Black blood in his veins and entertains the notion of walking away from his White lover, the picture generated a strong revulsion among African Americans, overshadowed by the hubbub accosting *The Birth of a Nation*.

War-related matters carried over after the armistice. The Red Cross Canteen Committee continued its services, attending the wounded soldiers transiting through the area. The Civic Club's Hostess House scheduled a Saturday dance and Sunday supper. To quicken long runs and avoid congestion, the Harrisburg Railways Company retained skip stops. Felix M. Davis, its superintendent, thought riders "would be annoyed with the resumption of stops at every half square and the contingent slowing down of the service."

Attention turned to federal plans for Middletown and Marsh Run. One observer thought the bases would remain or last for ten years.

Discussion resumed about remembering veterans. Mayor Keister supported the proposition, saying prudent "consideration in the selection of an appropriate memorial will result in the erection of a monument which will be worthy of a city such as ours." Harrisburgers expressed a readiness to organize and take donations. The *Courier* suggested twin masonry towers bordering Capitol Park and a "Soldiers' Bridge" across the Susquehanna. Rabbi Louis J. Haas wanted an up-to-date and favorably furnished "Harrisburg's War Memorial Hospital."

The city expected the continuation of wartime prosperity. A pent-up domestic market and repeated munitions orders stimulated steel plants. The Harrisburg Pipe and Pipe Bending Company anticipated unbroken war contracts since Washington desired preparedness. A Green Street resident looked forward to war's regulations being lifted and advocated, "Let those who desire whisky and beer have it and permit its manufacture."

But peacetime upset the outlook. A week after the armistice, the federal government voided the Pipe firm's contract for shell casings. Yet the next day, the Central Iron and Steel Company reported little impact from Washington's policy change.

Firms protested increased tax assessments. The Pipe Bending Company's counsel stated the concern's "officials think the boost…is enormous and is based, in part, on the fact that the company was compelled to pay $26,000 for a tract of five and three-quarter acres which was bought when the company began making munitions." Likewise, the Lalance-Grosjean tin mill requested a lower appraisal.

The wartime harmony between labor and capital broke down. Craftsmen at the munitions-producing Harrisburg Manufacturing and Boiler Company went on strike. The walkout lasted several weeks.

The commonwealth sustained casualties at home as well as abroad in 1918. From January through October, industrial accidents accounted for 2,893 deaths and 155,735 injuries. Railroad workers in particular experienced hazardous labors.

Conversion to peacetime meant jobs aplenty. War plant employees needed to return to their former towns and lines. Analyzing the labor

Soldiers and Sailors Memorial Bridge. *Courtesy of PennLive.*

scarcity, one observer believed, "The problem to-day is mainly one of immediate transfer of workers to their old trades and as near their home communities as it is possible."

A livestock shortage hampered agriculture. Too many draft animals ended up in France. Expressing the want for horses and mules, a person following farm issues reasoned, "It is up to us to encourage breeding and also to study tractors."

A School of Commerce ad pondered a woman's destiny: "Will she train herself to meet the demands which war placed upon the women and girls of America, and which will not be lessened when peace comes?"

Cliff Sterrett's *Polly and Her Pals* illustrated Delicia's response to Polly's question about the excitement of wartime employment: "Yep! The war has suttially [*sic*] gave us gals a place in the sun." Brigg's *Ain't It a Grand and Glorious Feelin'?* celebrated domestics returning to home service.

The *Telegraph* applauded women for their war labors. Conceding that homecoming servicemen "must be given every consideration and provided with employment as good, or better, than they ever had before," still "it does not follow that in thus caring for the soldiers the women workers shall be thrown upon their own resources."

The insurance industry faced challenges. The Central Pennsylvania Association of Life Underwriters met at the Engineers' Club and mulled over "Insurance During War Times and the Future of the Insurance Business."

Automobiles came into their own, becoming a necessity. But great consideration had to be taken when purchasing. Car dealer M.L. Mumma assured, "The mechanical excellence of the New Series 19 Studebaker Bix Six insures [*sic*] low maintenance and upkeep expenses."

The National Association of Wholesale Ice Cream Manufacturers prepared for peace, holding its annual convention at Chestnut Street. After remarks by Mayor Keister, the delegates talked over reconversion

Memorial to World War I women. *Photograph by Christine L.G. Ross.*

issues, giving scrutiny to sugar supply, milk commodities and market considerations. They confronted a "critical ammonia situation" and anticipated federal restraints.

Vendors advertised desires that conservation had inhibited. The United Ice and Coal Company pitched new housing. The Goldsmith's firm promoted furniture "that will add cheerfulness and comfort to any home and impress your boy with the fact that 'all was well' while he struggled 'over there!'" Alongside tapestry, the Mary Sachs's store carried fashionable wear, noting "the effect of the war's ending may be seen in the richer gowns and coats offered prominently in the better shops."

Men, money and materials sufficed for construction, forecasting "the greatest building boom Harrisburg has ever seen." The Penn-Harris Hotel neared completion. The *Telegraph* praised "all concerned that this great place of public entertainment has been pushed through under the most discouraging circumstances." With construction limits terminated, necessary housing began despite the absence of government permission. The *Courier* proposed "a new and modern hospital" as the foremost imperative. The paper also wanted pressure on the Pennsylvania Railroad to erect a station by its tracks at Walnut Street.

The Susquehanna River came in for discussion. Interested parties advanced dam construction for electricity and dredging for navigation, the latter projecting "Harrisburg [would be] a maritime as well as a railroad traffic center" plus "the third most important city in the State and would greatly enhance property values and make for the general prosperity for the community." The *Courier* supported a new toll-free bridge. It called likewise for an upgraded waterfront, a canoe storage and a Hargest Island beach.

Officials contemplated an Italian Park project. The McKee-Graham estate, owner of the twenty-five-acre tract, decided to yield control to the city planning commission, which could develop the area into an inexpensive civic haunt.

War-contracted industries reeked fumes. The *Courier* wanted something done about the smoky infest.

Despite Mayor Keister's assurances, Harrisburg turned out to be anything but clean. Without confiding in city law enforcement and "without favoritism," federal, state and military police pounced on disorderly houses. They apprehended two hundred culprits in shady spots like the "Bucket of Blood," operated by Sadie Hood; the Alva Hotel, adjacent to the Pennsylvania Railroad Station; and the China Diner on Market Street. Raids on dens at Cowden, North Third, James, Mulberry, North Seventh, State, East and Washington Streets corralled teenage boys and short-skirted damsels, as well as wedded women and men, all accused of "wilfully [*sic*] aiding and abetting [*sic*] prostitution within ten miles of a government camp," a wartime violation.

Thievery plagued war gardens. Green thumbs reported repeated robberies. Authorities accused James Reigan of looting a Fifteenth and Verbeke Streets lot. Shirley B. Watts, project superintendent, fired off summons to two young women for heisting produce from a Bellevue Park's school plot. Federal officials promised policing aid.

Notwithstanding depredations, Watts told the chamber of commerce that war gardens grew $9,484 worth of produce, $2,000 above 1917. The yield came from citizen plots, school grounds and backyards.

In the war's closing days and beyond, writing to servicemen remained foremost. The Red Cross urged cheery reports from home about "how the house and garden look, the talk of the neighbors, and who has been the latest one to enlist; how the Liberty loans and Red Cross drive made out." However, "never, never" unleash a sea of troubles. Beatrice Fairfax advised letters to an stranger in uniform as a courtesy. Annie Laurie recommended correspondence in spite of unacknowledgement, admonishing one girl, "Would you stop just because the man who is away on such an important mission hadn't time to write you?" and awakening her with, "Why goodness me, child, the boys in front aren't on a vacation."

Edmund Vance Cooke gave poetic quality to a homesick soldier's heartfelt plea:

Write to me, dear one, write to me;
Write to me every day!
Every line's a delight to me,
Every least sentence you say.

Anything, everything, sad or convivial,
All is important and nothing is trivial
What is The Boy saying? Saying right now!
Is Uncle Ike's "miery" better?
Is the rubber plant dead? Do the Brown's keep a cow?
Which word did you kiss in your letter?

So write to me, dearest, write to me,
Tattlings and tid-bits and tatters,
Nothing is trifling or trite to me,
Every least little thing matters.
Everything of you is shareable,
But silence, and that is unbearable.

Songs emotionalized separations. "Dear Old Pal of Mine" suggested a soldier's desolation and yearning:

All my life is empty, Since I went away
Skies don't seem to be so clear
May some angel sentry, Guard you while I stray
And fate be kind to join us some sweet day.

"Bring Back My Soldier Boy to Me" evoked an enlistee's leaving and his girl's longing:

Soldier boy, you've gone away,
In my heart I hope and pray,
That you will return someday.

My soldier boy
While you're over there,
This will be my pray'r,

Oh! Bring back,
Oh bring back my soldier boy to me,
Watch him, protect him.

The American serviceman's susceptibility to Parisian enchantment became likely. A letter to Annie Laurie revealed worry about unanswered correspondence, lamenting, "I am afraid he is in love with some French girl." The *Evening News* carried a front-page image of doughboys beaming at mademoiselles. The Troup Music House retailed the coquettish "Oui, Oui, Marie," a "speedy song, full of snap and go":

> *Poor Johnny's heart*
> *Went pitty-pitty-pat*
> *Somewhere in sunny France*
> *He met a girl by chance*
> *With a naughty, naughty glance*
> *She looked just like a kitty kitty cat*
> *She loved to dance and play*
> *Though he learned no French when he left the trench*
> *He knew well enough to say, he knew well enough to say*
> *Oui, oui Marie*
> *Will you do this for me? Oui, oui Marie*
> *And I'll do that for you, I love your eyes*
> *They make me feel so swoony, you'll drive me loony*
> *You're teasing me*

A wit quipped, "American soldiers who marry in France probably will find the French mother-in-law about the same as the American article."

Edmund Vance Cooke's "The Homeward Track" portended the soldiers' reunion:

> *O, we've been looking over as we sent the boys across*
> *And pride and hope have mingled with sober sense of loss*
> *But now the road which led away becomes a homeward track*
> *And all our eyes are straining till the boys come back;*
> *Till the boys come back,*
> *Till the boys come back,*
> *Surely there'll be singing when the boys come back;*
>
> *Every face is beaming,*
> *Every heart is dreaming;*
> *Dreaming, its delight because the boys come back.*

Indeed, the soldiers were returning. The USS *Harrisburg* made port on November 15, conveying wounded from the Continent. A Scottish shipyard had constructed the city's namesake thirty years earlier as an Atlantic liner. The U.S. Navy procured it in 1898 and christened it *Yale 2*. It transported troops during the Spanish-American War. Decommissioned and restored to line service, it registered as *Philadelphia*. It was obtained by the navy in 1918 and commissioned in May, and officials renamed it USS *Harrisburg*. It carried soldiers and provisions to Europe and, after the armistice, brought boys home.

The municipality expressed pride and thanks for the designation. The *Evening News* credited Secretary of the Navy Josephus Daniels for the "pleasant compliment," saying, "He must realize the superb part the city played in prosecuting the war." Without dissent, councilmen approved Mayor Keister's proposed gratitude for the honor.

Teutonics came in for condemnation up to and after the armistice. The Colonial's *To Hell with the Kaiser* screened "acts of bloodtingling revelations, that picture the Hun in his hellish degeneracy, and shows the Kaiser in just the place you would like to see him." A cartoon titled *Until Every Beast Has Fled* illustrated a victimized woman symbolizing Belgium fighting off a huge German with blood dripping from his hands.

Harrisburgers devised the Kaiser's punishment. One individual believed "Wilhelm ought to be boiled in oil, another believed he ought to be left to die in a little boat in an icy sea and still another thought he ought to be turned over to the women of Belgium." One more, after having difficulty transiting post station doorways, jested, "He ought to be made [to] spend the remainder of his life going in and out through the new doors of the Harrisburg post office." He added, "If you've tried them on a busy day you'll understand."

Innocuous happenings spurred doubts about loyalty. German speakers suffered penalties in Sioux Falls, South Dakota. An accented voice on a telephone call in Harrisburg during the armistice celebration asked, "Vat, please is all dis noise apout?" This convinced some "there are still some pro-Germans hereabouts." The *Telegraph* editorialized a solution for "these yellowbacks," suggesting, "Why not invite all pro-Germans in the United States to go back home—and provide them with free passage in trans-Atlantic cattleboats?"

One German native affirmed his attachment to the United States. The well-recognized musical enthusiast Professor J.H. Kurzenknabe migrated at the age of fourteen. The seventy-eight-year-old Camp Hill resident dashed off the ditty "Columbia's Heroes March Across the Rhine." Despite his

America's mothers also serve by bearing and waiting. *From the* Evening News. *Courtesy of PennLive.*

German birth, he felt compelled to compose the aforementioned because "for sixty-four years America has been my home and been good to me and… some time when I go on the Long Sleep I will be laid in its soil and I did not want the smallest particle of ground to touch a disloyal man."

Teutonism accounted for Germany's misdeeds. Imbued in a militaristic culture, the country's nineteenth-century society, according to the *Telegraph*,

The USS *Harrisburg* brought doughboys home. *From the* Patriot-News. *Courtesy of PennLive.*

had "been crushed by the military teachers, who took the children at the cradle and instilled into their hearts and minds the damnable doctrines that almost ruined civilization and are about to destroy the forces that set them in motion." Ten years after the war, Erich Maria Remarque wrote in *All Quiet on the Western Front* of Professor Kantorek's summons to German youths for duty.

An anti-Bolshevik mood gripped Harrisburg. Eathen T. Colton, YMCA labor chief concerning Russia, recounted that country's plight before the chamber of commerce and the War Work Committee. The current regime fails to represent the populace; instead, it consists, he maintained, "of a desperate little party of radicals who seized power at the point of the bayonet and have controlled the nation by sheer brute force." But their authority appeared diminished. The *Telegraph* thought the Bolsheviks more reprehensible than the Romanovs and castigated them as "an utter failure." The paper caricatured Russian Reds as a threat to global tranquility and predicted they would go the way of the German Hohenzollerns.

Dry sentiment prevailed in the city. Reopened dives with loudmouthed patrons agitated many. Police arrested bootleggers, boozers and soused soldiers. The Orpheum enacted a play version of Timothy Shay Arthur's *Ten Nights in a Barroom*, the leading literary force of the nineteenth century temperance movement and the "greatest argument for prohibition ever presented." A druggist promised wives burdened with drinking spouses that Prepared Tescum Powders, if deposited one dose "twice a day in coffee, tea or any liquid," would remedy the alcoholic tendency.

The war's end shifted reflection to education. Harrisburg straggled compared to other cities in an update of schooling. In particular, teachers' compensation needed to complement what "the wealth of the State and its importance in the commercial and industrial life of the nation would warrant its people in giving to them." The University Club at Front and Market Streets planned to meet and discuss postwar topics, giving attention to the educational requirements of returning soldiers.

The city could look forward to a period of marvelous music. The conflict interrupted creative compositions with maestros uniformed or stunned by combat's terrors. The *Courier* promised "with the healing of the scars of battle, genius will receive a loftier inspiration than ever before."

Mechanicsburg's B.F.M. Sours's "Peace" ushered the beginning of a new era:

> *Blow the whistles, ring the bells,*
> *Joy, O joy the wild din tells!*
> *Foes are silenced, guns are dumb;*
> *Ring the bells, for peace has come!*
>
> *Blow the horns, and shout the joy!*
> *Gladness? Yes, without alloy—*
> *Pure and stainless gladness, given*
> *By the listening God in Heaven*
>
> *Happiest tidings these since them*
> *Angels told by Bethlehem*
> *Save the gladness know to those*
> *Who first heard that Christ arose*
>
> *Truce is signed; the war will cease;*
> *Soon will come the fuller peace;*
> *God is listening from His skies*
> *For the praise that shall arise*
>
> *That the boys—our loved—are saved*
> *Where the foremen's flags had waved—*
> *That the lands oppressed are free*
> *For a holier life to be.*
>
> *Blow the whistles, ring the bells,*
> *Joy, O joy the wild din tells!*
> *Kaiser's banished, Christ alone*
> *Shall be King upon a throne.*

APPENDIX

These Harrisburgers gave their all:

Sergeant William C. Arnold
Private Earl E. Aurand
Corporal Raymond Axe
Private Charles W. Barker
Bugler Raymon L. Beard
Corporal John Harry Beshore
Private Charles F. Bricker
Private James W. Brightbill
Private Guiseppe Carboni
Private Percy A. Chronister
Corporal Isaac Cohen
Wagoner Eugene R. Davis
Private Ralph Diveley
Private James V. Dunlevy
Lieutenant James G. Elder
Private Henry Franklin Emswiler
Corporal George W. Fitzpatrick
Corporal Ada Genslider
Major Rexford Mason Glasppey
Corporal William O. Gorner
Private Frank P. Hawk

Corporal Robert H. Hoke
Lieutenant David J. Honert
Private Louis E. Houseal
Private Charles M. Houser
Sergeant Ray E. Johnson
Lieutenant Donald Johnston
Private Fred E. Jones
Private Robert James Kirby
Private Charles F. Krebs
Private Alfred Joseph Lilley
Private Burtnette Price Long
Private George E. Long
Private Walter W. Lower
Private Lee W. Monyer
Sergeant Edward Rock Murray
Private Francis Xavier Naughton
Corporal Jacob A. Nauss
Private William Shannon Noggle
Private John Christian Peifer
Private Amos C. Reese
Private Herman Ray Rhoades
Private Benedetto Salvadori
Private John F. Sattler
Private Sylvester P. Sullivan
Private William James Taylor
Private Roy A. Thomas
Private Frank H. Titzel
Private Charles Edward Weitmyer
Private John H. Young

BIBLIOGRAPHY

Books

Allport, Gordon W. *The Nature of Prejudice*. Garden City, NY: Doubleday Anchor Books, 1958.

Arnold, Catharine. *Pandemic 1918: Eyewitness Accounts from the Greatest Medical Holocaust in Modern History*. New York: St. Martin's Griffin, 2018.

Barry, John M. *The Great Influenza: The Story of the Deadliest Pandemic in History*. New York: Penguin Books, 2018.

Bauer, Ludwig. *War Again Tomorrow*. Translated by W. Horsfall Carter. New York: Duffield and Green, 1932.

Berg, A. Scott, ed. *World War I and America: Told by the Americans Who Lived It*. New York: Literary Classics of the United States, 2017.

Bristow, Nancy K. *Making Men Moral: Social Engineering During the Great War*. New York: New York University Press, 1996.

Commager, Henry Steele, ed. *Documents of American History*. 3rd ed. Crafts American History Series, edited by Dixon Ryan Fox. New York: F.S. Crofts, 1947.

Haulsee, W.M., F.G. Howe and A. C. Howe. *Soldiers of the Great War*. Vol. 3. Washington, D.C.: Soldiers Record Publishing Association, 1920.

Herring, Hubert. *And So to War*. New Haven, CT: Yale University Press, 1938.

Kazin, Michael. *War Against War: The American Fight for Peace, 1914–1918*. New York: Simon and Schuster, 2017.

Kennedy, David M. *Over Here: The First World War and American Society*. Twenty-Fifth Anniversary Edition. New York: Oxford University Press, 2004.

Leab, Daniel J. *From Sambo to Superspade: The Black Experience in Motion Pictures*. Boston: Houghton Mifflin, 1975.

Maynard, Richard A., ed. *The Black Man on Film: Racial Stereotyping*. Hayden Film Attitudes and Issues Series. Rochelle Park, NJ: Hayden Book Company, 1974.

———. *Propaganda on Film: A Nation at War*. Hayden Film Attitudes and Issues Series. Rochelle Park, NJ: Hayden Book Company, 1975.

Meyer, G.J. *The World Remade: America in World War I*. New York: Bantam Books, 2016.

Morison, Samuel Eliot, and Henry Steele Commager. *The Growth of the American Republic*. Vol. 2. New York: Oxford University Press, 1962.

Peck, Garrett. *The Great War in America: World War I and Its Aftermath*. New York: Pegasus Books, 2018.

Preston, Andrew. *Sword of the Spirit, Shield of Faith: Religion in American War and Diplomacy*. New York: Alfred A. Knopf, 2012.

Remarque, Erich Maria. *All Quiet on the Western Front*. Ullstein A.G., 1928. Reprint: New York: Crest Books, 1964.

Rosen, Marjorie. *Popcorn Venus*. New York: Avon, 1973.

Rudwick, Elliott M. *W.E.B. DuBois: Propagandist of the Negro Protest*. Studies in American Negro Life, edited by August Meier. New York: Atheneum, 1969.

Sisson, William. *Serving Christ and Community: A History of Market Square Presbyterian Church, 1794–1992*. N.p., n.d.

Spinney, Laura. *Pale Rider: The Spanish Flu of 1918 and How It Changed the World*. New York: Public Affairs, 2017.

Steinmetz, Richard H., and Robert D. Hoffsommer. *This Was Harrisburg: A Photographic History*. Harrisburg, PA: Stackpole Books, 1976.

Taylor, Jackson. *The Blue Orchard*. New York: Simon and Schuster, 2010.

Thirty Years of Lynching in the United States: 1889–1918. New York: National Association for the Advancement of Colored People, 1919.

Tresolini, Rocco J. *American Constitutional Law*. New York: Macmillan, 1959.

Weigley, Russell F. *The American Way of War: A History of United States Military Strategy and Policy*. Wars of the United States Series. Bloomington: Indiana University Press, 1973.

White, David Manning, and Richard Averson. *The Celluloid Weapon: Social Comment in the American Film*. Boston: Beacon Press, 1972.

Newspapers

Courier, April 1, 1917–November 24, 1918.

Evening News, April 3, 1917–November 25, 1918.

Harrisburg Telegraph, April 2, 1917–November 23, 1918.

Patriot-News, October 10, 2019, and April 9, 2020.

Sunday Patriot-News, December 23, 2018; March 29, 2020; January 17, 2021; and November 13, 2022.

Articles

Bruce, Robert B. "America Embraces France: Marshal Joseph Joffre and the French Mission to the United States, April–May 2017." *Journal of Military History* 66 (April 2002): 407–41.

Goodman, Adam. "Defining America: The Bureau of Naturalization's Attempt to Standardize Citizenship Education and Inculcate 'the Soul of America' in Immigrants during World War I." *Journal of American History* 109 (September 2022): 324–35.

Hogan, David W., Jr. "Head and Heart: The Dilemmas of American Attitudes Toward War." *Journal of Military History* 75 (October 2011): 1,021–54.

Latham, James. "The Kaiser as the Beast of Berlin: Race and the Animalizing of German-ness in Early Hollywood's Advertising Imagery." *West Virginia University Philological Papers* 50 (Fall 2003).

Pope, Steven W. "An Army of Athletes: Playing Fields, Battlefields, and the American Military Sporting Experience, 1890–1920." *Journal of Military History* 59 (July 1995): 435–56.

Book Reviews

Beaver, Daniel R. "Review of *Soissons 1918*, by Douglas V. Johnson II and Rolfe L. Hillman Jr." *Journal of Military History* 64 (2000): 563–64.

Hodges, Adam J. "Review of *The Espionage and Sedition Acts of World War I: Using Wartime Loyalty Laws for Revenge and Profit*, by Daniel G. Donalson." *Journal of American History* 100 (2013): 863–64.

Kieran, David. "Review of *Smoke 'Em if You Get 'Em: The Rise and Fall of the Military Cigarette Ration*, by Joel R. Bius." *Journal of American History* 107 (2020): 780.

Kuhlman, Erika. "Review of *The Sexual Economy of War: Discipline and Desire in the U.S. Army*, by Andrew Byers." *Journal of American History* 107 (2020): 520.

Mari, Nagatomi. "Review of *Over Here, Over There: Transatlantic Conversations on the Music of World War I*, edited by William Brooks, Christine Bashford and Gayle Magee." *Journal of American History* 108 (2021): 626–27.

Wierzbicki, James. "Review of *Dangerous Melodies: Classical Music in America from the Great War through the Cold War*, by Jonathan Rosenberg." *Journal of American History* 108 (2021): 198–99.

Internet

Digital Commons @ Connecticut College. "If He Can Fight Like He Can Love, Good Night Germany!" https://digitalcommons.conncoll.edu/sheetmusic/1629/.

Etsy. "Salt of the Earth by Mrs Alfred Cecily SIDGWICK." https://www.etsy.com/listing/985222978/salt-of-the-earth-by-mrs-alfred-cecily.

Genius. "Oui, Oui, Marie." https://genius.com/Arthur-fields-oui-oui-marie-lyrics.

IMDb. "*A Daughter of France*." https://www.imdb.com/title/tt0008994/.

———. "*The Eagle's Eye*." https://www.imdb.com/title/tt0009029/.

———. "*The Kaiser, the Beast of Berlin*." https://www.imdb.com/title/tt0009252/.

———. "*The Little American*." https://www.imdb.com/title/tt0008188/.

———. "*The Man Without a Country*." https://www.imdb.com/title/tt0008259/.

———. "*Mothers of France*." https://www.imdb.com/title/tt0008359/.

———. "*The Spirit of '17*." https://www.imdb.com/title/tt0009641/.

———. "*The Star Spangled Banner*." https://www.imdb.com/title/tt0794369/.

———. "*The Thing We Love*." https://www.imdb.com/title/tt0009691/.

———. "*To Hell with the Kaiser!*" https://www.imdb.com/title/tt0009706/.

———. "*The Wasp*." https://www.imdb.com/title/tt0131129/.

Library of Congress. "Sitting Knitting: All Day Long She Sits and Knits." https://www.loc.gov/item/2013567780/.

Lyrics Vault. "Olive Kline: 'Bring Back My Soldier Boy to Me.'" https://www.lyricsvault.net/php/artist.php?s=46770#axzz8IDlqX3gf.

The Parlour Songs Academy. "'Smile and Show Your Dimple,' Lyrics." https://parlorsongs.com/content/d/dimple-lyr.php.

ReSounding the Archives. "When Yankee Doodle Learns to Parlez Vous Français." https://resoundingthearchives.org/when-yankee-doodle-learns-parlez-vous-fran%C3%A7ais.

Sheet Music Singer. "Dear Old Pal of Mine." https://www.sheetmusicsinger.com/dear-old-pal-of-mine/.

The Silent Film Still Archive. "*Hearts of the World* (1918)." https://www.silentfilmstillarchive.com/hearts_of_the_world.htm.

Traditional Music Library. "World War One (WW1) Song: 'A Soldier's Rosary,' J.E. Dempsey." https://www.traditionalmusic.co.uk/ww1-songs/a-soldiers-rosary-j-e-dempsey.htm.

University of Illinois Digital Collections. "Lafayette." https://digital.library.illinois.edu/items/888fcf00-c561-0134-2373-0050569601ca-7#?

———. "My Belgian Rose." https://digital.library.illinois.edu/items/c23250c0-c560-0134-2373-0050569601ca-c#?

———. "Your Lips Are No Man's Land but Mine." https://digital.library.illinois.edu/items/aac3dbe0-c56e-0134-2373-0050569601ca-4#?

University of South Carolina Libraries Digital Collections. "Cheer Up, Mother." https://digital.tcl.sc.edu/digital/collection/jbgrtwrsm/id/1908.

Unpublished Material

Hays, Kenneth C. Email to author. April 12, 2023.

ABOUT THE AUTHOR

Rodney J. Ross was born in Harrisburg. He attended Forney Elementary, Edison Junior High School and John Harris High. He earned a bachelor's degree at Shippensburg State Teachers College in 1962. The Pennsylvania State University awarded him a master's degree in 1967 and a doctorate in 1973. Prior to retiring in 2017, he taught for seven years in the Harrisburg School District and forty-seven at the Harrisburg Area Community College. He has written academic articles, book reviews and encyclopedia entries. His first book, *Harrisburg in World War II*, was published by The History Press in 2021. He is currently researching Harrisburg's preparation for entry into the Second World War, 1939–41. He and his spouse, Aida, reside in Lower Paxton Township with their rescued shih tzu, Prince, and their adopted boxer, Rylah.

Visit us at
www.historypress.com